ROYAL ENFIELD
The Complete Story

Mick Walker

The Crowood Press

First published in 2003 by
The Crowood Press Ltd
Ramsbury, Marlborough
Wiltshire SN8 2HR

www.crowood.com

This impression 2014

British Library Cataloguing-in-Publication Data
A catalogue record for this book is available from the British Library.

ISBN 978 1 86126 563 0

Dedication
This book is dedicated to my American friends
Bob McKeever and Arvid Myhre.

Typeface used: Bembo.

Typeset and designed by
D & N Publishing
Lowesden Business Park, Lambourn Woodlands, Berkshire.

Printed and bound in India by Replika Press Pvt. Ltd.

Contents

Acknowledgements

When The Crowood Press first suggested I do a book on Royal Enfield, I was not too enthusiastic. However, this all changed as I began to consider the task. At first it appeared that the Redditch marque could not be compared to the more well-known British names such as BSA, Norton or Triumph. However, as readers will discover, in many ways the Enfield story is even more interesting. Not only has this long-established brand name outlived the vast majority of its contemporaries but, in addition, for the first half of the twentieth century Royal Enfield was, as often as not, in the very forefront of technical development – something that is very much overlooked today, when most people consider the company as a producer of sound, but run-of-the-mill, bikes.

Actually, Royal Enfield was a real innovator, with its developments often showing other, more well-known names, the way ahead. As this book shows, the company manufactured a wide range of engine sizes and types, including models for both sport and general transport, the military and police services, plus many component parts such as brake hubs, which it sold to other producers within the motorcycle industry. Then there was the non-bike industry production. This included pedal cycles (for almost the entire life of the Redditch works), automobiles (in the early years of the twentieth century), garden lawn mowers and a wide range of military equipment during both World Wars. Yes, Royal Enfield has a proud history and in the process of compiling this book I met a large number of people who helped in some way, on both sides of the Atlantic, with their knowledge and enthusiasm.

First of all my American friends Bob Mckeever and Arvid Myhre, in whose homes in Maryland and Florida, respectively, I wrote the majority of the text; Mick Page of Burton Bike Bits, who is a mine of information, particularly on the GP5 racer; John Szoldrak, who I met whilst he was racing a 500 Bullet at Daytona; Joseph G. Kimble; Lee Cowie; Roger Barlow; Billy Woolnough; Geoff Leather; and Tom Kerr, who provided literature and information on the American Indian Enfield's of the 1950s. Also to World Champion Bill Lomas, who provided information and photographs of his Enfield involvement.

Finally, but certainly not least, my good friends Mike Williams-Raahaege and Peter Rivers-Fletcher of the current British importers Watsonian–Squire, plus Jim Darcy of Charnwood Classics.

Many of the illustrations came from my own archives, with the balance coming from several enthusiasts plus Bill Snelling, and John and Barry Pook of Pooks Motor Bookshop.

In compiling *Royal Enfield The Complete Story* I made several new friends, met up with a couple of friends who I hadn't seen in years and in the process changed my view of the Enfield from one of passing interest to genuine enthusiasm. And I hope the reader will gain as much enjoyment, as I have had writing a story that spans over a century.

Mick Walker
Wisbech, Cambridgeshire
October 2002

1 Origins

If one counts the current Enfield India operation, Royal Enfield is the world's longest surviving motorcycle marque. In addition, throughout much of its life Enfield was a real pioneering company, often at the very forefront of new design and technology. But what of its origins, you may ask? Well, these go back to the middle of the nineteenth century, when the firm of George Townsend & Co. was formed in the tiny village of Hunt End, near the Worcestershire town of Redditch. George Townsend's operation specialized in sewing needles and machine parts.

Enter the Bicycle

As with many similar engineering concerns, Townsend's firm kept the business by tackling many other projects, although they retained their special skills for needle manufacture. Thus it was that during the 1880s they became involved with the burgeoning pedal-cycle trade. Their work in this field was to provide much useful experience for the new era of internal combustion engined vehicles, which was just around the corner.

By 1890, George Townsend & Co. had become a limited company, and was manufacturing its own brand of bicycle, together with many component parts and accessories for sale to the cycle trade.

Several changes were to occur over the next couple of years, with Albert Eadie becoming managing director and Robert Walker Smith works manager, whilst the company was re-registered under the Eadie Manufacturing title. It was also during this same period that the brand name Enfield was first applied to its products – this being due to contacts with the Royal Small Arms Factory in Enfield, Middlesex.

This contact between Eadie Manufacturing and Royal Small Arms was to result not only in the creation of Enfield Manufacturing Company Limited, but also the word 'Royal' subsequently being added to its name; this all taking place in 1893. It was this Royal Small Arms connection that was responsible for the famous trade mark, 'Made Like a Gun'.

By 1896, the New Enfield Cycle Company had been formed to embrace both the bicycle manufacturing division of Eadie and the sales arm of Enfield. A further twelve months on and the 'new' section of the title was dropped and The Enfield Cycle Company was officially launched – a name it was to keep throughout its many years, whilst located in the Redditch area.

Corporate Affairs

During this early period in Royal Enfield's history, it may come as a surprise to learn that there was a close association with BSA (Birmingham Small Arms). This came about because the Eadie firm itself continued to manufacture not only bicycles, but also, in due course, motorcycle components for BSA – and in 1907, Albert Eadie left the Enfield scene entirely to become a member of BSA's board of directors. This left Robert Walker Smith in charge of The Enfield Cycle Co., but in fact he too was also a director of BSA until he resigned, due to a conflict of interests, in 1909.

The First Enfield Motor Vehicle

As for The Enfield Cycle Co. itself, its first motorized vehicle, a prototype quadricycle, made its debut in 1898, followed the next year, 1899, by production of De Dion-powered tricycles and quadricycles. One of the latter vehicles took part in the well-known 1,000 mile (1,609km) trial of 1900, thus beginning what was to become a long Enfield tradition, with the sporting connection being maintained once the company entered the motorcycle world, which it did in 1901.

The First Motorcycle

The first Royal Enfield motorcycle was constructed with its engine mounted over the front wheel and driving the rear one via a crossed belt. Then came the machine with the engine at the rear of the saddle tube, followed in 1903 with the source of power being located in the more usual central position – just forward of the bottom bracket and the pedals. Also, this was the first motorcycle that illustrated both the pioneering Enfield spirit of future years and a classic marque trade mark – the latter being an oil container within the engine; an advanced feature at the time. There was also a gear primary reduction to a countershaft, with chain drive to the rear wheel.

In fact, as will become apparent, the Enfield concern was not afraid of adopting new ideas as and when they were invented. However, Royal Enfield soon reverted to the more usual direct belt drive, and even produced a range of conventional single-cylinder machines with mechanically operated side-valves.

Four Wheels

Then came a period when Enfield concentrated its efforts on four wheels, producing not only complete automobiles but also component parts for other manufacturers. The first car was built in 1901 and the much increased activities saw the size of the Hunt End works constantly increasing in area. This activity led to an entirely new factory being constructed within Redditch itself, the resulting Hewell Road site, which opened in 1907, eventually covering 24 acres (9.7ha) and Enfield's home for the next sixty years.

V-Twins

By 1910 the company had decided to concentrate its efforts on two wheels and, in particular, V-Twins. Initially Royal Enfield used either Swiss MAG or British JAP power units. And, once again displaying a pioneering spirit, the Redditch concern was in the forefront of innovation by adopting the countershaft gearbox and chain drive – which appeared in 1911. By now the automobile side had been wound down and, beside motorcycles, The Enfield Cycle Co. was very well-known for its manufacture of cycle and motorcycle components, which included brakes and hubs. These were supplied to other motorcycle firms – and continued to be an important source of revenue to the company for the next half-century. At one time they even made frames for the likes of the Scott marque.

The first Royal Enfield motorcycle appeared in 1901 and was constructed with its single-cylinder engine mounted over the front wheel. The rear wheel was driven by a crossed belt.

The most notable early production Royal Enfields were V-Twins. This example dates from 1914, featuring 600cc, inlet-over-exhaust, enclosed valve gear, hand-operated oil pump, two-speed countershaft gearbox and chain final drive.

This Royal Enfield is an experimental ohv V-Twin with exposed valve gear and pushrods. The sole prototype was constructed in 1913.

The Model 180

In 1912 Royal Enfield built the first of its famous Model 180s. Powered by 770cc side-valve JAP-engined V-Twins, these proved popular sidecar machines, Enfield often supplying them as a complete outfit.

The Model 180 not only features chain drive and a two-speed gearbox, but was the first British motorcycle to employ the famous Enfield rubber cush drive system in the rear wheel, to minimize chain snatch. Later this innovation was first to be sold and later copied by countless other motorcycle manufacturers down through the years. Essentially it was a separate hub with a series of rubber blocks (vanes) and provided the chance of greatly increased chain life.

In 1913 Royal Enfield had produced its own 3hp (425cc) ioe V-Twin engine, having previously employed bought-in Swiss MAG or British JAP power units. Reduced to 350cc for the 1914 TT, it was the first British production engine to feature dry sump lubrication with an automatic geared oil pump.

In the 1913–14 Enfield V-Twin, the lubricating oil was contained in a glass tank attached to the frame tube that ran from the seat to the rear of the engine. Strange as it may seem, this worked perfectly and also had the added advantage of providing an instant visual check of the oil level.

Dry Sump Lubrication

In 1913 another pioneering step was made, when Royal Enfield introduced its own 3hp (425cc) ioe (inlet over exhaust) engined V-Twin. This was the first British production motorcycle to feature dry sump lubrication with an automatic-geared oil pump; this coming at a time when everyone else was using the Pilgrim-type hand-operated pump with its total loss lubrication system. In Enfield's V-Twin, the pump fed oil under pressure to the big-end bearing via a hollow crankpin, returning the lubricant from the crankcase to the glass oil tank beneath the saddle. Glass may seem a strange material, but at least it did have the advantage of allowing a visual check, not just if oils were there, but that the system was operating!

The 425cc ioe V-Twin put out, for its time, a very healthy 14bhp, which helped propel the 312lb (141kg) machine to a maximum speed (solo) of 55mph (88km/h).

Reduced to 350cc, an example of the V-Twin almost won the 1914 Junior TT in the Isle of Man in the hands of F.J. Walker. He led the race until delayed by punctures. Then, after crossing the finishing line, the luckless Walker crashed fatally into a barrier that had been placed across the road to prevent slower riders going for another lap.

A 350 Enfield V-Twin similar to the one ridden into third position in the 1914 Junior TT by F.J. Walker.

Next came a 225cc single-cylinder two-stroke (*see* Chapter 5). First produced in 1914, the 225L (Ladies) featured an open-frame. The three-port engine featured a deflector piston, outside fly-wheel, and two-speed, hand-operated gearbox. The open frame was created so that the machine could be easily ridden by women wearing long skirts, which were all the fashion at the time. There was a barrel-shaped fuel tank, which was located to the rear of the steering head. This model continued to be offered until 1929 – whilst Enfield still listed a 225cc two-stroke until well into the 1930s.

The Great War

The First World War (known as The Great War) began during 1914. When hostilities broke out, it was not long before Royal Enfield was called on to supply motorcycles to the British War Department.

In true pioneering spirit, many of the early Royal Enfields were, for their period, extremely innovative, and none more so than this 1915 675cc in-line three-cylinder two-stroke prototype; it was probably the world's first with this configuration and engine type.

Notable was a series of large displacement JAP-engined V-Twins equipped with a sidecar – these performed a variety of duties including machine-gun mount and even ambulance. Besides also selling the military large numbers of bicycles, Royal Enfield was involved in a contract to supply the Imperial Russian Army with a number of its V-Twins.

The Smith Family

Robert Walker Smith had been appointed managing director in 1923. All his three sons served in the war – and amazingly, considering the carnage of this awful conflict, all survived, including the oldest, Major Frank Walker, who had served as a Royal Flying Corps pilot in France.

Actually, more than probably any other family in the British motorcycle industry, the Smiths of Royal Enfield were an exceedingly close-knit team. Not only did 'Major Frank', as everyone called him, take over the reins when his father died in 1933 (after serving as assistant managing director, after joining the firm in 1919), but all the brothers were keen motorcyclists and trials riders. This not only gave them a hands-on approach, but meant that they were quite often involved with developments of new innovations and models –

and that the Enfield Cycle Co. was one of the very best British motorcycle companies to work for. Unlike the really big names, such as AMC, BSA and Triumph, Enfield was a place where everyone connected with the operation felt he or she was wanted. In Steve Wilson's excellent six-volume *British Motor Cycles*, Royal Enfield's post-war trials star Johnny Brittain recalled how Major Frank Smith had deeply appreciated both his and his father Vic's roles as ambassadors, for both company and country, at events such as the annual International Six Days Trial, commenting 'they [Enfield] were a pioneering little company and I really enjoyed riding for them. We never had a cross word in fifteen years!'.

This was also true of key engineers such as E.O. (Ted) Pardoe and R.A. (Tony) Wilson Jones, who both joined The Enfield Cycle Co. during the 1920s and were to be involved from then until the 1950s and 1960s, respectively – again compare this to the comings and going in the vast majority of the motorcycle industry, which often involved the great personalities of their day. With these other marques it was almost akin to the frequent new signing – often with financial considerations – which are made in the soccer world of today. But at Royal Enfield it was different; brand loyalty really did count for something.

As is revealed in Chapter 3, Royal Enfield motorcycles were widely used in the First World War; a Redditch-built machine (V-Twin) is seen here during the conflict.

2　The Inter-War Years

As related in Chapter 1, Royal Enfield had supplied various specialized military motorcycles to the British armed forces during the Great War of 1914–18, and was even awarded a contract to build bikes for the Imperial Russian Government during the same period.

The Redditch concern thus emerged into the sunlight of peace – and after the appalling carnage of the First World War it really was an appreciated peace – in a reasonably healthy financial state.

Guided by the Smith Family

Guided by the Smith family, Royal Enfield pursued a policy of keeping its product line in the realms of what the man-on-the-street could afford. Thus, during the early post-war era it stayed clear of exotic designs, which meant that when the years of depression came after the Wall Street stock market crash of 1929, the company was far less affected than the majority of other motorcycle manufacturers. Another real asset was its engineering arm, which provided additional stability. All-in-all, Royal Enfield was a well-run

ship – and lean enough to make rapid adjustments where necessary. Maybe Royal Enfield did not quite acquire the charisma of marques such as Norton or Triumph, but it still managed to do good, profitable business, which was to ensure its survival when many other similar size marques went to the wall during the inter-war years.

Design Expertise

The factory was also helped by the arrival of Ted Pardoe during the immediate post-war period. In 1924 he was responsible for a newly designed 346cc (70 × 90mm) side-valve single. This was a vital creation, as it gave Enfield an important self-sufficiency; before this many of the engines that powered its range had come from the like of JAP and Vickers. The 350 was joined in 1927 by a larger 488cc (85.5 × 85mm) side-valve single. By sharing the same bore and stroke as the 976mm single-valve V-Twin, the beginning of the modular policy began. This provided a commonality of design and an interchangeability of components parts.

In 1925 Royal Enfield considered two designs of ohv engine to replace its existing JAP type. One of these featured needle-bearing overhead rockers, grease lubricated; the other with semi-enclosed rockers on plain bearings, oil-mist lubricated. The latter (seen here) was put into production for the 1926 season; the engine displaced 346cc.

ROYAL ENFIELD
MADE LIKE A GUN

Trade Delivery Outfits

THE ROYAL ENFIELD 9·76 h.p. Motor Cycle with its great flexibility and ample reserve of power is most suitable for tradesmen's use. The powerful twin-cylinder engine has mechanical lubrication. Transmission is by roller chain with Sturmey-Archer 3-speed Gear, handlebar-controlled Clutch and Kickstarter. Internal Expanding Brakes (with 8" drums) are fitted to both wheels and Enfield Cush Drive in rear hub.

In the Six Days' Trial for Commercial Sidecars the Dairyman's Outfit illustrated completed the course without loss of marks and obtained a Special Certificate of Merit.

Our complete Motor Cycle Catalogue will gladly be forwarded post free on request.

THE ENFIELD CYCLE CO. LTD.,
Head Office and Works: REDDITCH.

Birmingham Showrooms:
274a BROAD STREET.

London Showrooms:
48 HOLBORN VIADUCT, E.C.1.

Between 6 and 11 July 1925 this Royal Enfield V-Twin-engined Dairyman's Outfit took part in the ACU Six Days' Trial for Commercial Sidecars, completing the arduous course without loss of marks and obtaining a Special Certificate of Merit. The inter-war years was a period when the sidecar reached its zenith.

Close-up of the 1929 488cc ohv Enfield engine. This featured twin ports, exposed valve gear, coil springs, hand gear-change and iron head and barrel.

The 1930 Model Range

Royal Enfield's range for 1930, announced in September 1928, consisted of thirteen motorcycles:

- 225cc (64 × 70mm) two-stroke single Model A;
- 225cc (64 × 70mm) side-valve single Model B;
- 346cc (70 × 90mm) side-valve single Model C;
- 346cc (70 × 90mm) side-valve single Model F;
- 346cc (70 × 90mm) side-valve single Model G;
- 346cc (70 × 90mm) overhead-valve single Model CO;
- 488cc (85.5 × 85mm) side-valve single Model D;
- 488cc (85.5 × 85mm) side-valve single Model H;
- 488cc (85.5 × 85mm) side-valve single Model HA;
- 488cc (85.5 × 85mm) overhead-valve single Model E;
- 488cc (85.5 × 85mm) overhead-valve single Model J;
- 488cc (85.5 × 85mm) overhead-valve single Model JA;
- 488cc (85.5 × 85mm) side-valve V-Twin Model K.

This was, of course, sound economic policy and has since proved a key feature to help owners or restorers of the Redditch marque down through the years. Today, together with newly made Enfield India motorcycles, it means an easier life for Royal Enfield fans than is the case for many rival brands.

Wilson-Jones Arrives

The second vital arrival in 1925, was that of Tony Wilson-Jones, at the age of twenty-four, as head of development. It was also this man who was largely responsible for the setting up and running of the company's apprentice training scheme: up to forty youngsters were recruited into the apprenticeship scheme each year. This was to ensure a good level of skilled labour – and was to play a vital role in the firm's continued success in future decades.

During 1928 Royal Enfield had adopted saddle tanks and centre-spring girder front forks – one of the first companies to do so. This meant that the bikes had a modern appearance; this, together with a comprehensive range, meant continued sales – even when the dark days of depression arrived in Great Britain towards the end of 1930.

The Model A

The Model A was the smallest (and cheapest) machine in the range and many machines made their debut on the eve of the First World War in 1914. The Model A two-stroke engine featured a mechanical oil pump – an advanced feature, even during the early 1930s. As with the whole 1930 range, it was equipped with a girder fork featuring twin-tension springs. The Model A came with a three-speed, hand-change gearbox and the traditional Royal Enfield detachable rear mudguard and carrier.

The next machine was the Model B. This also come with a 225cc displacement but was a side-valve four-stroke, while the Model C featured an inclined 346cc unit, also with side-valves. It is important to mention that this employed the classic 70 × 90mm bore and stoke dimensions, giving 346cc — something continued through into the three-fifty bullet, and still retained in the Madras-made model of today! This, as already mentioned, was to be a feature of the Enfield factory over the years, helping with a continuity of production so vital for, what was after all, a relatively small company.

The Model D was a 488cc side-valve and the Model E its other counterpart; again, three-speed gearboxes were specified, although four-speed were available as options.

Inclined Cylinders

The next batch of motorcycles were new for the 1930 model year — all featuring inclined cylinders and dry sump lubrication. The oil was circulated by twin plunger pumps driven by a shaft in the timing cover, itself operated by a worm on the crankshaft. The lubricant was carried within a compartment cast integrally into the front of the crankcases — a feature to be used by Enfield for many years. These models were: the F 350 side-valve; the G was the same displacement but ohv; H came with 488cc side-valves; and J was the ohv version of the 488cc motor.

The range was headed by the Model K with its 976cc side-valve V-Twin power-plant. Like the Model A two-stroke, the K was an old design and largely intended as a sidecar tug, but over the years it had been continually updated and by now sported the new-style front forks and improved braking.

Early in 1930 the Model CO was added to the range with its inclined 346cc ohv engine.

A Model K 976cc V-Twin and bullet-shaped aluminium sidecar from the mid-1930s, when both the V-Twin and the sidecar were very much in vogue.

DETAILS THAT MAKE for ROYAL ENFIELD PERFECTION

Journal Bearing Hubs

THE hubs of all Royal Enfield Light-and Medium-weight motor cycles are fitted with single row, deep groove journal ball bearings as illustrated. These give far better service than the old type of cup and cone bearings, and, owing to their special construction, are adequate to deal with both radial and thrust loads. An additional advantage is that these bearings never require any adjustment, neither are they capable of being adjusted. Thus incorrect adjustment, which so frequently causes failure of cup and cone bearings, is rendered impossible.

The use of this type of bearing is but one of many instances of detail design which make Royal Enfield machines so reliable and such remarkable value.

The outstanding quality of the Royal Enfield is the result of untiring experiment and research. Herein lies your safeguard, for no part, however minute, can find a place in the Royal Enfield specification until it has undergone drastic tests on road and track. Nothing is skimped — every machine has a most complete specification and is good for many years strenuous service. In short, the details that make for Royal Enfield perfection ensure your safety, comfort and convenience and keep your running costs down to a minimum—and the Royal Enfield Gradual Payment Scheme helps you to buy your machine.

Fill up the coupon below and despatch it at once. A halfpenny stamp only is necessary if the envelope is unsealed.

3·46 h.p. Two-port Model CO £43 5s.

(Electric Light, £5 10s. extra.)

ROYAL ENFIELD

MADE LIKE A GUN

London Showrooms .. 48, Holborn Viaduct, E.C.1
London Service Depot .. 5, 7, 9, Hatton Wall, E.C.1

To The Enfield Cycle Co., Ltd., Redditch.
Please send Free Catalogue "E."

A 1930 advertisement for the twin-port Model CO Enfield costing £43 5s, with electric lighting at an additional £5 10s.

Later that spring came the HA and the JA; these latter machines were very much a case of providing as wide a range of models as possible, without having to resort to brand-new designs. An 'L' added to any of these prefixes denoted the de luxe option.

Longer Stroke

For 1931, the Model J was redesigned as the J31, this now having a 499cc engine size – with the long-stroke dimensions of 80 × 99.25mm and a twin-port cylinder head. The H31 used the same 99.25mm stoke, but with the cylinder bore increased to 85.5mm, giving 570cc.

Four-Valve Head

The most radical newcomer was the JF31; this used the J dimensions with a four-valve cylinder

Four-valve Royal Enfield Model LF. This 488cc (85.5 × 85mm) engine ran from 1932 until the end of 1934. Note the exposed valves and heavily finned crankcase.

head. The valves were arranged in a pent-roof fashion, meaning that the valve gear was more complex than that found on other Enfield singles of the era.

For the 1932 model year, the big news was the arrival of a new 248cc engine size, with a bore and stroke of 64 × 77mm, it was offered in both side-valve and overhead-valve guises, under B (sv) or BO (ohv) model prefixes. In January 1933, the V-Twin was given a larger 1,140cc engine (for export only) by lengthening the stroke to 99.25mm.

The Bullet Name Arrives

It was around this time that the first use was made of the now-famous Bullet name – this was applied to the range of ohv singles in 248, 346 and 488cc engine sizes. For 1934 it was very much a case of careful development rather than entirely new engineering practices.

Three Valves

The big news for the 1935 model year was the three-valve Model LO.

This came from the success achieved by the new 148cc (56 × 60mm) ohv machines, which had made such a good impression with the buying public over the preceding months – thanks in no small part to their entirely enclosed valve gear. It was thus decided to extend this to the larger 488cc engine size.

Various valve layouts were tested and after much thought it was decided to use a three-valve layout with vertical valves. The reason for this set-up was that it was felt that the new cylinder head would provide an almost identical level of performance to the earlier four-valve one, but with an increase in silence, neatness and reliability.

There was a pair of smaller inlet valves and a single larger exhaust valve, so the valve heads lay in a roughly triangular flat space and the head was of the pent-roof formation. This resulted in a very compact combustion space – permitting a 6:1 compression ratio with a flat-topped piston.

A big advantage over the three-valve head was that in the three-valver the valve gear was totally enclosed. A large, flat inspection cover at the very top of the cylinder head gave access to the entire upper pushrod mechanism, making tappet adjustment a simple matter. The adjusting nuts were housed in a box at the base of the cylinder barrel and could be accessed after removing a square plate (as tappet adjustment is still made on the current Bullet singles).

The lower part of the engine followed conventional Enfield practice: crankcase carrying a large oil container, the oil being circulated on the dry sump system by two separate plunger pumps.

Another modern feature of the Model LO three-valver was its four-speed, foot-operated gearbox.

The frame of the LO followed the by now well-known Enfield duplex-cradle type, having forged cradle sides, whilst the cush hub and detachable rear mudguard were retained. There

Drawings showing details of the 1935 three-valve model LO cylinder head and valve arrangement.

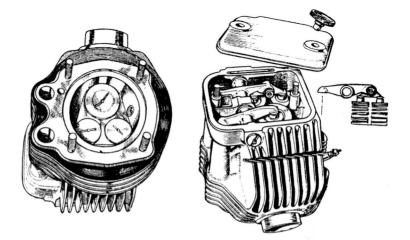

In September 1934, Royal Enfield announced its new three-valve 488cc single. This featured enclosed valve gear and was only produced for the 1935 season.

were, however, other notable features, for the 6½in (16.5cm) brake drums were malleable castings with deep cooling ribs, whilst the rear-wheel spindle was of the knock-out type, and although the wheel was not of the quickly detachable type, the inner tube could be entirely removed for repairs with the wheel *in situ*!

Other features of what, at that time, was Royal Enfield's most advanced motorcycle included the company's very practical side-stand, 3.25 × 26 tyres, Terry de luxe dished saddle, large rubber lock-stops, an instrument panel and shock-and-steering dampers for the girder front forks. The engine's cylinder was inclined forward at 20 degrees. With full electric lighting – by then a feature of all Royal Enfield's production range – the price of the Model LO was £59 7s 6d.

Vertical Cylinders

When the 1936 range was announced in July 1935, the big news was the introduction of the first machines with a new style of vertical cylinders. This was to become very much a feature of Royal Enfield motorcycles over the forthcoming years – and a feature of all the company's post-Second World War designs, including the Bullet series and the parallel twin family.

In general layout, except for the top end of the engines, the design followed normal Enfield lines with a gear train to drive the camshafts and a rear-mounted dynamo or magdyno, dry sump lubrication, with the oil housed in a forward extension of the crankcase, and fully enclosed valve gear.

Model G and Model J

There were two standard two-valve models, the 346cc G and the 499cc J, the latter featuring new 84 × 90mm bore and stroke dimensions. Both came with coil ignition and four-speed, foot-operated gearboxes. The frame sported a single top and down-tubes with duplex rails passing under the engine; at the front was a set of pressed-steel blade girder forks.

There was also a third model: this was the JF Bullet. There had, on this machine, been a return

to a four-valve head, like the older LF Model.

The remainder of the four-stroke-single range continued with inclined cylinders, much as before.

April 1936 witnessed the introduction of a more sporting version of the G and J known as the Competition Models, which were intended for both the competitor and the road user. These came with a tilted silencer (also a feature of the original post-war Bullet), the purpose of which was to provide increased ground clearance. Also part of the specification was knobbly tyres and narrow-section, chrome-plated steel mudguards. An interesting feature was the provision of lifting handles either side of the rear wheel – for easier retrieval when the rider dropped his mount in the trials section.

V-Twin Redesign

For 1937, the long-running side-valve V-Twin was completely updated. The displacement was rounded out at 1,140cc for the home market, as well as overseas sales. The cylinders featured detachable heads (both in iron) and enclosed valve gear, with the crankcase having been redesigned to incorporate dry-sump lubrication.

In the main, the lubrication system followed Enfield practice, the oil supply being carried in a separate crankcase compartment. There were, however, no fewer than four oil pumps, all of the oscillating-plunger variety. One of these fed the big-end bearings, and another the front cylinder. A third pump drew oil from the crankcase and delivered it to the timing gear, and the fourth drew from a predetermined level in the timing case, and returned the oil to the main compartment.

The four-speed gearbox was still hand-operated and – as before – either hand or foot operation could be provided for the clutch. The engine and transmission of the big vee was carried in a full duplex cradle frame, the front down-tubes passing on each side of the oil container. An oil-bath chain case was fitted, but the clutch was in a separate compartment, so as to be kept clear of oil. One big-end was of the forked type, but both con-rods were entirely separate – each featuring its own pair of roller bearings.

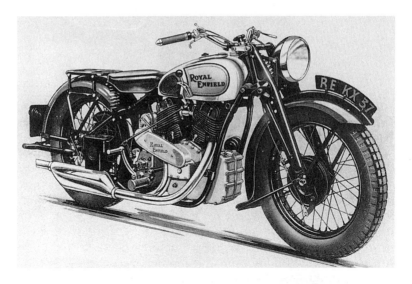

Official factory illustration of the 1937 1,140cc side-valve KX V-Twin with alternative chromium-plated fuel tank.

In January 1935 the Model K 976cc side-valve V-Twin cost £65 17s 6d in solo form. The spec included a four-speed hand-change gearbox and fully enclosed valve gear.

The 1,140cc SV V-Twin was the only one of the larger Royal Enfields on which the magdyno was chain driven (the others being by gears). This lay behind the seat-frame down-tube, with its chain being easily accessible for adjustment.

It also worth noting that at this time Royal Enfield also marketed their own range of side-cars, ranging in price between £15.00 and £25.00, and that the 1937 model range saw wide use being made of an Enfield rubber-mounted handlebar, which permitted the bar to be adjusted for both height and angle.

Two-Valve 500

For 1938, Enfield sold its 500 singles in both four- and two-valve guises – the two-valver being intended as a sporting, well-mannered,

fast roadster capable of 75mph (120km/h), and the four-valve engine giving an additional 5mph. Both were of the twin-port engine type. There was also a new 350 single-port model with enclosed valve gear.

All-Aluminium Bullet

At the 1938 London Earls Court Show, one of the highlights was an all-aluminium 350 Bullet single – the press and public were both smitten. When interviewed in January 1939 about the new design, Enfield's Tony Wilson-Jones said that the reason they chose a 350cc job with an alloy head and barrel was for 'improved cooling, a considerable reduction in weight, and a 350cc because it is probably the most useful size of engine at the present time'.

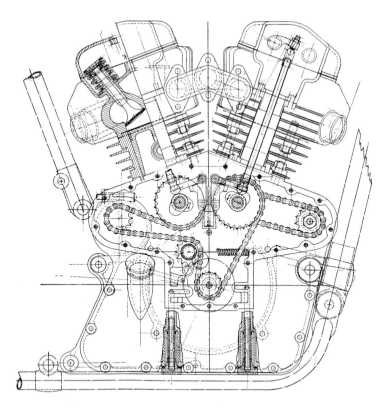

Many designs, although tested, did not reach production status. For example, in 1934 a prototype transverse V-Twin engine of 500cc with shaft drive performed well, but was deemed too expensive. This was then redesigned in 1937 as a 692cc V-Twin with the engine in the conventional position (shown). This latter type employed a chain-driven timing gear that proved utterly reliable. A simplified version of the timing was adopted for the vertical-twin designed after 1945.

The late 1930s 1,140cc side-valve KX V-Twin engine. It featured four oil pumps, all housed in the oblong timing gear cover. The gearbox was a bought-in Albion with Royal Enfield logo.

Explaining the New Design

In many ways the 1939 Bullet 350 was where the origins of the post-war model came from. For example, for the first time it used two rocker boxes. When questioned about this Wilson-Jones replied: 'Well, that involves several points. The wide angle between the valves [90 degrees] necessitates the two rocker boxes, and this same wide angle provides room for the hard valve-sect inserts; it also permits better gas flow and consequently higher volumetric efficiency.'

A Specialized Cylinder

The use of an aluminium cylinder barrel was not entirely new to Royal Enfield, as it had been tested with considerable success on the works' trials machines for the previous two seasons (1937 and 1938). The cylinder was lined with 'Vacrit', and pressed into position – the manufacture of the liner and its insertion being carried out, not by Royal Enfield, but by specialists, Hepworth and Grandage.

Die-Cast Crankcases

Die-castings were employed for the two halves of the crankcase, which included the oil 'container', and the oilways were formed in the castings. A slight taper on the crankshaft flywheel rims caused excess oil to fly off the flywheels into a small sump at their base (not the oil container!).

Heat-Treated Y-Alloy

Both the cylinder and head were of heat-treated Y-alloy (a copper, nickel and aluminium alloy). Both valves were of the semi-tulip shape, designed to permit good gas-flow, and both had a port of opening of 1⅜in (3.5cm) and a lift of ⁵⁄₁₆in (0.8cm). However, whereas the inlet valve was made of KE1029, a silicon–chrome alloy, the exhaust valve was of KE965, which retained much superior tensile strength at high temperature. Both valves operated in phosphor bronze guides and there were dual springs for both valves. The high dome piston, also in Y-alloy, had three rings (two compressors, one oil scraper) and the gudgeon pin operated in a bronze small-end bush.

The single carburettor of the KX engine sits between the vee of the cylinders; other features include primary chain case, massive aluminium crankcase and magdyno behind the rear cylinder.

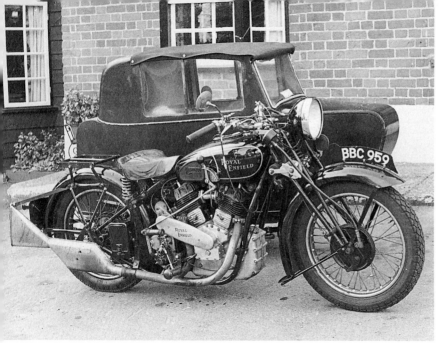

Although available as a solo, Enfield's big V-Twin was really at its best when acting as a sidecar tug. Either way the 1,140cc KX was an imposing motorcycle.

BELOW: *The single-port ohv two-valve Model G was introduced for the 1938 season and in many ways can be considered as the father of the post-war Bullet range.*

Testing the All-Alloy Bullet

When *The Motor Cycle* tested the new all-alloy Bullet 350 in its 6 July 1939 issue, it began by saying: 'Modernity has always been the keynote of Royal Enfield design and the 350cc overhead-valve Bullet is undoubtedly among the out-of-the ordinary machines of today.'

The maximum speed of 69.3mph (111.5km/h) was obtained on a wet track and under gusty wind conditions – the tester saying: 'Given better weather the speeds, at last in top gear, would probably be improved.'

In the areas of starting (hot or cold), comfort, road-holding, clutch operation (light and free from drag), noise and brakes (outstanding), the new Bullet received top marks. The only negative note concerned oil tightness: 'A certain amount of oil leakage took place from the crankcase and the kickstarter, but the top half of the engine remained absolutely dry.' As far as performance, an ability to maintain high cruising was noted:

On the open roads speeds of 60mph [97km/h] and higher could be held indefinitely without any protest from the engine, and the only indication of high revs was a slight fork spring vibration at 60mph. The ability of this engine to withstand full-throttle speeds and indefinitely was extra-ordinary, though probably this characteristic was due in large measure to the light-

alloy cylinder and head, which resulted in remarkably cool running.

The price, in July 1939, including UK taxes, was £63 10s with electric lighting, horn and Smiths speedometer.

War Stops Play

Then in early September 1939, following Germany's invasion of Poland, war was declared – effectively ending normal peacetime pleasures for the next six years. As is related in Chapter 3, Royal Enfield was one of the first British motorcycle factories to put their production over to the War Department (WD), and continued to be a major supplier to the military during the years of conflict.

3 War Department

The Lee Enfield 0.303 rifle is famous the world over – and as explained in Chapter 1, the Royal Enfield brand name did have an association with the gun-making concern during its very earliest days, but otherwise the two are unconnected, except that both were major suppliers to the British War Department (WD) during both World Wars of the twentieth century.

The Motorcycle for Military Use

In years gone by, the horse was the prominent means of transport for troops in the field. However, as the internal combustion engine was developed and became increasingly reliable, so military planners began to appreciate the potential of the motorcycle. As with all new technology, there were those who had a vested interest in maintaining the status quo. The cavalry, in particular, was none too keen, when the motorcycle was considered as a possible substitute for horses. But the advantages of the motorcycle were to be clearly demonstrated during the military manoeuvres that took place in the years preceding the outbreak of the First World War in 1914, resulting in their widespread adoption by various countries such as France, Germany, Austro-Hungary, the USA and Great Britain.

With a slogan 'Built Like a Gun' it was perhaps hardly surprising that Royal Enfield machines were widely used during what was termed as The Great War. The use of motorcycles continued to gain pace as the conflict unfolded. Enfields

A Royal Enfield V-Twin sidecar outfit outside the Redditch factory in 1917 – the sidecar was used as a gun platform. During the First World War, besides the British forces, Royal Enfield motorcycles were also employed by the Belgian and Russian military services.

were often employed as sidecar tugs, notably as machine-gun mounts and for ambulance duties. The Redditch concern even received a contract for its motorcycles from the Russian Government.

The Inter-War Years

During the immediate post-war period, large numbers of military motorcycles were sold as surplus to requirement, in sales throughout Britain. Enfield like other motorcycle marques went back to its civilian customers. The development of military bikes was then largely forgotten until the mid-1930s, when the threat of another world conflict awakened government interest.

Whilst the majority of machines used during the First World War had been ones originally intended for peacetime duties with the general population, now it was often the case that purpose-built bikes were required for military service.

Another trend was that during the Second World War, which began in September 1939, the sidecar was largely replaced (except by the Germans) by four-wheel jeep-type vehicles. Instead the motorcycle was employed as a solo, for duties such as escort, despatch rider (DR) and even, in Royal Enfield's case, a collapsible, disposable lightweight with airborne parachute troops.

The Flying Flea

Although not the most numerous of Royal Enfield's Second World War offerings, the most well-known and best remembered is without doubt the 'Flying Flea'.

The Flea owed its existence to the Germans who, in 1938, had instructed DKW to cancel its Dutch concessionaire, after his company refused to get rid of its Jewish owners, Stokvis and Zonen. Instead the Dutch company simply took an example of the 98cc DKW RT to Enfield, who they asked to make the same machine but with an engine displacing 125cc. Royal Enfield's designer, Ted Pardoe, obliged by building what amounted to a faithful reproduction of the original, right down to the front fork with its rubber bands – and originally used on the mid-1930s works DKW SS250 *renn* racing motorcycle.

The actual mechanics of the Flea (known as the RE125 in its post-war civilian guise) are outlined in Chapter 5, but suffice to say that the engine was of unit construction with a vertically split crankcase containing the three-speed gearbox, as well as the crankshaft. With bore and stroke dimensions of 53.79 × 55mm, the cubic capacity was just under 125cc.

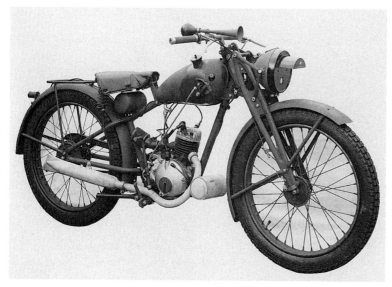

Based on a pre-war German DKW design, Royal Enfield's WD/RE 'Flying Flea' served with the Allied airborne troops on D-Day, being carried into action in both aircraft and gliders, and it proved its worth, with its riders being able to direct operations as required.

A flywheel magneto provided both the ignition and lighting from a pair of coils, whilst the points cam was located at the extreme end of the crankshaft. Gears were selected by hand, whilst the kickstart lever folded away at the exhaust header pipe and the silencer ran along the offside.

On many Fleas, two silencers were employed: the first, a cylindrical device set across in front of the crankcase; and the second, the normal tubular one on the offside. Engine lubrication was by a petrol–oil mixture.

The engine assembly was mounted in an extremely basic tubular rigid frame equipped with blade girder forks, using rubber bands as a suspension medium.

In its military guise, the Flying Flea came with only the most rudimentary of equipment: a saddle, skimpy mudguards, rear carrier, cylindrical toolbox and lighting equipment.

The 'Birdcage'

The 'Birdcage' refers to a steel tubular cage into which the Flea was fitted for its airborne role. A parachute was attached to the cage and, to aid packing, the handlebars turned easily, as they were held by a cycle-type stem bolt, with a built-in wing nut. Its fuel tank cap featured a screw-down vent and so could easily be put into service. Besides its role with paratroops, the tiny Enfield also went into action: it was carried in aircraft and gliders; it was taken aboard tanks to act as a mobile means of transport; and it was even used in beach-landing attacks – particularly the Normandy 'D' Day landings, where its riders were able to direct operations, as required. All-in-all, the Flying Flea – or the land-based Flea – served an important role, which had largely been ignored before the War Department had the idea of employing an ultra-lightweight in the front line and dropping with airborne forces. Actually, this did not occur until 1942 – the tooling for the civilian model having stood in storage since the outbreak of hostilities in the autumn of 1939.

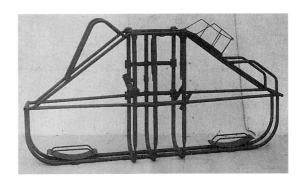

ABOVE RIGHT: The tubular steel 'birdcage' in which the Flying Flea was carried when dropped by parachute.

A 125cc WD/RE two-stroke machine in its tubular crate. To aid packing, the handlebars turned easily, as they were held by a cycle-type stem bolt, with a built-in wing nut. The fuel tank featured a screw-down vent, which could be instantly released when put in service.

Enfield was lucky indeed, as it already had an ideal basis for what the military had in mind on the stocks and little development work was needed to put it into wartime production. Actually, the 'Birdcage' took more time than the actual motorcycle did to transform from civilian commuter to military war-horse (or should that be pony?).

Three-Fifty Singles

The bulk of the 55,000 motorcycles manufactured by Royal Enfield during the war years were of 346cc (70 × 90mm) and based on pre-war models. Two versions were produced, the ohv CO and the less numerous side-valve C; but in reality, apart from the cylinder barrel and head, the two machines were identical.

In traditional Royal Enfield practice, the vertically split crankcases included the oil container for the dry sump system. This meant that, unlike the vast majority of other British four-stroke designs, there was no external, separate oil tank. Other features included: plain small and big-ends, a floating bush being used for the big-end; a train of gears on the offside in the timing chest, which turned the camshafts and drove the mag-dyno assembly, the latter being positioned at the rear of the cylinder barrel. The twin oil pumps (and filters) were located below the crankshaft gear.

The valve gear was fully enclosed on both models, whilst the head and barrel were both manufactured from cast iron. On the overhead-valve engine the one-piece rockers were retained in split clamps, which were assembled on studs beneath an aluminium cover. A plate at the off-side of the cylinder barrel provided access to the tappet adjusters at the lower end of the pushrods; below these were flat-faced tappets. A similar plate on the side-valver did an identical job.

Unlike the later post-war Bullet range, the four-speed foot-operated gearbox (of either Albion or Burman manufacture) was mounted separately on plates, and was chain driven from the engine. It is also worth pointing out that machines fitted with the Burman 'box' lacked the cush-drive centre of the Albion. Burman-equipped CO models were prefixed CO/B.

The ohv CO, in particular, was a good performer and in many ways was a rival to the Matchless G3/L, with one notable exception: suspension. The AMC bike benefited from the addition of the excellent teledraulic front forks, whereas the Redditch-built machine had to make do with girders. It was not until the post-war period that either bike gained rear springing.

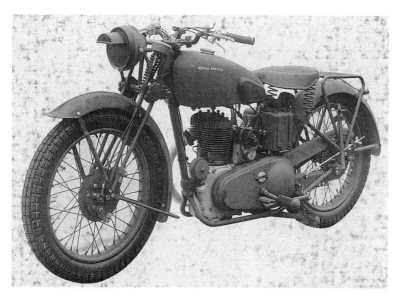

Besides its ohv models, Enfield built a considerable number of the 346cc WD/C side-valve singles during the war period.

One of the WD/CO ohv 346cc singles in full wartime specification, including headlamp blackout, speedometer, air cleaner (canister on top of tank), panniers and pillion pad.

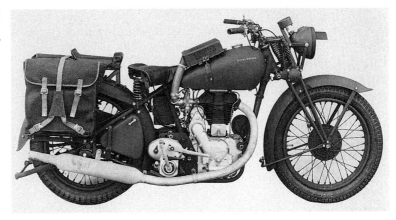

Miscellaneous Offerings

Besides its Flying Flea two-stroke ultra-light-weight and the pair of 350 singles, the Redditch-based company also constructed some 2,000 examples of the 248cc (64 × 77mm) Model D. Intended for training rather than frontline duties, this was another side-valve single and did not have much in the way of performance.

There was also a batch of 570cc Model L side-valvers for the Royal Navy – for shore duties such as communications and escort work.

The remaining military Enfields of the era were prototypes. The most interesting was a 348cc (52 × 82mm) side-valve twin. The appearance of the engine was unconventional to say the least, the two iron cylinders cast as one iron block and laid backwards, even though the fins remained horizontal. Only a single example was built in 1944 and featured the valves, carburettor and exhaust pipes all at the front; the cylinder head gave the appearance of having been laid on at a strange angle – as an afterthought. Unlike other Enfield four-strokes, there was a separate, conventional oil tank outside the engine. The gearbox, a foot-operated Albion four-speeder operated with both drive chains (primary and final) enclosed in a single extended casing, the final (rear) chain being tensioned by a jockey sprocket. The rigid frame had girders up front and 17in (43cm) tyres were employed of exceedingly wide 4.50 section. Development took up several months, but the

twin, together with several single-cylinder prototypes, was not awarded a contract. In addition, a very few WD models were constructed with an early version of the telescopic front fork later adopted for the ohv Model G in the immediate post-war period (*see* Chapter 4).

Other Wartime Products

In addition to producing some 55,000 motorcycles for military service during the Second World War, the Enfield Cycle Company was also called upon by the British authorities to manufacture a variety of special instruments and apparatus to use against enemy forces. They included:

- predictors for use with Bofors anti-aircraft guns;
- oil motors for operating Bofors guns, ship stabilizers, searchlight controls, fuse-setting and the like;
- diesel-engined 5.6KVA generator sets for testing aeroplane and radar equipment;
- gyroscopic sights for Oerlikon and other guns;
- ressetter boxes for gun sights;
- anti-vibration mounts for gun sights;
- armour-piercing shot for 40mm anti-tank guns;
- petrol-driven pump units for operating guns;
- straight-line cams for use in precision instruments;
- self-synchronizing equipment for 40mm guns;
- lag-compensating for self-sectoring equipment for gun sights;
- tubular crates for enclosing motorcycles to be dropped by parachute.

Sterling Service

Generally, the various production military bikes built by Enfield during the Second World War were well received, carrying out vital duties reliably and efficiently. The term 'sterling service' comes to mind as an apt description. Besides the army and navy, the Royal Air Force also used batches of CO ohv and C sv 350 singles. In addition, Royal Enfield was also employed by certain Civil Defence Units, these being mainly employed for communication duties.

An RAF Leading Aircraftman astride a 499cc WD/J2 in May 1941. This machine, developed from the pre-war Model J, featured a twin port ohv single-cylinder engine with foot-change gearbox, girder forks and a rigid frame.

BELOW: *Besides the British Army and Navy, Royal Enfield motorcycles, such as this 500 WD/J2 seen here in the spring of 1941, were also extensively used by the Royal Air Force during the Second World War.*

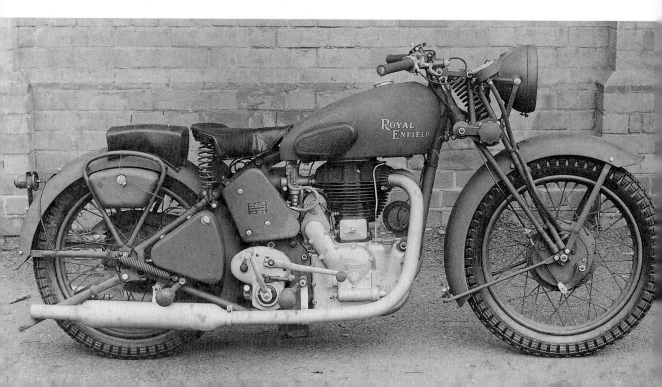

ABOVE: Dispatching a consignment of overhead valve WD/J2 models from Royal Enfield's Redditch works in 1941.

As well as its motorcycle production, Royal Enfield built a wide range of products during the war years, including pedal cycles, armaments and this 250cc twin-cylinder generator assembly.

ABOVE: *A line-up of six 499cc WD/J2 overhead singles at the Redditch works in May 1941.*
BELOW: *Typical immediate post-war advertisement for ex-WD (War Department) motorcycles, Royal Enfield in particular. This advertisement is dated 5 May 1950.*

Into Civvies

Like other British marques, when peace finally came the various ex-WD Royal Enfield machines were sold off to dealers in large numbers, but unusually the factory itself was fully involved and bought back many bikes, which were fully reconditioned and sold to the Enfield dealer network. Why? Well, in a transport-starved post-war Britain, where virtually every newly made motorcycle went for export to earn vital foreign currency for the war-ravaged British economy, anything with an engine and two wheels was saleable.

Thus the advertisements at the rear of either the Blue 'Un (*The Motor Cycle*) or the Green 'Un (*Motor Cycling*) carried masses of trade advertisements with illustrations of the various models, for a machine-hungry public who snapped them up in their thousands. In fact, in Enfield's case, the immediate post-war factory brochures actually carried the reconditioned ex-WD bikes alongside the latest civilian models. Usually these were finished in black with gold lining, with the wheel centres in black to match. Even as late as the early 1950s, this trend continued until sufficient supplies of newly built bikes at last were released for the home market. Then, almost overnight, the ex-WD machines lost favour, many being either run into the ground or simply locked away in the family garden shed and forgotten. The survivors were, like other old bikes, often lovingly restored

as the classic bike scene prospered from the late 1970s onwards. Today, the military motorcycle scene is a thriving niche market, with its own set of enthusiasts, many of whom attend the various military vehicles' rallies held throughout the summer months at various venues.

4   The Post-War Bullet

Without the shadow of a doubt, the most famous name in the history of the Royal Enfield marque is that of the Bullet. The subject of this chapter is the swinging arm Bullet, the first examples coming in February 1948, when the works trials team of Charlie Rogers, George Holdsworth and Jack Plowright made an unannounced debut appearance at the Colmore Cup Trial (*see* Chapter 7) on a trio of brand new machines equipped with oil-damped, pivoted-fork rear suspension. Subsequently to become known as the swinging arm Bullet, successors to these original prototype machines are still being built today, over half a century later, in Madras (Chennai), India.

Origins of the Name

The origin of the Bullet name is however considerably older then its 1948 debut – dating from September 1932, when three new sports models (in 248, 346 and 499cc engine sizes) were added to the Royal Enfield range. Common to all three, even in those early days, were foot-change four-speed gearboxes, which embodied an external gear-position indicator, an oil compartment integral with the crankcase, dry-sump lubrication and, naturally, the rubber block cush-drive rear hub pioneered by Royal Enfield in their Model 180 V-twin of 1912. Chilled-iron valve guides, and nitrided valve stems, were features very much in advance of contemporary motorcycle engineering.

The Model G

That 1932 Bullet series, however, featured an inclined cylinder, exposed valve gear, Pilgrim oil pump and chain-driven magneto; so, for the true ancestor of the post-war model, it is necessary to turn to the 346cc (70 × 90mm) Model G, first revealed to the public in August 1935.

Features of the newcomer included a vertical cylinder, cast-in pushrod tunnel, totally enclosed valve gear, magneto driven via a train of gears, and a unique double-ended eccentric oil pump. This then was the starting point for the engine assembly that was eventually to form the basis of the military WD/G and WD/CO models during the Second World War and, indeed, the Model G, which was to resume peacetime production after the end of the war.

Post-War Production Begins

When Royal Enfield announced its peacetime production plans in the autumn of 1945, it was seen that, besides the 'Flying Flea' RE 125cc two-stroke, initial production would be centred around a pair of ohv singles, based on the WD/CO 350, one having a 346cc engine, the other a 499cc unit; these being coded Model G and J, respectively.

A New Alloy Connecting Rod

The main alteration to the Model G three-fifty, as compared to the earlier engines, was the floating of a new RR56 bush in the big-end eye, and, as the bearing between and the crankpin, a floating bush of aluminium-tin alloy. A feature of the newly revised engine was its remarkably low vibration figures. The big-end bush, crankpin and connecting rod assembly is illustrated on page 37.

Telescopic Front Forks

But the really big news was the new hydraulically damped telescopic front forks. Having a stanchion (fork tube) diameter of 1⁷⁄₁₆in (3.65cm), these provided a total movement of 6in (15.25cm). The bottom members (sliders) carried the wheel spindle in

Making their debut in the autumn of 1945, at least on civilian models, Royal Enfield's own designed and manufactured telescopic front fork placed the Redditch marque at the very forefront of motorcycle design. The forks shown here are fitted to a 1948 Model G.

a split-clamp type of fixing arranged at the front of the fork (leading axle type), which, apart from the question of the spacing of the fork bearings, enabled the Enfield design team to fit drain plugs – acting as level plugs – at the base of each leg.

As can be seen from the drawing of a fork leg (*see* page 36), the main spring was anchored at both the top and the bottom and had a guide member – a fibre-block 'steady' bush – screwed into the spring halfway up. Screwed into the base of each stanchion was the valve port and passing back and forth through this, as the forks operated, was a rod, drilled down the middle and anchored, at the top end, to the spring by means of a scroll and stud. This rod was provided with a double taper on its exterior. On the lower portion there was a longer slow taper. This, of course, was for absorbing the impact; as the fork closed up, so the passage for oil through the valve port was gradually closed. The part of the rod that occupied the valve port with the forks in their normal, static-loaded position was parallel, so there was a relatively free movement at 'dead centre' and the forks thus reacted to minor road irregularities (the drawing on page 36 shows the forks in this position). Immediately above this position there was a steep taper, a very short one, in the opposite direction; for the rebound. The forks were filled with oil up to the level of the slantwise hole immediately above the steep taper.

The oil was poured into the fork leg at the top after removal of an acorn-type nut. The oil in each leg was filtered via a multi-thickness gauze. In addition to acting as a filter for the oil, this gauze filtered the air; when the forks operated there was a displacement of air. The Enfield design team had provided for this by incorporating a breather system. Before this arrived, during early testing, particles of dirt were found in the oil following a dusty run. At the top of the damper rod was a simple type of flap valve – on rebound, oil was forced through this valve – the tapers on the rod being determined after considerable experimentation. The result of Enfield's work was one of the most effective of all early telescopic fork designs.

NOVEMBER 27, 1947.

MOTOR CYCLING

READ WHEREVER
MOTORCYCLES
ARE RIDDEN

Editor:
GRAHAM WALKER

FEATURES OF *Exclusive* ROYAL ENFIELD DESIGN

★ THE ROYAL ENFIELD
PATENT
NEUTRAL FINDER

The Royal Enfield Patent Neutral Finder removes the one possible objection to the modern foot-operated gear control — the difficulty sometimes experienced in finding neutral.

Without affecting the normal action of the foot-control this device enables neutral to be "selected" instantly and positively from top, third or second gears. The clutch has only to be lifted and the Neutral Finder pedal pressed firmly against its stop. . The neutral position thus found is the normal one between bottom and second gears so that the rider is all set to engage bottom gear when he wishes to move off again.

Royal Enfield

Enfield's exclusive patented neutral finder – from a 1947 advertisement.

A 1948 advertisement showing the Model G 350 single with telescopic forks, rigid frame and iron head and barrel. Also shown is the company's famous 'Made Like a Gun' trademark.

"THE END OF YOUR QUEST!"
Royal Enfield

The Really New Motorcycle

This is the Royal Enfield " 350 Bullet " Standard Model, and here are some of the Exclusive Royal Enfield features which make it so much of a success.

1 DETACHABLE REAR MUDGUARD which gives access to the whole of the tyre without removing wheel from frame when dealing with a puncture.

2 SPRING FRAME. Without increasing wheel base or weight, the Royal Enfield Spring Frame supplies perfect lateral rigidity and does not impose a strain on wheel spindle. It provides the rider with smooth speed and cushion comfort.

3 AIR CLEANER. Clean air is supplied to the carburetter by its passage through this scientifically designed air cleaner. This ensures long life for the cylinder and piston.

4 NEUTRAL FINDER. Foot pressure on lever enables "neutral" to be positively selected from second gear when the machine is at rest, or from top, third or second gear when the machine is moving.

PRICE: 350 c.c. BULLET, £140 . 0 . 0.   Plus Purchase Tax, £37 . 16 . 0.

THE ENFIELD CYCLE CO LTD. Head Office & Works. REDDITCH.
LONDON SHOWROOMS AND SPARES DEPOT. 221. TOTTENHAM COURT ROAD. W.I.

A December 1949 advertisement showing the recently released ohv Bullet roadster. The four key features of its design (from factory eyes at least) were: detachable rear mudguard, spring frame, air cleaner and neutral finder.

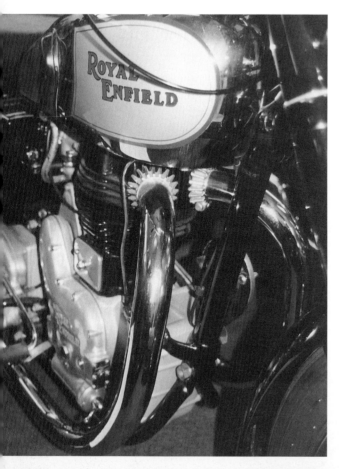

ABOVE: *Manufactured in-house, the Enfield telescopic front forks were hydraulically damped, featuring a breather at the top of each fork leg; its operation is described in the main text.*

LEFT: *Close-up of the model J2 power unit, showing to advantage the twin-port, twin-exhaust layout of this big single.*

BELOW: *The twin-port 499cc ohv Model J2 of 1949. Except for its civilian paint job, chromium plate and polished alloy, plus teles, it is almost the same bike that was supplied to the military during World War Two.*

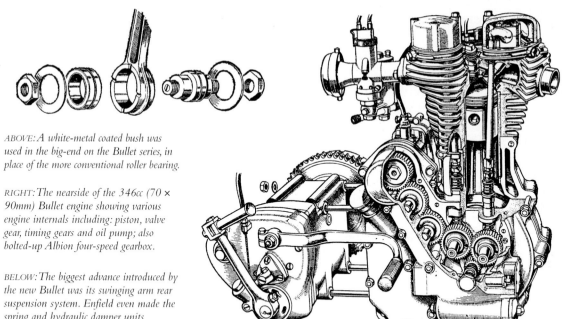

ABOVE: *A white-metal coated bush was used in the big-end on the Bullet series, in place of the more conventional roller bearing.*

RIGHT: *The nearside of the 346cc (70 × 90mm) Bullet engine showing various engine internals including: piston, valve gear, timing gears and oil pump; also bolted-up Albion four-speed gearbox.*

BELOW: *The biggest advance introduced by the new Bullet was its swinging arm rear suspension system. Enfield even made the spring and hydraulic damper units themselves.*

Neutral Selector

An interesting feature of the new models was the first use of the now familiar Enfield neutral finder. This was essentially an over-riding control, which enabled the rider to go from top, third or second gear to neutral simply by pressing down a pedal. This pedal was mounted on the end of the shaft to which the gear indicator was attached – the gear selector shaft. However, with this system it was not possible to select neutral whilst in bottom gear.

Compared to the military model with its girder forks, the new telescopic fork equipment three-fifty Model G was lighter – 356lb (161kg) against 358lb (162kg). In this guise, except for very minor charges, the G Model remained until the G2 (the Bullet) made is bow in 1948 (the G was finally discontinued in 1954).

The New Bullet Arrives

After making its debut as a works trials mount, the production swinging arm Bullet, the G2 debuted towards the end of 1948. And although it might have resembled the existing Model G, it was in many ways a new motorcycle, and one which was to outlive every other British competitor.

Designer Tony Wilson-Jones spent some four years conceiving the swinging arm Bullet and it was to be his and Royal Enfield's crowning achievement. What made the post-war Bullet such an outstanding design was its ability, as Don Morley once described it, 'to plonk and go'; in other words, the Enfield single had both torque and power, and thus rates up there with the two other immortal British singles of the same era: the BSA Gold Star and Velocette. But perhaps the

---

1949 Bullet 350

Engine	Air-cooled overhead-valve semi-unit construction, single with vertical cylinder, alloy head, cast-iron cylinder
Bore	70mm
Stroke	90mm
Displacement	346cc
Compression ratio	6.5:1
Lubrication	Dry sump
Ignition	Lucas magdyno
Carburettor	Amal 1in (2.5cm) 276
Primary drive	Duplex chain
Final drive	Chain
Gearbox	Albion, four-speed, foot-change
Frame	All steel, tubular construction
Front suspension	Royal Enfield telescopic forks
Rear suspension	Swinging arm, Royal Enfield hydraulic units
Front brake	Drum 6in (15cm)
Rear brake	Drum 6in (15cm)
Tyres	3.25 × 19 front and rear
General Specifications	
Wheelbase	54in (1372mm)
Ground clearance	6¼in (159mm)
Seat height	29½in (749mm)
Fuel tank capacity	3½gal (16ltr)
Dry weight	350lb (158kg) with oil and 1gal (4.5ltr) petrol
Maximum power	18bhp @ 5,750rpm
Top speed	74mph (119km/h)

Swinging Arm Experiments

The question of rear suspension at Royal Enfield had received attention even before the outbreak of the Second World War and in the spring of 1939, a prototype machine was produced with short leaf springs forming extensions to the normal chainstays and backstays. These springs were connected by plates carrying the wheel spindle so arranged that the latter moved in an arc, thus maintaining constant chain tension.

Originally rubber bushes were employed at the pivot points but these imparted, as Enfield designer Tony Wilson-Jones revealed in 1958, 'a jelly-like feeling to the handling', and were replaced by phosphor bronze bushes. Further experience showed that the short leaf springs were over-stressed, but even so, actual suspension at the rear end was good enough, whilst it lasted, to show up deficiencies of the link-type front forks in much the same way as the vastly superior telescopic front forks provided post-war revealed shortcomings of the unsprung (rigid) frame.

In early 1946, Wilson-Jones and his team of engineers created another form of rear suspension. This featured two short swinging arms carrying the rear spindle and joined together by a U-shaped member butting against the end of a large leaf-spring mounted parallel to the seat-frame tube of the machine.

In combination with telescopic front forks this gave an excellent ride, but Wilson-Jones always 'had a feeling that the design was wrong somewhere' and was therefore 'not sorry' when the seat tube broke close to the clamping point of the leaf spring and the project was abandoned.

At this time, the majority of motorcycles in production embodying any form of rear suspension used plunger-type springing and there was, as Wilson-Jones described it, 'a strong demand at a high level [the directors] to use this type on the Royal Enfield machines'. However, Wilson-Jones was convinced (largely by a paper by Phil Irving – an Australian who worked for several firms including Vincent) that this type of springing was inferior in every way to the swinging arm variety – the latter not only provided a much larger range of movement and reduced flexing stress on the rear-wheel spindle, but also called for less accuracy in manufacture of component parts.

Originally the damper units (or 'spring boxes' as they were called in the 1940s) were made at the Enfield Redditch works. However, these assemblies were to prove a problem. Actually there were several types. The first used the spring in tension as well as compression and aimed at progressive hydraulic damping on the bump stroke only, whilst the second (later) version employed the spring on compression only, providing hydraulic damping on the rebound stroke, so, and again to quote Tony Wilson-Jones, 'we wisely decided that the manufacture of hydraulic damper units was the job for the specialist [either Armstrong or Girling]' and called on the services of the proprietary manufactures.

With swinging arm rear suspension, as with so many new innovations in the first half of the twentieth-century motorcycle industry, Royal Enfield was a true pioneer. Whilst Enfield was creating, developing and putting into production such a major advance in motorcycle design, the likes of BSA, Norton and Triumph were largely content with the status quo.

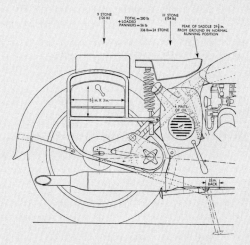

Drawing of the experimental 'short-arm' rear suspension tested by Royal Enfield in 1946.

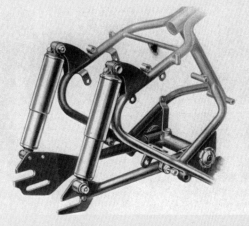

The swinging arm rear suspension adopted for production by Royal Enfield after making its debut on a trio of trials machines in the Colmore Trial during early 1948.

RE's biggest plus was that the Bullet was created as a 350, not a 500. This meant it was 30lb (13.5kg) lighter than the AJS/Matchless ohv single (swinging arm models) and 60lb (27kg) lighter than BSA's swinging arm B31, which arrived in 1956. In fact, except for the Bullet, virtually every other British heavyweight single was conceived as a five-hundred – hence the additional pounds in weight.

A Brilliant All-Rounder

As with BSA's Gold Star, the Enfield Bullet was a brilliant all-rounder – roadster, trials iron, scrambler and even racer – it could perform all these tasks with an ability few others could match. The prototype machines, which had made their debut in the Colmore Trial during February 1948, had caused a sensation by their use of swinging arm rear suspension, then unheard of for trials use (although Irishman Billy Nicholson's McCandless rear suspension BSA had put up some good performances). The other works teams such as BSA, AMC and Norton were still wedded to rigid frames for their mud pluggers.

As described in Chapter 7 (*see* page 90), the Bullet also proved its worth in the ISDT in 1948, not only winning gold medals, but also being part of the victorious British Trophy Squad.

Fundamental Differences

Although the factory trails prototypes had much in common with what had gone before, this was very much related to details, rather than major features. For example, the oil pump layout remained the same, as did the dry sump oil container in the crankcases – and the use of an Albion-made gearbox. However, the big items were not – compactness being a major priority, together with comfort and handling.

Even though the bore and stroke remained unchanged at 70 × 90mm and the alloy con-rod, the layout of the timing gears running up to a rear mounted magneto, together with the duplex oil pumps and filtering system remained the same, this could not be said of the crankcase – for the oil compartment was now behind the crankshaft flywheel chamber, with the filter neck and cap for the oil relocated to the rear of the timing cover, instead of its previous forward location.

Unlike the existing Model G (which was to continue in production until 1954), the original Bullet prototypes featured an aluminium cylinder with a cast-iron liner. This was deeply spigoted into the crankcases – so far in fact that the barrel joint was above the tappet inspection plate and the latter item became attached to the crankcase rather then the barrel, as on the earlier engines.

The timing gear remained the same with flat-footed tappets operating in pressed-in guides to operate aluminium pushrods with hardened ends and screw-type adjusters. In his redesign, Wilson-Jones had made detail changes to the timing pinion and oil-pump worm, both of which were machined as part of the mainshaft, which was keyed into the flywheel and held to its taper by a nut. He also recast the timing cover, there now being a bulge to allow for the auto-advance mechanism to be fitted to the magneto drive pinion, if required. Although on the works trials' bikes a racing-type magneto was specified, Wilson-Jones had left enough space to enable a magdyno on the forthcoming street version.

The crankshaft flywheels were polished steel running on a plain phosphor bronze bush on the timing side and a couple of ball race bearings on the drive side. The latter side of the crankcase was webbed internally to provide additional strength and to ensure that the bearing housing was rigid enough for sustained competition usage.

An Aluminium Head

Like the cylinder barrel, the head was of alloy, the latter featuring cast-iron valve seats. The barrel and head were held down by five long studs in the crankcase, supplemented by a case to barrel fixing between the pushrods and another above it from the cylinder to the head. The valves featured hardened caps and operated in pressed-in phosphor bronze guides and used duplex coil springs retained by collars and cotters. Each valve had its own rocker cover, with one-piece rockers.

On the Model G there was a single oil connection, whereas in the G2 Bullet the pipe was fitted with a tee-junction, thus branching out to supply each valve's rocker spindle.

Lubrication

The new Bullet's lubrication system was conventional Enfield practice and the breather worked through the drive-side mainshaft, which contained a non-return disc valve, but not in the primary chaincase. The engine sprocket nut featured an extension that mated up with a recess in the chaincase cover – from this a drilled passage led downwards through the cover wall to the atmosphere.

The Gearbox Mounting

Designer Wilson-Jones had already shortened the crankcase assembly by transferring the oil container and repositioning the filler neck to suit. But he went a stage further in creating a more compact motorcycle, by giving the rear of the crankcase a flat face and mounting the Albion gearbox housing flush against this – thus doing away with the traditional spacing of the gearbox found on most British bikes, including earlier Enfields, up to that time.

There was a quartet of long mounting studs locating and bolting the gearbox to the crankcase assembly. Thus the Bullet became a semi-unit construction (a design feature also found on the twin cylinder range), with fixed chain centres so the primary drive was by a duplex chain with a slipper tensioner running in a two-piece aluminium chaincase (also copied with the twins). This assembly was sealed at the joint by a circular rubber gasket, which was fitted into a groove in the rear section, whilst the outer casing was retained by a single bolt.

The Clutch

The Bullet's clutch featured Ferodo-made discs riveted to the sprocket drum, and three plates with cork inserts. This was operated, not by the traditional Enfield long lever, but by a quick thread worm, the assembly being secured to the outside of the gearbox outer cover. As for the gearbox itself, on the original prototype machines the neutral selector lever had been dispensed with.

The Swinging Arm Frame

Tony Wilson-Jones had not simply been at work on the power unit, but the bike as a whole. He already had the recently introduced telescopic front forks, so his attention was levelled at the frame.

The old rigid frame (Enfield never produced a plunger, unlike Norton, BSA and Ariel, for example) was deemed out of date, so a new assembly with swinging arm rear suspension was created. This featured single top and front down-tubes, the latter ending in a small cross-tube to which the tops of the front engine plates were located. These (on the trials prototypes) were combined with a substantial underside bashplate and to further plates and a cross-bolt, which passed through the base of the gearbox shell. A single saddle tube supported a further cross-section tube, which featured end-plates that attached to the top of the gearbox.

The rear loops ran from a junction of the saddle and top tubes out and rearwards to support the top of the Enfield-made rear shock absorbers (featuring silent bloc bushes) before turning downwards to pass beneath the swinging arm pivot point and on to join the rear engine plates. Bracing tubes ran from just above the fork pivot to the saddle tube and plates in the resulting area supported the swinging arm itself. This was a formed steel casting onto which was brazed the pair of tapered swinging arm legs, the whole assembly pivoting on plain phosphor bronze bushes on a hardened steel spindle.

At the front were the aforementioned telescopic forks, whilst both wheels sported single-sided Enfield-made brakes with 6in (15cm) drums. The rear hub had the standard Enfield cush-drive; chain adjustment being carried out by serrated snail cams either side of the wheel spindle. The front tyre was 21in (53cm) and rear 18in (46cm).

On the prototypes, knobbly competition tyres were specified, whilst the gearing was for trials use – the ISDT mounts differing in detail. And, in truth, there were still some areas under development during that year, but by the time the 1949 model range was announced, not only had the specification been finalized, so the company could announce a roadster, but there was a whole range of Bullets available in various guises including trials and scrambles trim (later a racing variant would be added).

To achieve this diverse selection, although the same basic package was used throughout, there were varying details to such items as compression ratio, gearing, tyres, exhaust and wheel sizes.

An Iron Instead of Alloy Cylinder

One area that did see modification between the works development trials machines and the production bikes was the cylinder barrel, which was changed from alloy to cast iron. This was because the weight saving of the aluminium component with its iron liner, compared to an all-iron one, was minimal; and because of the exceptionally deep spigot. Cooling was improved by continuing the barrel fins onto the crankcase mouth.

The roadster version of the Bullet employed the existing front mudguard headlamp and air cleaner from the Model G plus 3.25 × 19 tyres on both wheels; this first version also had a swept-up exhaust (later the production roadster was to have a flat type). In addition the roadster was the only one of the 1949 Bullet range to feature a neutral selector mechanism. The road-going model was also equipped, as standard, with a pair of toolboxes (one each side), and centre and prop stands. The roadster also had a magdyno, whereas the competition versions had a racing magneto (Enfield offered trials customers the option of ordering their motorcycle with the roadsters magdyno and lights – at extra cost).

The trials bike featured wide ratio gears, a high-level exhaust and a carb inlet shield in place of the air cleaner. Other trials model details included different mudguards (in aluminium), tyres and security bolts on both wheels.

For scrambling, a straight-through exhaust pipe was fitted, together with ultra-lightweight guards (different again from the trials version), a close ratio gear cluster, motocross tyres and a choice of no less than three different compression ratios. All three 1949 Bullets cost £171 9s including UK purchase tax.

'Long-Type' Dynamo

For the 1950 model year, the Enfield development team decided to fit a new 'long-type' dynamo, which allowed a greater output to be generated (between 45 and 60W). In addition, there was now a polished aluminium speedometer console panel; forged front fork ends, which were now welded (not screwed) to their sliders; the front mudguard was changed from one featuring valances to one with a deep single section; and an upswept silencer of more cylindrical appearance.

More changes arrived for the 1951 season. The plain timing side-bearing bush was supplemented by a single row caged roller race located inboard of the aforementioned bush. Whilst the oil-pump worm, previously integral with the timing side mainshaft, was now detachable. The timing pinion, also previously integral, was now keyed onto the shaft by the internally-threaded oil-pump worm.

In mid-year, the oil feed, previously delivered to the big-end on the pump's delivery stroke and the piston skirt on the return stroke, was delivered to the big-end on both strokes, thus improving lubrication to this vital component.

'A Cobby Five-Hundred'

The Motor Cycle in the 20 November 1952 Earls Court Show issue, referred to Royal Enfield's new, larger Bullet as 'a cobby five-hundred for the sportsman'. Actually, it had already been on sale in export markets for several months. This was an important step in the evolution of the Bullet, as several of the upratings done for the bigger engine were also introduced into the 350 production.

For a start, the 350 engine sprocket became a splined fit on the drive-side crank mainshaft instead of a taper and key. This move also entailed a revision of the crankcase breather. Previously, with the engine breathing through the mainshaft, it had been found to promote clutch-plate sticking problems, caused through oil fumes leaking into the primary chaincase; also crankcase pressure build-up tended to cause oil leaks. To solve these glitches, there was now a separate disc-type breather with a banjo union, fitted to the nearside of the crankcases, with oil-mist directed in the area of the final drive chain. In addition, the oil return pipe and plug in the crankcase base now incorporated an oil non-return valve where, previously, the plug had been.

Also the drive-side main bearings previously fitted a spacer between outer, fixed ports only. Now a spacing tube was fitted between the sprocket and outer main bearing, with a large diameter bore cork washer running on this instead of the axle. The outer bearing was now located by a circlip, and a thrust washer fitted between the inner main bearing and crank flywheel.

Frank Sheene, father of double 500cc World Champion Barry, on Quarter Bridge Road in the 1952 Junior Clubman's TT – 350 Bullet-mounted Frank finished 60th.

The 350 Bullet engine, circa 1953, with rear-mounted magdyno for sparks and lighting; note also the aluminium head and cast-iron cylinder barrel.

TOP: *The metal tank badge gave the early Bullet models a quality feel.*

ABOVE: *A 1955 350 Bullet with double-sided aluminium front brake and optional factory soft panniers. Note casquette-type headlamp with small sidelights.*

Shared Components

On both the 500 and 350 Bullet models there were some components that were new for 1953 and shared by both models. A visual feature was the new design of tank badge; this was in the shape of a wing and was both chrome plated and painted – previously there had simply been a Royal Enfield logo on either side of the petrol tank. The front brakes of both the 350 and 500 sported floating cam spindles, whilst the Enfield-made rear shocks were no longer equipped with a drain plug at their base.

For the 500 Only

The most important improvement between the 350 and the 500 was the latter's larger 7in (18cm) rear brake. Smaller features only found on the bigger Bullet included a new rear number plate with a Lucas stop-tail light and red reflector – the stop-light switch being housed in the nearside toolbox. Finally, the headlamp featured an under-slung pilot light.

Testing the 1953 500 Bullet

When *The Motor Cycle* published a road test of the new 500 Bullet on 30 July 1953, they found it offered 'a loping gait' and 'as a result of the engine's excellent torque and flywheel characteristics, main-road cruising speeds were effortlessly maintained on average gradients without the need for appreciable increase in throttle opening'. Furthermore, 'with the exception of a slight period from 60 to 65mph, there was no perceptible engine vibration'. This lack of vibes on the 500 Bullet (and to an even greater extent on the 350 version) is, in the author's opinion, one of the Redditch-built motorcycle's most endearing features, comparing most favourably as it does when mentioning the likes of Ariel, AMC (AJS and Matchless), BSA and Norton singles of the same era.

The Motor Cycle test lavished praise on the handling of the machine, saying: 'The steering of the Bullet was first class, being precise and rock steady at all times. At high or low speeds the machine could be banked over without the least tendency for the front wheel to waver; in strong, gusty winds, and on wet city cobbles, stability was of a high order.'

The suspension, both front and rear 'were somewhat hard by modern standards' but, 'the degree of comfort was improved when a pillion passenger was carried'.

The Motor Cycle achieved a maximum speed of 78mph (125km/h), and 60mpg (4.72ltr/100km) at a steady 60mph (96km/h).

Features that received criticism concerned the clutch (a shade heavy in operation) and a front brake that required adjustment 'after extended heavy usage', whilst 'at the conclusion of 1,500miles [2,414km] of hard riding the exhaust pipe had blued considerably near the port and slight oily messiness was apparent around the oil-filter cap'. From the author's own experiences with the early single side brakes fitted to both the 500 and 350 Bullet models, these were without doubt the weakest features of the whole design. It is also worth mentioning that the original Enfield India 350 used these brakes – with the same poor performance.

The Casquette Arrives

A notable feature of the 1954 Bullet singles was the arrival of the now famous Royal Enfield casquette, with twin pilot lights. This encased both the speedometer and headlamp assemblies. Another notable change was from Enfield's own rear suspension units to bought-in Armstrong components.

For the 500 only, a stiffened-up swinging-arm was now fitted, the previous bracing tubes and welded-in steel gusset plates being replaced by brazed-on malleable lugs. Also only on the 500, there was an aluminium centre stand.

Meanwhile the 350 was given the cast-aluminium front-fork sliders (which had already been fitted to the 500 and the twin-cylinder models.)

From mid-1954, from gearbox numbers 39654 (350) and 40212 (500), the gearbox end cover was tidied up, whilst the rear pedal and kickstart crank were positioned on a co-axial shaft. Finally, the

previous worm-gear operation of the clutch pushrod was replaced by a clutch fulcrum lever enclosed within the cover.

An Extensive Range

When the 1955 Enfield range was announced during October 1954, *The Motor Cycle* described it as 'extensive', going on the say: 'In the comprehensive range of Royal Enfield models are machines to suit the requirements of almost every type of rider. The choice is wide indeed, ranging as it does from a one-fifty two-stroke to a 692cc overhead-valve vertical twin, and the variety is such that the utility rider, the tourist, the sporting rider, the sidecar man and competition enthusiast are all catered for.'

Dual Front Stopper

The really big news for the Bullet singles was the adoption of the 6in (15cm) dual front brakes; previously only available on the 672cc Meteor Twin as standard equipment, although they were listed as a cost option for 1954 on the Bullet series.

The hub employed two separate cast-aluminium drums, each of which incorporated a spoke flange and with a cast-in, chromidium–iron insert to provide the braking surface. Both drums were pressed over a tubular steel sleeve, which housed the ball-journal wheel bearings. The brake plates were in die-cast aluminium alloy and were provided with anchor slots. Compensated twin cables, operated from a single handlebar control, actuated the cam levers. Besides giving a larger braking area than the previous single-sided cast-iron hub, an added advantage, or so Enfield claimed, was that the dual brakes provided better directional stability under heavy braking than a single brake. This was correct, providing that both brakes operated together; unfortunately on many machines this was not to be the case. However, when the dual unit was set-up properly, the results could be extremely promising by the standards of the time.

There were also a number of detail changes on the 1955 346cc and 499cc Bullet models. To enable full advantage of improved quality fuels, the smaller engine had been given a compression ratio of 7.25:1, compared to the previous 6.5:1. Redesigned cams, incorporating quietening ramps, were fitted in both engines, resulting in a marked decrease of mechanical noise. On both bikes, too, there was a new air cleaner, within an oval container, a new dual seat as standard equipment, whilst the frame was modified in the area of the swinging arm pivot.

The 350 was given the aluminium centre stand of the 500. Then, in March 1955, on the 500 only, a full-width rear hub and QD wheel (from the twins), together with a revised rear chainguard were fitted.

A Revised Cylinder Head

From June 1955, a revised cylinder head was designed for the 350, with the inlet valve size increased to 1⁹⁄₁₆in (4cm), gas-flowed inlet port, the valve seat radiused into the port and with the throat of the valve blended into the port. At the same time the previous stub fitting of the exhaust header pipe was changed to a push-in fit.

1956: A Year of Major Change

Compared to what had gone on in recent years in the evolution of the Bullet range, 1956 was to prove a major landmark, with a myriad of modifications and innovations.

- From engine numbers 38101 (350) and 14194 (500), there came a new, lighter, higher, all-welded frame, together with a wider swinging arm (the latter to permit the fitment of a wider section rear tyre).
- A large, pressed steel box with detachable side panels contained a Vokes air filter element, tool kit and battery.
- Amal 376 and 389 Monobloc carburettors for the 350 and 500 models, respectively.
- A boxed-in rear number plate.
- Revised dual seat, slimmer and raised at the rear, and attached to a tubular loop.
- Lucas SRI magneto and 70W crankshaft-mounted alternator in a revised primary chaincase. These replaced the previous mag-dyno assembly.
- Combined horn and dipswitch on handlebar.
- Folding kickstart lever.
- Full-width QD rear wheel, previously standard on 500, now only optional on both 350 and 500. Revised rear chainguard to suit.
- Size of tappet feet increased and tappets changed from two-piece to one-piece.
- Small oval 'Royal Enfield' plate on timing side outer casing, replaced previous stamped-in 'Royal Enfield'.
- Plastic circular winged tank badges and revised knee grips, now plain; and a revised fuel tank mounting; screw-in chromed side panels for tank sides.

For the 350 Bullet Only

The smaller Bullet's engine was strengthened and brought into line with the 500. Externally, the oil container was given finning, whilst internally the 350 crank flywheels were now spaced further apart, and the nuts securing them changed from the original ¾ Whitworth to the slimmer, smaller diameter ¹¹⁄₁₆ Whitworth. As with the ⅝ of 500, the engine sprocket became a parallel press fit from the inside of the flywheel, with a locating key and flange at the inner end (on both engine sizes the outer end now carried an extension for the newly introduced alternator rotor). The width of the big-end bearing was increased from ¾in (2cm) to the 1in (2.5cm) of the 500. The main bearings became an inner roller (now a non-lipped component), plus outer ball on the timing side again, as on the larger engine. The timing side's plain out-rigger bearing stayed in place – its function mainly being to act as a seal to stop oil drawing from the timing cover into the crankcase. It should be noted that the connecting rods of the two engines remained different to each other. Also, the 350's oil pump cover changed in shape from rectangular to oval – as it had been on the 500 from the beginning – with the retaining screws down from six to four. With the same pump as the 500, the 350 bottom end became one of the most robust in the business.

It is also worth saying that the 1956 350 Bullet was virtually as quick as the 500 (both around 80mph or 129km/h flat out). The main difference between the two units was a need to rev on the smaller engine, whilst the 500 gave a much lazier ride. However many, including the author, prefer the smaller Bullet, thanks to its sweeter nature. As for prices, the 350 Bullet came out at £204, the 500 version £12 more at £216; both figures including UK purchase tax. Production of trials, scrambles and short-circuit racing versions was still continued.

Minimal Changes

After such a busy development period leading up to the launch of the 1956 Bullet range, it was perhaps unsurprising that the following year, 1957, there was very little change.

The only change made was that the previous policy of offering the QD rear wheel incorporating a full-width alloy hub and chromium-plated tank side-panels as cost options was altered to include them as part of the standard specification.

In addition, the former circular pattern air filter was superseded by a larger, more efficient D-shape device. There was no doubting that by now the Bullets were amongst the most attractive of all the more sporting British singles. Perhaps they did not have the glamour of the BSA Gold Star or the charisma of the new Velocette Viper/Venom, but nonetheless they were fine motorcycles. And they were, in general, reliable, hard wearing bikes too, the best of the entire Royal Enfield range.

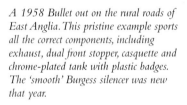

ABOVE RIGHT: Geoffrey Hay with the sole Dreamliner prototype built in 1956; this used a 350 Bullet as its base. Tests indicated a maximum speed improvement of 11 per cent and a 30 per cent average greater fuel economy, but its futuristic looks meant that the less radical Airflow was adopted a couple of years later.

A 1958 Bullet out on the rural roads of East Anglia. This pristine example sports all the correct components, including exhaust, dual front stopper, casquette and chrome-plated tank with plastic badges. The 'smooth' Burgess silencer was new that year.

The 1958 Bullet was an attractive motorcycle, and it seems a pity that this model was not selected for production in India instead of the 1955 series.

This photograph clearly shows Bullet details such as the tappet inspection cover, oil filler cap, kickstart/gear levers and the neutral finder.

A feature of the late 1950s/early 1960s Royal Enfield models was the famous casquette, which held the instrumentation and lighting equipment; it was a contemporary of the Triumph nacelle. Also evident in this view are the dual front-brake compensator and other controls including the choke lever.

Details in this close-up of a 1958 Bullet front wheel, include aluminium full-width dual front brake, mudguard stays and leading axle front forks.

The minimal changes policy largely continued for 1958. The only mechanical update came in the shape of the gearbox sleeve gear being modified from a plain steel to a bushed component. Cosmetically, there was a new 'smooth' shape Burgess silencer (shared with the twins), saddle portions of the dual seat were now highlighted by the use of white piping and a new type of Armstrong-made rear shock absorber was fitted (but still non-adjustable).

The 'Bighead'

The next big update of the Bullet series came for the 1959 model year, and chief amongst these was a new cylinder head for the 500. Known as the 'Big Head', due to its bigger appearance, the design of the rocker gear no longer resembled that of the 350 in which the rocker arms were integral with their spindles and these spindles operated in split bearings. Instead, the redesigned head featured bushed rockers which operated on shafts located between the rocker-box walls, lubricating oil being fed to the shaft ends by external pipes. Small inspection covers replaced the earlier rocker-box components. The new cylinder head embodied a down-draught inlet tract, inclined to the right (offside) of the machine at an angle of 18 degrees from the longitudinal centre line, and the inlet valve head

For the 1959 model year, the 350 Bullet received revised engine internals, 7in (18cm) brakes, both single-sided, full width aluminium hubs, 17in (18cm) wheels, larger tank and chromium-plated mudguards.

In 1959 the 500 Bullet gained a new alloy cylinder head with cast-in rocker boxes (called the 'Big Head') and then, in 1960, the adoption of coil ignition (shown).

diameter was increased to 1¹⁵⁄₁₆in (5cm). As with the unit construction 250 Crusader Sports, the cams had a quick-lift profile, valve springs being of the two-rate pattern with light-alloy top covers and the valve stem tips case hardened.

Featuring a compression ratio of 7.25:1, the 1959 500 Bullet saw its cylinder head and barrel (still aluminium and iron, respectively) clamped to the crankcase by six long set-screws, which engaged with helicoil thread inserts in the crankcase castings.

On the 500, the rear tyre size was now 3.25 × 19. For the 1959 season, the 500 and 350 models were both given:

- redesigned centre stands (still in aluminium);
- new engine plates;

- chromed steel mudguards;
- new, all chromed fuel tanks: 4¼ gallon (19ltr) on the 500 (as per Constellation trim) and 3¾ gallon (17ltr) for the 350 (as per Crusader Sports);
- Airflow streamlining and rear chain enclosure as optional extras.

For the 350 Only

- Meteor Minor 500 twin-cylinder telescopic front forks.
- 17in (43cm) wheels front and rear (giving reduced seat height).
- 7in (17cm) single SLS, single sided, full-width front brake.
- 7in (17cm) rear brake (as on 500).
- Gearing increased to: 14.3:1, 9.5:1, 7:1, 5.2:1 (top).
- Higher lift cams.
- Amal Monobloc carb size increased to 1¹⁄₁₆in (2.7cm).
- Compression raised from 7.25 to 7.75:1.
- Modified exhaust header pipe (sweep).
- New, longer silencer.

88mph (142km/h) Top Speed

In their test dated 16 March 1959, *The Motor Cycle* put one of the updated 350 Bullets through its paces. Performance was impressive, with a maximum one-way speed of 88mph (142km/h) being recorded. The conditions were a light following wind, with the rider wearing a two-piece riding suit and overboots. The test's headline ran: 'An exciting, high performance mount with a strong appeal to the discriminating sporting rider.'

Braking came in for particular praise:

An excellent feature of this model, which contributed to its ability to put up good averages, was its braking. The brakes are of 7in [17cm] diameter and as the data panel shows [from 30mph (48km/h) to rest, 29ft 6in (9m)], were remarkably effective. Indeed, full application of the front brake caused the tyre to protest audibly on a dry road surfaced with coarse granite chippings. Operation was light and progressive and was amply sensitive for either wet or greasy conditions. Both brakes retained their efficiency during long journeys in heavy rain and did not lose their adjustment during the 1,000-odd miles covered in the test.

It is worth comparing the above with the braking criticism of the 1953 Bullet made on page 45, to see the big strides made in this area of Royal Enfield.

In fact the only negative comment of *The Motor Cycle* 1959 350 Bullet test came with: 'It was advisable, prior to the first start of the day, to free the clutch plates by means of the kickstarter if first gear was to be engaged quietly.' Otherwise it was praise all the way, with the test concluding: 'To sum up, the Royal Enfield Bullet is a lively, likeable mount possessing a whole host of features to commend it to the enthusiastic rider.'

It is also interesting to report that the Lucas SRI rotating-magnet magneto embodied an automatic advance and retard mechanism. So, unlike those models equipped with the old-fashioned mag of earlier years, the rider was not faced with having to continually adjust or retard the ignition by means of a handlebar-mounted lever. Also, adjustment of the contact breaker on the 1959 Bullet could be effected simply by undoing three screws and removing the plastic end cover, leaving the points exposed.

Coil Ignition is Adopted

For the 1960 Bullet models, the big news was the adoption of coil ignition with the crankshaft-mounted Lucas RM15 alternator. The contact breakers were mounted behind the cylinder in a distributor unit, with the ignition switch located on the offside of the toolbox.

To improve wear and operation of the clutch, neolangite-bounded plates were introduced. There was also a revised casquette with the pilot lights now set further apart.

For the 350 Bullet only, the following changes were introduced:

- Previously, the valve springs had tapered collets and steel top and bottom plates, and stem

cops, these were altered to semi-circular grooves and larger collets, with smaller valve springs using dual collets at the top and steel components at the bottom. The valve ends were now hardened as on the 500.
- The 3¾gal (17ltr) tank had its fixing modified at the rear to a spring clip retainer which snapped around the sleeve on the top tube.

As in previous years, the 500 Bullet could be supplied ex-factory in sidecar trim at no extra charge. Compared with the solo specification, the modifications comprised lower gear ratios, reduced front-fork trail and heavier duty springing at both front and rear. In addition, sidecar specification models were also fitted with a steering damper. When buying a 500 Bullet (or for that matter any of the twin-cylinder models), it is as well to check that this is not a former sidecar tug. Not only will items such as gearing and suspension be incorrect for solo use, but a sidecar machine will also, most probably, have had a harder service life. It is also worth pointing out that besides the 350 Bullet, Royal Enfield also sold the cheaper, lower specification 350 Clipper from 1956 until the early 1960s. Much confusion surrounds this model as there were several versions. For example, from 1960 the Redditch company put the Bullet engine (with alloy head) into the Clipper chassis, with only a lower 6.75:1 compression ratio, the 17in (43cm) wheels, painted 'guards and tank, plus old-fashioned BSA type Burgess silencer, to tell it from its more expensive and sporting Bullet.

Called the Clipper II, it was much nearer the Bullet than the original austere older Clipper I brother. The latter, which ran from 1955 until the end of the 1950s, was equipped with an iron cylinder head, lower 6.5:1 compression ratio, and 18in (46cm) wheels (1955–57) or 19in (48cm) wheels (1958–59), plus a single sprung saddle.

The final two years of the original Bullet series (as opposed to the New Bullet unit model, which arrived at the end of 1962) saw little development – and slow sales. The new decade had brought with it big changes to the British motorcycle industry. After record sales totalling some 350,000 machines in 1959, the following years were ones of decline, hastened by the arrival of severe foreign competition and a change in buying habits, which saw the lightweight all-dominant – not helped by the British Government introducing a new law, which restricted novice riders to a maximum of 250cc. In fact it was this, together with the removal of favourable tariffs for British bikes in Commonwealth countries, which in hindsight was a real reason for the decline of a once great industry, including Royal Enfield.

The New Bullet

With all the above in mind, one has to wonder why Enfield bothered at all with the 350 class – and even more so why it wasted valuable money at development facilities on a new model based on the unit construction Crusader model, but retaining the original Bullet's 346cc (70 × 90mm) measurements. And it wasn't simply a case of

slapping on a bigger top end. The New Bullet was given revised internals and an uprated gearbox. It weighed in at 310lb (140kg) and produced 22bhp at 6,500rpm. Other details of the newcomers specification included coil ignition (with alternator), 17in (43cm) wheels and Crusader cycle parts. The compression ratio was 7.5:1. Although the New Bullet continued until it was dropped in August 1965, its poor sales never covered its development costs. So the unit Bullet only hastened Enfield's ultimate demise, a sad end to what had been a glittering career for a much revered name. However, all was not lost for the famous Bullet name. An earlier licence agreement with India ensured the Bullet, in name at least, would rise from the ashes. Its existence at the beginning of the twenty-first century is a testament to its sound design, which had outlived not only its brothers but the rest of the great British motorcycle industry of years gone by.

The three-fifty Bullet as it was for the 1959 season; a handsome bike with good performance.

5　Two-Strokes

The most famous Royal Enfield two-stroke was the RE or Flying Flea, conceived just as war was about to begin in 1939, and owing much to a German DKW design. Post-war, the RE was developed from its original 125cc engine size to 148cc as first the Ensign and eventually the Prince. Production came to an end in the early 1960s. Other notable Enfield 'strokers' included the Villiers-powered Turbo Twin of the mid-1960s, and the GP5 racer of the same era (*see* Chapter 9).

However, many forgot that some of the above were the first of their type at the long-running Redditch works, because even before the First World War reared its ugly head, Royal Enfield had become well versed in the black art of two-stroke engine design.

The 225L

The first 225L (ladies model) made its debut in 1914 and was offered until as late as 1929, with an open frame and round barrel-shaped fuel tank (a conventional model with a flat tank was also offered). The three-port, two-stroke engine with deflector piston, outside flywheel and two-speed gearbox gave modest performance. The open frame was designed to be ridden by those of the fairer sex – wearing, as was the fashion, long skirts. Leg shields, which were standard, gave excellent wet-weather protection. Weight was 150lb (68kg).

Model A

Introduced for the 1930 model year, the Model A used an updated 225cc (64 × 70mm) engine, with three speeds and a mechanical pump, the latter being an advanced feature for its time. With the arrival, during late 1930, of the Great Depression in the United Kingdom, following the New York Wall Street stockmarket crash of October 1929, Royal Enfield's management decided on a further update of its 225cc two-stroke and production stopped between October 1930 and April 1931, when it was relaunched as the A31.

The first Royal Enfield two-stroke made its debut in 1914. This 1924 Model 201A Ladies with a 225cc (64 × 70mm) twin-port-exhaust engine was a development of the original.

'Naked' version of the 225cc twin-exhaust-port single, showing details such as the tank-mounted hand-change gearbox and rear-mounted magneto.

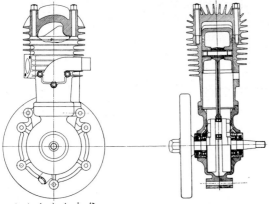

Factory drawings of the 225cc two-stroke single-cylinder engine, circa 1928.

Suspension-wise it retained its girder front forks featuring twin tension springs, traditional Enfield detachable rear mudguard and carrier.

The engine was redesigned and now featured an inclined cylinder and aluminium head but retained the old bore and stroke measurements, mechanical oil pump and outside flywheel on the offside (right). A dynamo was clamped into the engine plates behind the crankcase and driven by chain. It carried the contact breaker points for the coil ignition on its end and the whole machine was finished in a maroon livery.

Model Z

A change in tax rates for motorcycles saw Enfield introduce the Model Z in March 1932. The engine displaced 148cc (56 × 60mm) and was named Cycar. This uniquely styled lightweight featured enclosure of the engine unit, and partial enclosure of the rear section of the machine; it also sported leg shields, girder forks (with pressed steel blades) and rear carrier as standard equipment.

The frame of the Cycar was part of the enclosure and was manufactured from pressed steel sheet. The hand lever for the gear change protruded through a slot in the above pressings. The entire rear mudguard was QD (quickly detachable) in traditional Enfield fashion.

Within this unique frame was Enfield's neat two-stroke single-cylinder engine with its inclined cylinder, and a non-detachable head. Ignition was by a crankshaft-mounted flywheel magneto. The carburettor was on the offside, the exhaust on the left. Some models came equipped with a battery as standard equipment.

For its time, the Cycar was an extremely modern design and pre-dated post-war bikes such as the LE Velocette, Aermacchi Chimera and Ariel Leader.

The 1934 version of the long-running 225cc two-stroke. By now it had a single-exhaust-port cylinder, magdyno, blade girder forks and a three-speed gearbox.

A change in tax rates for motorcycles saw Royal Enfield introduce the Model Z in March 1932. Named the Cycar, this featured a 148cc (56 × 60mm) engine and was a uniquely styled lightweight commuter machine, which offered comprehensive enclosure.

Model X

In April 1933 another two-stroke model was added to the Enfield list. Coded X, this was essentially the Cycar power unit with its cylinder vertical, mounted in a lightweight duplex tubular frame. A dynamo was mounted in the engine plates to the rear of the crankcase, but it retained the flywheel magneto and many of the mechanical features of the Z. Thus the Model X had three speeds, blade girder forks and small-diameter drum brakes.

For 1934, the Model A received a redesign. This saw the machine go over to petroil lubrication, a one-piece head and barrel, and single exhaust system – although it retained the original model's coil ignition, dynamo and girder front forks.

A Redesign

In 1936 the 148cc two-stroke was axed. By 1939 the Model A had been changed considerably. Still 225cc, it now featured a revised engine with vertical cylinder, a new frame, the brake pedal moved over to the nearside, and the option of tubular girders instead of the pressed steel blades and covers for both the dynamo and outside flywheel.

The Dutch Connection

Royal Enfield had the Dutch company Stokvis & Zonen to thank for its most famous two-stroke: the RE or 'Flying Flea'. The RE came about in response to a request from Holland, which came from a company in Rotterdam that had been importing the German DKW RT98 model, with some considerable success. The problem came in 1938 when their import agreement had been cancelled, due to the firm having Jewish owners. They responded by asking the Redditch-based Enfield concern to make its own version of the RT98, but with the engine capacity raised to the 125cc class. This was to be marketed in Holland under the Royal Baby (RB) brand name.

By April 1939, prototypes had been received in Holland and soon afterwards production authority given. Unfortunately, just as the first production batch was ready for delivery, the Second World War began. The result was that Great Britain had a fully developed ultra-lightweight; one, it was soon discovered, particularly suitable for use by airborne troops in the field; hence its title the 'Flying Flea'.

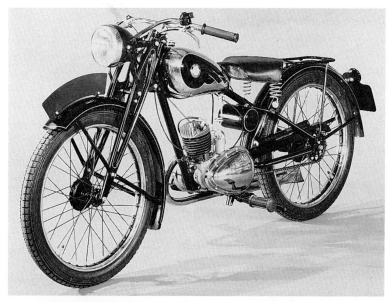

One of two prototypes of the Royal Baby displayed at the Rotterdam Show in April 1939. Produced by Royal Enfield for the former Dutch DKW importers, it was based on the German factory's RT98. Featuring a 125cc engine size it was subsequently built by Royal Enfield in both civilian and military guises as the RE and 'Flying Flea', respectively.

Royal Baby outside the Redditch works; with Royal Enfield management circa spring 1939.

The Flying Flea

In the 12 October 1939 issue, *The Motor Cycle* was able to announce the newcomer's arrival, describing it as a 'well equipped 125 machine with engine-gear unit and other interesting features'. *The Motor Cycle* was also able to claim 'this little machine to have a maximum speed of from 40 to 45mph [64–72km/h] and a petrol consumption at 25–30mph [40–48km/h] of 130-140mpg [2ltr/100km]'.

The Engine

The newcomer had many points of interest, being a particularly neat and modern machine compared to similar size British motorcycles of the same time – and was the work of Ted Pardoe. Chief amongst these features, however, was the engine assembly, which was of the unit construction type, with the engine and transmission in one assembly. Although many claim it to have been 126cc (due to official handbooks and the like giving this figure), the bore and stroke measurements were actually 53.79 × 55mm, giving a shade under 125cc.

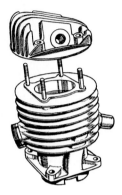

Cylinder head and barrel from the original 1939 RE 125; the piston (not to scale) featured an unusual type of deflector, whilst the cylinder had two ports.

1946 RE 125	
Engine	Air-cooled two-stroke single with piston-port induction, alloy head, cast-iron cylinder
Bore	53.79mm
Stroke	55mm
Displacement	125cc
Compression ratio	5.75:1
Lubrication	Petroil
Ignition	Miller flywheel
Carburettor	Amal $^{11}\!/_{16}$in (1.74cm) 223
Primary drive	Chain
Final drive	Chain
Gearbox	Three-speed foot operated
Frame	All steel, tubular construction
Front suspension	Royal Enfield undamped telescopic fork
Rear suspension	Rigid
Front brake	Drum 4in (10cm)
Rear brake	Drum 5in (12.7cm)
Tyres	2.75 × 19 front and rear
General Specifications	
Wheelbase	49in (1245mm)
Ground clearance	6in (152mm)
Seat height	26½in (673mm)
Fuel tank capacity	1.75gal (8ltr)
Dry weight	139lb (63kg) with 1gal (4.5ltr) petroil mixture
Maximum power	3.5bhp @ 4,500rpm
Top speed	47mph (75km/h)

Launched in October 1939, the RE 125 came about thanks to the Dutch Royal Baby project.

OPPOSITE: *An August 1949 advertisement showing the final version of the original RE 125, before a change was made for 1950 by the fitment of telescopic front forks.*

The slightly inclined cylinder featured two transfer ports leading tangentially into the bore; the gases being deflected upwards to an aluminium piston which, in place of the new usually humped deflector, had a specially formed recess in the rear of the crown. The piston was specially heat treated, with a fully floating gudgeon pin.

The big-end was of the roller-bearing type, whilst the crankshaft was supported by a pair of ball race bearings on the drive side and a single one on the flywheel side. On the latter there was also an outrigger bearing, whilst each crank flywheel shaft had plain bushes forming compression seals.

Miller Flywheel Magneto

Ignition was taken care of by a specially supplied Miller flywheel magneto of the six-pole type, which doubled up as the lighting supply. This gave a 6V, 27W output for the ignition and 24W headlamp and a 3W output for the tail-lamp bulb. The headlamp featured a dip switch (on the handlebars) and a rubber-mounted tail-light assembly.

A needle-type Amal carburettor, again specially made for the RE, came with an air cleaner, and a choke for starting. Lubrication was petroil, with a ratio of 24:1.

Detachable Cylinder Head

Unlike many two-strokes at this time, the cylinder head was detachable. Made in aluminium, this was held down by four bolts, with no gasket being used. The head featured a release valve and a 14mm spark plug angled towards the nearside. The barrel was in cast iron.

A cylindrical silencer featured three unequally spaced rear-pointing cones in its rear section, the exhaust gases passing through a series of ½in (1.27cm) holes at the end.

Gearbox

In unit with the engine was a three-speed gearbox, with ratios of 6.95, 10.8 and 20.3:1. This was operated via a hand lever on the offside of the fuel tank. Completing the transmission was a single-plate cork clutch, oil-bath primary chain and an exposed final-drive chain.

Frame and Front Forks

A simple diamond frame was constructed in circular steel tubing, whereas the front fork was quite unusual, being built up from two pressed steel girders linked top and bottom to the steering head by a series of rubber bands – a system pioneered by DKW from the mid-1930s. The RE's specification was completed by 4 and 5in (10 and 12cm) diameter drum brakes, front and rear, respectively.

The wheels were fitted with 2.50 × 19 Dunlop cord tyres, there was a single sprung saddle and a canister-type tool container.

MODEL R.E. 125 c.c.

HANDIEST OF ALL!
WEIGHS ONLY 135 lbs.

MAXIMUM ECONOMY

SPEEDS UP TO 45 M.P.H.

Helping to save precious dollars the Royal Enfield 125 c.c. Model R.E. has a consistent petrol consumption of over 130 m.p.g. and is the lightest motorcycle of its class.

With a background of 10 years PROVED PERFORMANCE—thousands were used by Airborne troops during the War and since then thousands more have pleased motorcyclists at home and overseas—the stamina and possibilities of this model must be experienced to be believed.

PROVED PERFECT!

The Lightest 125 c.c. MOTOR CYCLE

PRICE 125 c.c. Model R.E.	£58 . 0 . 0	
Plus Purchase Tax	£15 . 13 . 3	
Lightweight Speedo.. ..	£3 . 3 . 6	
Plus Purchase Tax on Speedo	17 . 2	

Royal Enfield

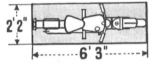

2' 2" 6' 3"

It can be housed easily in a comparatively small space.

The full story of the machine's military career is charted in Chapter 3, but it is interesting to note that because of supply difficulties the first examples that reached the War Department were supplied with cup-and-cone wheel bearings; whereas the civilian RE model, like the later WD machines, had journal bearings and, therefore, the need for periodical hub adjustment was eliminated.

Ex-WD Machines

Like some of its other models, Royal Enfield repurchased many of the military Flying Fleas and put them back into civilian guise at the end of the hostilities. In 'civvies' they were sold off over the next few years to the transport-starved British public. For example, as late as 1950, Marble Arch Motor Supplies of London were offering 'ex WD 125cc Royal Enfield's for immediate delivery at £58'. Further description said: 'These machines have had practically no use and are mechanically as new. Finished in sparkling maroon with gold lined tank.'

Torrens' Report

'Torrens' (Arthur Bourne), reporting in the 8 November 1945 issue of *The Motor Cycle,* described the 125cc Royal Enfield as:

> Capable of going places impossible to any wheeled or tracked vehicle. This does not matter to the ordinary purchaser, but what will appeal to him is the extraordinarily easy handling and the supreme confidence the machine gives on greasy roads and the like. I know of no machines on which I am happier when the conditions are really bad.

Torrens also found 'the machine to be amongst the quietest two-strokes', whilst 'those rubber-band front forks I have found entirely satisfactory – as good as the forks of any lightweight I know', and far better than most. And in summing up he said: 'It is a mount that has served the Army well, and now should make a big name for itself in "Civvie" Street.'

Unfortunately, even though in many ways an excellent machine, the Enfield two-stroke was to suffer from the arrival of the BSA Bantam – another DKW-based design – when it was launched later that decade.

Telescopic Front Forks

As the 1940s came to a close, telescopic front forks came very much into vogue – even on ultra-lightweight machines. So even though its DKW-derived rubber-band forks were one of the machine's best features, these were discarded

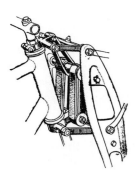

DKW-derived 'rubber-band' front suspension, simple but very effective, found on the RE 125 until the end of 1949.

Undamped telescopic front forks replaced the DKW-type rubber-band girders for the 1950 season. They used the outgoing girder pick-up points.

Bill Lomas with the Royal Enfield development 125cc racer, circa 1949 – built from a standard roadster, at Cadwell Park.

in the interest of sales appeal for the 1950 Royal Enfield 125cc. The new telescopic forks specified for the machine featured no damping or rebound springs, being, like the new BSA Bantam, of the most basic design.

Other changes for the 1950 season were: a larger capacity fuel tank, up from 1½ to 1¾gal (6.8–8ltr), a silver-grey paint job, and 2.74 × 19 tyres. Price, including UK purchase tax, came out at a shade under £74.

A New 125

In November 1950, a new RE 125 was announced (known as the RE2). This came in response to falling sales from the outgoing model (even though it had been updated with telescopic forks only 12 months earlier).

The centre of attraction was the newly designed and much neater engine assembly. It would be true to say that it showed much DKW RT125/BSA Bantam influence.

Die-Castings

The new four main sections to the lower half of the new RE 125 engine were all aluminium alloy pressure die-castings. The two middle sections formed the crankcase and gearbox shell; the outer sections comprised covers for, respectively, the clutch and primary drive on one side and on the other, the generator and the kickstart, plus the gear selector mechanism.

As was the case with the original, the crankshaft was built-up with the forged mainshaft units pressed on the crankpin. The pin was parallel and shouldered, was of case-hardened nickel steel and had a journal diameter of 0.723in (1.8cm) to provide greater rigidity. Supporting the crankshaft were four large-diameter ball race bearings situated close together, two on either side.

The Clutch

In order to provide the lightest possible operation – and valuable additional flywheel effect – thereby making the engine smoother than before, the clutch was fitted to the nearside. Still of the single-plate variety, it was unusual in having springs that were interposed between the pressure plate and the drive plate. To free the clutch, the back plate (or drum) was pushed away from the friction plate.

The clutch comprised four main components: a steel drum, which was slotted on its outer rim in the conventional manner; a light alloy friction plate with cork inserts, to which was riveted (on a phosphor bronze-bushed boss) the engine sprocket; next to this was the splined drive plate, which was fitted to a boss locked up on a taper to the gearbox mainshaft; and, finally, there was an outer pressure plate, which was retained in the clutch drum by means of a circlip and which after short inward travel, bore up against a step machined on the inside of the rim of the drum. Operation of the pressure plate (which was pushed inward) was by means of a worm housed in the outer cover. The six springs were located in flange cups interposed between the pressure plate and the driving plate so that, because of the pressure on the circlip, the tendency was to push the drum away from the engine thus bringing it into contact with the friction plate. When the clutch was withdrawn, pressure was taken off the circlip, thus relieving the friction pressure.

Footchange Operation

Like the DKW RT125 and the BSA Bantam, the latest Royal Enfield RE 125 featured a three-speed footchange gearbox in unit with the engine. The RE was unusual in that it had a cross-over drive. Another unorthodox feature was that the drive between the mainshaft, which was of case-hardened steel, and the second gear pinion was by way of four radially disposed pegs in the shaft engaging with slots machined in the end of the pinion. The gearchange pedal was on the same side (right) as the kickstart lever.

Flywheel Generator

Incorporated into the ignition system of the 1951 RE 125 was a new Miller-made, 40W flywheel AC generator. This provided low-tension current for energizing the primary winding of an ignition coil (mounted to the frame under the tank), and low-tension current for the lights. The three generator coils (housed in the offside outer cover) formed the stator unit. The rotor was fitted on the taper and keyed, and consisted of the conventional bronze flywheel with a steel centre riveted in, and with the soft-iron pole-pieces bolted in.

The rear of the flywheel was flat and the rim narrow. The contact breaker was easily accessible by simply removing two screws, being situated in the outer cover clear of the stator coils. The cam was mounted on the end of the mainshaft.

Cast-Iron Cylinder Barrel

The cast-iron cylinder barrel was deeply spigoted into the crankcase, to a depth of 1⅜in (3.5cm). The design of the transfer ports had been revised, these now being formed further round on the sides of the barrel and in such a way that the gases were swirled upwards and rearwards, resulting in improved performance. With a power output of 4.5bhp the new engine was some 0.75bhp more than the outgoing unit. The two-ring piston was manufactured in silicon alloy, with a semi-dome crown. Once again the gudgeon pin was retained by circlips and of the fully-floating type, manufactured in case-hardened steel.

Spark plug and compression release holes were disposed at 180 degrees to each other in the separate light alloy cylinder head, which featured a hemispherical combustion chamber.

The carburettor was an Amal ¹¹⁄₁₆in (0.7cm) instrument.

An Opportunity Missed

It was in the area of chassis design where Royal Enfield really missed the boat. When BSA launched its DI Bantam, it was soon possible to have plunger rear suspension as a cost option. However, and probably for cost reasons, Royal

Enfield chose to stick with a rigid frame. In retrospect what they should have done was produce the RE 125 with a brand new swinging arm frame – which it had already introduced on larger models, such as the new Bullet and 500 Twin. In fact, the author would have gone a stage further and given the machine four instead of three speeds. This surely would have given the little Enfield a distinctive edge in the ultra-lightweight sales war over the early 1950s. Instead Enfield paid the price by always running a poor second behind the top-selling BSA product.

The undamped telescopic front forks introduced the previous year were retained, but modifications were carried out in the method of fixing the fork legs to the steering lugs.

For 1952, the only changes were cosmetic – the wheel rims, previously dull-chromed, were now enamelled grey, whilst the cast-aluminium crankcase outer covers were polished instead of matt-finished.

The Ensign Arrives

At the end of 1952 Royal Enfield launched the Ensign model. This employed a 148cc (56 × 60mm) version of the RE2 engine. Running on a compression ration of 6.5:1 (5.5:1 on the RE2), the Ensign produced 5.25bhp.

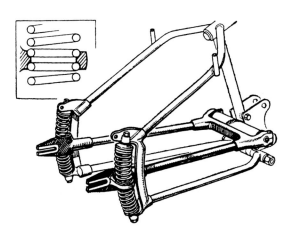

The 1953 148cc Ensign rear suspension. Although extremely basic, it was nonetheless the first of its type on an Enfield two-stroke.

The biggest change was to the frame. At first glance this appeared to have plunger rear suspension with exposed springs, but in reality this was a pivoted fork. It was crude to say the least – the springs simply being held in place as on a plunger frame.

The Ensign's arrival signalled the end for the RE2, at least as far as production was concerned. However, due to existing stock, the smaller-engined bike was still available from dealers for several months more.

The 'new' Ensign itself was only to be offered for a few months before being axed in favour of the Mark II variant.

Ensign II

The revised version of the Ensign, the II version, debuted in autumn 1955. *The Motor Cycle* said, in a road test report of the Ensign II, in the 1 March issue:

> The Royal Enfield two-stroke has progressed greatly since its introduction as the Flying Flea of wartime fame. With the airborne troops who used it the machine was an immediate success, for it was very light (and thus easy to ride and manhandle), economical, sprightly and utterly reliable. During the intervening years the machine has changed. A redesigned engine, telescopic front fork, foot gear change and pivoted fork rear springing have brought it up to date and, indeed made it no longer an obvious derivative of its predecessor.

Earls Court Show Debut

The latest version, the Ensign II, made its debut at the 1955 London Earls Court Show. As soon as it was put on Enfield's stand, it was obvious that considerable changes had occurred. Most noticeable was the dual seat, followed by chrome-plated shrouds for the curved rear-suspension springs and a bright green paint job. The finning of the head and cylinder barrel had been made deeper, whilst the brake lining area had been increased by some 60 per cent in order to achieve improved performance and at the same time give greater brake lining life.

THE *New* **Royal Enfield**
ENSIGN II

featuring
NEW

* ENGINE
* BRAKES
* CLUTCH
* FORKS

New for 1956, the Ensign II featured a number of improvements …

… *notably improved front forks with larger diameter tubes, wider braking area and an improved engine featuring revised porting and combustion chamber, giving increased performance and economy.*

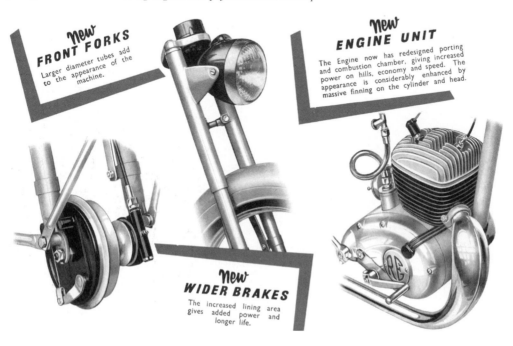

new FRONT FORKS
Larger diameter tubes add to the appearance of the machine.

new ENGINE UNIT
The Engine now has redesigned porting and combustion chamber, giving increased power on hills, economy and speed. The appearance is considerably enhanced by massive finning on the cylinder and head.

new WIDER BRAKES
The increased lining area gives added power and longer life.

In addition, the diameter of the fork sliders and cover tube had been increased, the clutch designed to give a longer life and to eliminate noise when it was held out of engagement, and finally the ports and combustion chamber had been modified to provide better overall performance.

Performance Figures

When tested by *The Motor Cycle* in March 1956, the 148cc Ensign II achieved a maximum speed of 51mph (82km/h) (still air; rider wearing a two-piece oversuit); the non-snatch minimum speed in third (top) gear was 13mph (21km/h). Weight, including 1gal/4.5ltr of fuel came out at 183lb (83kg), whilst fuel consumption at a constant 40mph (64km/h) was 96mpg (3ltr/100km). The test report ended with the following:

> General impression was that the Ensign II is an outstanding machine in its class, relatively inexpensive to buy (£105 8s) and cheap to run, and providing an all-round performance which makes town riding and long-distance touring equally pleasurable.

Rectified Lighting

New for 1957 was a second version of the Ensign II with rectified lighting; the disc-type metal rectifier being suspended from the frame top tube, thus being shielded from possible damage by the tunnel of the fuel tank. The battery was mounted on the offside of the machine, below the nose of the dual seat, whilst the ammeter was incorporated inside the Miller headlamps.

Ensign III

The III version of the Ensign was something of a deceit by Enfield, because it was not really a new model at all. Instead, for the 1958 model year, the previous Ensign model, which used the rectifier and battery, became the series III – even though the series II was also continued. The only real difference between the two was a cast aluminium fork crown, which supported a new, deeper headlamp, which was fitted to the speedo, in addition to the lighting switch and ammeter.

Actually, as was to become apparent, the only reason the II continued was to sell off existing stock, as it was dropped during the year.

The Prince

New for 1959, the Prince, although still a 148cc two-stroke, differed in several ways from the Ensign.

In the engine, circular flywheels were employed in place of the former bob-weights, and as a result, crankcase compression was raised, providing an

The final development of the Royal Enfield family of cheap-to-buy, cheap-to run commuter two-strokes; the 148cc Prince ran from 1959 until the end of 1962.

1960 Prince

Engine	Air-cooled two-stroke single with piston-port induction, alloy head, cast-iron cylinder
Bore	56mm
Stroke	60mm
Displacement	148cc
Compression ratio	6.5:1
Lubrication	Petroil, mixture ratio 24:1
Ignition	Miller flywheel magneto, 6V
Carburettor	Amal
Primary drive	Chain, in oil bath
Final drive	Chain
Gearbox	Three-speed foot-controlled
Frame	All steel, tubular construction
Front suspension	Royal Enfield undamped telescopic fork
Rear suspension	Swinging arm, twin Armstrong hydraulic units
Front brake	Drum 5in (12.7cm)
Rear brake	Drum 5in (12.7cm)
Tyres	2.75 × 19 front and rear

General Specifications

Wheelbase	48in (1219mm)
Ground clearance	6in (152mm)
Seat height	28½in (724mm)
Fuel tank capacity	3 gal (13.6ltr)
Dry weight	216lb (98kg) with 1gal (4.5ltr) petroil
Maximum power	7.5bhp @ 4,750rpm
Top speed	53mph (85km/h)

increase in power – 7.5bhp at 4,750rpm (against 6bhp at the same engine revolutions). To cope with the extra power, the gearbox (still a three-speeder) featured a beefed-up mainshaft and improved pinion tooth form; whilst a neoprene synthetic rubber shock absorber was incorporated in the sprocket on the gearbox mainshaft.

For the first time on an Enfield two-stroke, hydraulically damped near shock absorbers (of Armstrong manufacture) were specified, which were needed for the new swinging arm rear end. However, even though at long last the small Enfield had proper suspension front and rear, the Prince was no sportster. Instead it was very much in the commuter bike image, with fully enclosed final-drive chain and deeply valanced mudguards. The long tapered silencer was equipped with a detachable, light alloy tail piece, to aid removal of build up of carbon inside the exhaust system.

A Luxury Commuter

So what was the Prince? The answer quite simply was a two-stroke luxury model designed specifically for the person who was seeking inexpensive-to-buy, cheap-to-run transport – no more, no less.

This, the final model in a chain that had begun some 20 years earlier with the Dutch Royal Baby, retained virtually no features in common with those of its forebears. Over those two decades, year-by-year, step-by-step development had brought the ultimate expression of the Royal Enfield ultra-lightweight two-stroke single.

When *The Motor Cycle* tested an example of the Prince in the 7 January 1960 issue, it was described as: 'A stylish lightweight combining smart appearance with excellent economy and good all-round performance.'

Costing £119 10s, the Prince achieved a top speed of 54mph (85km/h) and 110mpg (2.57ltr/100km) at a constant 40mph (64km/h).

The only real criticism of the Prince concerned its clutch operation, which, as *The Motor Cycle* reported: 'Mounted on the crankshaft and therefore running at engine speed, the clutch did, however, take some time to slow down when upward gear changes were being made. It was not, as a result, easy to ensure quiet changes'.

Like the larger Royal Enfield four-strokes of the period, the Prince came equipped with a substantial cast-alloy centre stand.

From its introduction at the end of 1958, the Prince was to remain virtually unchanged, with only cosmetic details such as the fuel tank badges altered, during the production run which lasted until the model was axed in August 1962. By that time commuter sales were falling for bikes such as The Prince, not helped by an influx of machines from the Land of the Rising Sun, such as Honda's hugely successful C50 step-thru.

The Turbo Twin

Although the Enfield 125/148cc singles had already departed the scene, they were not to be the final two-strokes to leave the Redditch works. For a start, there were to be brand new competition mounts including the Scrambler of 1963/64 with its Villiers Starmaker engine (*see* Chapter 7) and of course the much more well-known GP5 racer (*see* Chapter 9). But as far as this chapter is concerned, covering the company's two-stroke street models, there is one last model to deal with: the Turbo Twin. This also broke fresh ground for Royal Enfield, as it employed a twin-cylinder powerplant. However, this was not an Enfield design, instead it was a bought-in 4T unit from Villiers of Wolverhampton. Featuring a four-speed unit construction gearbox, it was fitted into the existing Crusader chassis and, to be honest, the finished result looked as if this frame had been specially made for the Villiers motor.

Launched in 1964, the Turbo Twin was effectively a marriage of Crusader cycle parts with a bought-in Villiers 4T twin-cylinder two-stroke engine.

1964 Turbo Twin

Engine	Air-cooled Villiers 4T two-stroke parallel twin with piston-port induction, alloy head and cast-iron cylinder
Bore	50mm
Stroke	63.55mm
Displacement	249cc
Compression ratio	8.75:1
Lubrication	Petroil
Ignition	Flywheel magneto
Carburettor	Villiers 526/6
Primary drive	Chain
Final drive	Chain
Gearbox	Four-speed foot-change
Frame	All steel, tubular construction
Front suspension	Royal Enfield telescopic fork
Rear suspension	Swinging arm, with Girling hydraulic unit
Front brake	Drum 6in (15cm)
Rear brake	Drum 6in (15cm)
Tyres	3.25 × 17 front and rear

General Specifications

Wheelbase	52in (1321mm)
Ground clearance	6in (152mm)
Seat height	29in (737mm)
Fuel tank capacity	3.5 gal (16ltr)
Dry weight	298lb (135kg)
Maximum power	17bhp @ 6,000rpm
Top speed	80mph (129km/h)

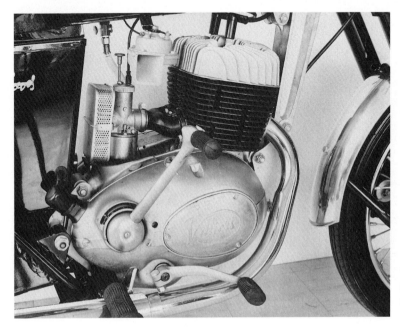

The Villiers 4T 249cc (50 × 63.5mm) twin-cylinder two-stroke engine (seen here mounted in a Greeves frame). It put out 17bhp at 6,000rpm.

Cost Cutting

The Turbo Twin did suffer to some extent, as a certain amount of cost cutting took place to bring it to production. This meant that the balance of the machine was the Clipper economy model, with paint instead of bright chrome on components such as fuel tank and mudguards (although a small number of the Sports versions were built with these features). Many observers do not rate the 4T engine as well as its earlier brother, the 2T. However, in Enfield's case it is difficult to judge, as the company only made a 4T-engined bike. This used the 249cc (50 × 63.5mm) piston port twin-cylinder two-stroke engine, which produced 17bhp at 6,000rpm. It should also be noted that the Turbo Twin Sports used the same engine tune. 'Sports' in this case meant looks rather than performance – with only chrome plate and lower bars to tell the standard model and sportster apart.

The first Turbo Twin (in Sports guise) went on sale during 1964. A price tag below £200 meant that the Turbo Twin was cheaper than machines such as the Crusader Sports or Super 5 from the same stable.

With a maximum speed of just over 70mph (112km/h) the Turbo Twin label certainly did not mean speed; instead it was related to the bike's ability to provide turbine smooth acceleration compared to the Enfield ohv 250 models. Where the four-strokes did gain, was by way of a higher maximum speed and lower fuel consumption figures.

By the middle of the 1960s, Royal Enfield was in deep financial trouble, due to rapidly falling sales, brought on by the ageing designs and Japanese competition – particularly in the up to 250cc category.

Rather surprisingly, the Turbo Twin was the next to last of all the Enfield 250 models to get the chop, surviving until October 1966 (only the Continental GT fared better).

Sadly Royal Enfield hit the financial rocks shortly afterwards, with production being transferred to Enfield Precision's Bradford-on-Avon works. But this did not act as a reprieve for any of Enfield's two-strokes. So the Turbo Twin was truly the last of a line, which had started all those years back in 1914, just prior to the outbreak of The Great War. During the intervening half a century, the Royal Enfield family of two-strokes had sold in their thousands, making friends all around the world. And in the process generated profits, which had helped the Redditch factory become a respected force in the motorcycle world.

Don Raybould's collection of Royal Enfield two-fifties. From left to right: 1965 Turbo Twin Sports; 1963 Turbo Twin; 1965 Turbo Twin Sports; 1963 Continental.

6   500 Twin

At the beginning of November 1948, Royal Enfield announced a brand new Twin. The work of Ted Pardoe, and to a lesser extent Tony Wilson-Jones, the newcomer was the Redditch company's own version of the popular British parallel twin, a fashion sparked off by the great success achieved by the arrival of Edward Turner's ground-breaking Triumph Speed Twin of the late 1930s.

Like Turner's creation, the Enfield Twin was a 500, but here, except for its general configuration, overhead valves and vertical cylinders, the resemblance ended.

Unlike the other twins by then emerging from other British factories, there were two separate cast-iron cylinder barrels (only AMC followed this route). Each featured its own light alloy cylinder head and integral rocker box. Another Enfield feature was that the skirts of the barrels were sunk very deeply (by over half their length) into the mouth of the crankcases.

The Enfield 500 Twin was announced in late 1948, the first production examples going on sale in early 1949. Many of its features, such as the dry sump lubrication carried in a container cast into the crankcase and the bolted-up Albion four-speed gearbox, followed existing company practice.

Modular Approach

In fact it would be true to say that Ted Pardoe (who was responsible for the engine) was very much influenced by Enfield's policy of a modular approach – aimed at keeping production costs to a bare minimum, whilst aiming wherever practical at a standardization of component parts' supplies. Another reason was that many of Enfield's existing design practices had been developed over a number of years, proving their work in the process.

There was, for example, the familiar arrangement of the oil compartment, cast into the crankcase assembly. Whilst this was not a wet sump system it did mean there was, unlike all other British four-stroke parallel twins of the era, no separate oil tank attached to the frame and separate from the engine. The oil pump was of the double-acting twin-plunger variety located in the timing cover. Both these features in fact copied the company's Bullet single.

1949 500 Twin	
Engine	Air-cooled, overhead-valve parallel twin semi-unit construction, with separate cylinder heads
Bore	64mm
Stroke	77mm
Displacement	496cc
Compression ratio	6.5:1
Lubrication	Dry sump, twin oil pumps
Ignition	Battery/coil
Carburettor	Amal 276 ¹⁵⁄₁₆in (2.4cm)
Primary drive	Duplex chain
Gearbox	Albion, four-speed footchange
Frame	All steel, tubular construction
Front suspension	Royal Enfield telescopic fork
Rear suspension	Swinging arm, twin Enfield-made with shock absorbers
Front brake	Drum 6in (15cm)
Rear brake	Drum 6in (15cm)
Tyres	Front 3.25 × 19; Rear 3.50 × 19
General Specifications	
Wheelbase	54in (1372mm)
Ground clearance	5½in (140mm)
Seat height	29½in (749mm)
Dry weight	390lb (177kg)
Maximum power	25bhp @ 5,500rpm
Top speed	80mph (129km/h)

What was different to the Bullet, however, was the position of the main oil filter – which now lay across the engine in a separate tunnel cast in the crankcase just below the Bullet-type oil-filler cap. Additionally, the filter was on the return side of the scavenge pump and filtered the lubricant as it returned to the sump (oil container). And there were no unsightly external oil pipes.

The engine's displacement of 496cc was achieved, in typical Enfield fashion, by utilizing the pre-war 64 × 77mm (248cc) Model S ohv single.

Vertically Split Crankcases

The crankcases were split vertically in line with the wheelbase of the machine, which was called the 500 Twin. The mouth of the crankcases providing an uninterrupted joint face for each cylinder base; but there was, in each half of the crankcase and finishing, of course, below the

joint faces, a central slot through which the connecting rod of the relevant cylinder could pass at the bottom dead centre during assembly of the crankshaft in the main bearings.

At the base of the crankcase was, as already mentioned, the oil sump (container); this was separated from the rest of the crankcase by a two-piece, corrugated gauze screen. Cleverly, the screen (filter) was corrugated to provide a greater area, and in order that the crankshaft flywheel movement would help push the oil through the filtering gauze.

Main Bearings

Both main bearings were of the same diameter. On the driving side there was a large, single-row ball race bearing, which located the end of the crankshaft. This bearing was pushed in from the outside against a shoulder and was held in place endways by the rear section of the primary chaincase. The primary sprocket was splined on to the crankshaft and held by a nut, whilst the inner ring of the bearing was held between the rear of this sprocket and a washer located against the crankshaft web.

On the timing side there was a roller bearing, which was pushed in from the inside and retained by a circlip. Any differential expansion between the case and the shaft was allowed for by sliding which could occur on the rollers.

One-Piece Crankshaft

The dynamically balanced, hollow crankshaft was a one-piece casting in aluminium iron, featuring a massive central flywheel with a balance weight; the crank webs were circular.

In the drive end of the crankshaft was a non-return, disc-type breather valve, which operated through an external pipe. Pushed into the timing-end of the shaft, which was a bored-out taper, was the sprocket for the simplex timing chain; keyed in, this sprocket was held against the taper by a bolt running though its centre and engaged a nut recessed on the inner face of the crank web. Knurled, and not having spanner flats, this nut was locked in position by a rod passing through the crank web radially and held into the nut by a grub screw at its outer end. The grub screw was locked by centre punching. Carried on the head of this bolt that held the timing chain sprocket against its taper was the worm drive for the cross shaft, which drove the oil pumps. The bolt was hollow and took the oil feed to the big-ends.

Cored Hollow Crankpins

Cored hollow crankpins were employed in the Enfield twin-cylinder engine, with steel discs closing the holes at each end, and were held in position by circlips. The timing side disc featured a small, spring-loaded, pressure-release ball valve. Oil-feed outlet holes for the big-ends were at 90 degrees to the crank throw. Lubricant was fed into the cored passage and then through the outlet holes.

Plain, Split Big-End Bearings

Plain, split big-end bearings were employed, manufactured in RR56, which was also the material used for the connecting rods. The little ends were plain (unbushed), with fully floating gudgeon pins located by circlips. These pins were of 3 per cent nickel case-hardened steel.

Slightly Domed Pistons

The aluminium alloy pistons were slightly domed, featuring the relatively low 6.5:1 compression ratio, but high dome pistons were available to special order. Each piston featured a full skirt, which comprised a form-turned taper and oval. There were two compression rings and a single slotted scraper.

Interchangeable Cylinder Barrels

The two cylinder barrels, of cast iron, were entirely separate and spigoted to a depth of 3in (7.6cm) into the crankcase. The barrels were interchangeable, which not only meant that if an owner struck problems he could buy a single cylinder and piston, but that there was not the extra cost to Enfield of right and left assemblies; again proving the soundness of the company's modular concept. Paper gaskets were used for the joints between the cylinder and the crankcase. Each barrel was held to the crankcase by five through-studs, which also secured each cylinder head. Copper–asbestos gaskets were used to seal the barrel–head joint of each assembly. An additional advantage of the separate barrels–heads was that these received a particularly effective flow of cooling air.

Aluminium Heads

Like the barrels, the heads were entirely separate, but in aluminium alloy, each featuring integral rocker boxes. Cast-in, cast-iron combustion chamber inserts were employed, which included the valve seats and plug bosses; there were also cast-in steel exhaust stubs.

Separate Camshafts

Two separate camshafts – exhaust in the front and inlet at the rear – ran in plain bronze bushes, and were driven at half engine speed by a ⅜in (1cm) pitch chain from the sprocket already mentioned. A jockey sprocket, running on an eccentric, was employed for chain tension, which could be adjusted simply by slackening a single nut, moving the slotted, quadrant-shaped extension of the eccentric and then retightening the nut.

Cradle-Mounted Dynamo

A new Lycas dynamo, measuring 3½in (8.9cm), was cradle-mounted. This was driven at engine speed by an 8mm pitch chain from a duplex sprocket on the inlet camshaft. Ignition was by battery/coil, through a vertical distributor assembly running at half engine speed and incorporating an automatic advance and retard. Electrical components, including switch, ammeter, voltage control and warning light were carried in a box alongside the seat tube; the ignition coil was mounted underneath the saddle of Enfield's new twin-cylinder challenger.

Flat Base, Inclined Tappets

The camshaft operated flat base, inclined tappets, which in turn operated solid, inwardly inclined 5½in long (14cm) pushrods; these in turn operating the rockers.

Tappet adjustment was in the valve end of each rocker, with the lock-nut beneath the rocker end. Each nut featured a conical seating and a shallow 'saw-cut' in order to tighten itself more securely. The pushrods operated in tunnels cast in the cylinder barrels and heads, whilst the tappet guides were pressed in, each guide having a thread for extraction purposes. The valves worked in pressed-in guides and each was retained to its seat by duplex coil valve springs retained by a collar and split cotters. Hardened valve caps were used. Valve head diameters were 1⅜in (3.5cm) inlet and 1¼in (3cm) exhaust.

Lubrication System

As already described, engine lubrication was controlled by two, double-acting, oscillating plunger pumps. The primary side of the feed pump drew oil from the sump compartment and supplied it directly to the big-ends. Released from the big-ends, the lubricating oil went by splash to the main bearings, cylinder walls and pistons, and hence drained down through the two-piece gauze screen into the sump.

Meanwhile, the secondary side of the feed pump drew oil from the compartment and delivered it to a single drilling in the timing side of the crankcase. This drilling branched into two cross-passages at the top of the crankcase. Each end of the cross-passages registered with vertical drillings leading up each cylinder barrel to the inside of the rocker spindles. In each rocker spindle were six outlet holes covered by the rocker itself.

Escaping past the rockers, the oil drained down the pushrod tunnels, through grooves in the tappet guides, and into the camshaft tunnels. At the timing-case end of each camshaft tunnel was a drain hole, through which most of the oil passed to lubricate the timing gear. The inlet (rear) camshaft tunnel broke through into the crankcase at points opposite the spigot portions of the cylinders. In each spigot, a hole registered with each break-through point, so that an additional supply of lubricant went to the rear of each cylinder and then drained through the gauze screen.

Fitted with a larger plunger, the return pump drew oil from the sump and returned it to the oil compartment. At the same time, this pump scavenged oil from the timing case and returned it to the compartment. In both operations, just prior to the oil reaching the compartment, it passed through a large felt filter. Bolted onto the offside of the crankcases was an accessible oil filter and cap.

The Gearbox

The Albion-supported gearbox of the 500 Twin was, like the new 350 Bullet single swinging-arm model of the same time, bolted directly to the rear of the engine; the gear ratios being 13.9, 9.0,

6.5 and 5.0 to 1. A curved, hard chromium-plated, slipper tensioner, adjustable from within the case, operated on the bottom run of the ⅜in (1cm) duplex primary chain. The primary drive, together with a four-plate clutch, was enclosed in a neat cast-aluminium chaincase (again as on the newly released Bullet), and the clutch operated by a quick thread worm.

Shared Cycle Parts

Many of the 500 Twin cycle parts were shared with the new swinging arm Bullet single, or at least displayed the same layout. This put the new Enfield parallel twin ahead of many similar models, the majority of which at that time had inferior plunger rear suspension. The specification included two toolboxes, a single sprung saddle, sprung front mudguard, detachable rear guard and an air filtration system, which was sandwiched between the battery carrier and a further box carrying electrical components. This latter feature, and the fact that the headlamp assembly was fork-mounted, meant that the headlamp shell was bare of controls, switches and instrumentation.

Tourer Rather than Sportster

It would be true to say that Enfield's new Twin had been conceived very much as a docile tourer,

rather than a sports bike. This showed up in the low compression ratio (6.5:1) and the power output of only 25bhp at 5,500rpm. On the road this endowed the 500 Twin with a maximum speed of 80mph (137km/h). Even so, as later events were to show, there was both a hidden performance potential and additional cubes to be exploited.

When announced in November 1948, the machine was priced at £196 17s, including UK purchase tax. But very few were actually sold in Britain during the first few months of production, the majority going to earn vital revenue in overseas markets.

Developments

For 1950, the wheel spindle lugs on the front forks were in one piece (to prevent oil loss), whilst there was now (like the latest Bullets) a neat high-polished cast-alloy facia enclosing the upper section of the fork legs and moulded to take the Smiths, rear-wheel-drive speedometer. Other notable differences were a special oil-wetted Vokes carburettor air filter and chromium-plated fuel tanks.

For the following year, 1951, the use of die castings for the crankcases reduced the weight of the 500 Twin down to 390lb (177kg). Thus modified, the Royal Enfield twin became one of the very lightest British vertical twins of its era.

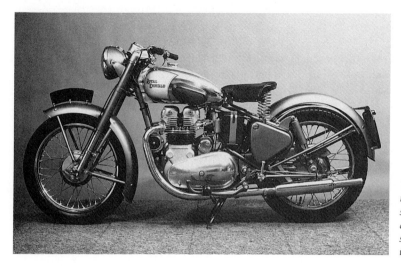

The 500 Twin in 1950 guise, much the same as when launched, but with small changes to the front mudguard and base of the front forks; its swinging arm rear suspension was inherited from the Bullet single.

Bolted-up Albion-made gearbox with separate shafts and pedals for gear change, kickstarter and neutral finder.

A 1951 500 Twin showing new front mudguard. Other changes for that year saw die-cast crankcases, revised fork ends and a reduction in weight.

The distributor unit was mounted on the dynamo. This housed the points and retard mechanism. A separate ignition coil was employed and the distributor assembly could be rotated in its housing to adjust the ignition timing.

Revised forks and mudguard of the 1951 500 Twin.

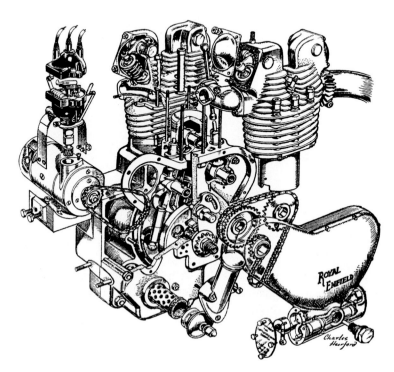

ABOVE: *Factory-fresh 1951 500 Twin showing the compact nature of the machine.*

The 500 Twin engine assembly. Like the Bullet single, the oil tank was built into the crankcase. Separate cylinders and heads were used, whilst a single chain was employed to drive the two camshafts. A much shorter chain was provided for the rear-mounted Lucas dynamo, the latter incorporating a car-type distributor.

Road Test Comment

During 1951, one of the latest Twins was put through its paces by *The Motor Cycle*, who had this to say:

> The machine has all the feel of a machine scaling under 400lb [181kg]. By far the most pleasing characteristic, however, is its delightfully sweet and silky power delivery at low speeds. The top gear minimum non-snatch speed is as low as 12–14mph [19–23km/h]. Low speed torque is exceptional for a modern 500cc twin and the machine will accelerate quite smoothly in top gear from speeds as low as 18–20mph [29–32km/h]. Acceleration, also, is outstandingly good. From slow idling to high revs, the pick-up is entirely clean-cut. Another feature contributing to sparkling acceleration is the instantaneous gear change. Clean and rapid upward or downward changes may be accomplished by the clumsiest novice with only an easy, decisive movement of the pedal. Top gear cruising speed appeared to be anything from 20mph [32km/h] to 70–75mph [113–121km/h] and even at the later figures there was a remarkable lack of fuss.

The tester went on the say:

> The standard of comfort and the handling properties were inordinately good judged against the highest modern standards. Excellent comfort too, was provided by the relationship between the saddle and footrests and the angle of the grips.

However, the brakes were deemed as 'not sufficiently powerful for the machine's performance', and the 'tank width across the knee grips is on the large side and the prop stand leg too long, except where there was a favourable camber'.

A Dual Seat Arrived

For the 1952 model year, Enfield made available (at extra charge) a Dunlopillo cushion dual seat. A pannier set was also made available as a cost option.

Some modifications had been made to the electrical system of the Twin. The ammeter and ignition switch had been removed to the headlamp, and the ignition coil moved to a protected position on the front portion of the rear mudguard. The metal box in which they were originally housed was replaced by a large air filter. The ignition switch had been transferred inside the tool box (with the key projecting to the front) and protected from the tool kit by a metal shield.

Making the Engine More Oil Tight

Previously, the rocker boxes had been lubricated from oil passages drilled in the cylinder and heads – unfortunately this feature also led to the possibility of oil leaking past the cylinder head/ barrel gaskets. Now the oil was fed from bosses just above the rear of the cylinder bases and led by means of external pipes direct to the rocker spindles. Another minor modification – also made to ensure fewer oil leaks – had been to provide two additional screws for decreasing the pressure between the crankcase in the area of the cylinder joint faces. These two ¼in (0.6cm) diameter screws were accessible after removing two plugs (which screwed into loose nuts in the offside of the crankcase and which should be removed only when the cylinders are to be lifted).

For 1952 the prop-stand operation had been improved by incorporating a return spring instead of the spring clips used previously.

Overshadowed by a New Bigger Brother

A new 692cc (called the 700) Twin arrived for the 1953 season (*see* Chapter 8). This meant that from then on the original smaller Twin was to be overshadowed (and outsold) by its new, larger brother. There was also, at the same time, a change to die-cast cylinder heads, which represented a considerable tooling investment. The new heads saw the valve seats shrunk in and fitted with a Y-shaped inlet manifold, instead of the original type.

There were also other small changes, shared by the Bullet-single, concerning the pilot lamp, stop and tail lamp, reflector, and floating brake cam spindle housings.

In 1954, the small Twin was fitted with proprietary rear suspension units and, for the first time, the famous headlamp casquette, with its twin pilot lights, one each side. This casquette was a die-cast aluminium cowl and enclosed the top section of the front forks and extended back to the steering head. The top surface acted as a mounting console for the speedometer, ammeter and lighting switch.

The 500 Twin was also offered with the option of the existing coil and distributor ignition system or a magdyno. If the latter was fitted, the magneto sat in the normal dynamo position and carried the dynamo on its back. This seems a curious move as other Enfield models at this time were being equipped with more modern alternators and rectified electrical systems. In order that the magneto ran at half the engine speed, the size of the second of the two sprockets attached to the inlet camshaft was halved. The dynamo speed was recovered by gearing up between the electrical instruments.

Improved Braking at Last

The poor braking performance of the 500 Twin was addressed for the 1955 model year with the adoption of the dual front brake. However, it should be pointed out that to achieve the full performance of this brake it was important to ensure that both brakes were operating together; otherwise braking power would be sadly missing –

even worse than on the original single-sided unit!

At the same time, the magdyno was standardized and a new gearbox end cover, with repositioned gear pedal, was adopted (shared with the Bullet range). Frame changes and an oval air cleaner body were also modifications copied from the singles.

During the spring of 1955 the Twin became available with the option of the quickly detachable rear wheel and, as on the singles, this was superseded by a full-width version for the 1956 series. At the same time, the Enfield development team upped the compression ratio to 7.25:1. The $^{15}/_{16}$in (2.4cm) carburettor size remained unchanged, but the Amal type was changed from 276 to 376, the main jet size rising from 150 to 230. This meant an increase of 2bhp to 27bhp and 500rpm extra (6,000). Smaller detail improvements came in the shape of a folding kickstart lever, a combined horn button/dipswitch and a new tank mounting.

More Radical Changes

The 1957 model year brought with it a more radical update, the dynamo finally being ditched in favour of a crankshaft-mounted alternator. This allowed a return to coil ignition with a distributor driven by chain from the camshaft. But the principal change was the adoption of the fullloop Super Meteor frame. There were also a number of styling changes.

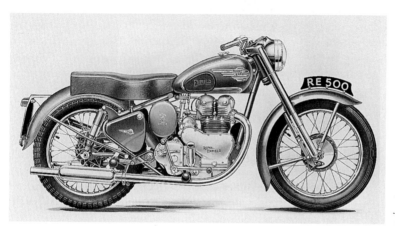

By 1955 the 500 Twin had gained a dual seat, die-cast cylinder heads, external oil feed to rockers, oval air-filter box, magdyno and double-sided front brake.

The Meteor Minor

Spring 1958 saw the 500 Twin at last given a name – the Meteor Minor. This was listed in standard and de luxe guises. Although it followed the same basic layout, it benefited from improvements in engine technology since the original had been launched a decade earlier.

This meant shorter stroke measurements of 70 × 64.5mm (the same as those of the new 250 unit single). The change also allowed the use of larger valves. Other differences of the short-stroke engine (still displacing 496cc) were the big-end bearings, which consisted of split shells running on a one-piece modular iron crankshaft (still rotating in a mixture of ball and roller bearings). The shape of the timing cover was altered, and a siamezed (two-into-one) exhaust system and smaller 17in (43cm) wheels (previously 19in/48cm) were fitted. In the braking department, at the rear, a 7in (18cm) hub was fitted and, on the standard model, a 6in (15cm) full-width assembly at the front. The de luxe version was given a larger 7in (18cm) full-width assembly at the front, together with a quickly detachable rear wheel – which was vital – as this model came with full rear-chain enclosure. The standard bike came equipped only with a single sprung saddle, whereas the Redditch factory was kinder with the de luxe – it had a more practical dual seat and pillion footrests, plus an air cleaner, stop light and prop stand, as well as a more deeply valanced front mudguard. A notable feature of the Meteor Minor de luxe was its pressed steel cowling, which effectively hid the distributor and air cleaner, plus components such as the tool kit and ignition switch; the nearside cowling housed the ignition switch.

1958 Meteor Minor

Engine	Air-cooled, overhead valve parallel twin semi-unit construction, with separate cylinders and heads
Bore	70mm
Stroke	64.5mm
Displacement	496cc
Compression ratio	8:1
Lubrication	Dry sump, twin oil pumps
Ignition	Battery/coil
Carburettor	Amal 376 Monobloc 1 1/16 in (2.7cm)
Primary drive	Duplex chain
Final drive	Chain
Gearbox	Albion four-speed foot-change
Frame	All steel, tubular construction
Front suspension	Royal Enfield telescopic fork
Rear suspension	Swinging arm, with Armstrong hydraulic unit
Front brake	Drum 6in (15cm)
Rear brake	Drum 7in (18cm)
Tyres	3.25 × 17 front and rear
General Specifications	
Wheelbase	53½in (1359mm)
Ground clearance	6in (152mm)
Seat height	29½in (749mm)
Dry weight	370lb (168kg)
Maximum power	30bhp @ 6,250rpm
Top speed	87mph (140km/h)

A new 500 Twin arrived in April 1958 and was given a new name, Meteor Minor. Major differences included shorter stroke 70 × 64.5mm dimensions, modified bottom end, siamezed exhaust system and 17in (43cm) wheels. The example illustrated is a 1960 de luxe model with 7in front brake and full chain enclosure.

More Power, Less Weight

With more power (30bhp at 6,250rpm) and less weight (370lb – 20lb less than before) maximum speed went up to just under 90mph (one magazine got 97mph – but with a strong following wind!).

To cope with the additional performance there was a new clutch; but even with the engine update, more power, less weight and an improved clutch, the Meteor Minor was not quite the smooth, gentlemanly machine its predecessor had been. The trade-off had been vibes replacing the previous soft power delivery, which had made the 500 Twin such a delight to ride in cruising mode.

In June 1958 the plastic 'Airflow' weather-shielding (first introduced in early 1958 on the 250 Crusader unit single) made its entry on the two Meteor Minor twins, as a cost option. Strangely, on the Airflow-equipped machines, the 7in (18cm) front brake was fitted to both the de luxe and standard bikes.

The Meteor Minor Sports

When Royal Enfield announced its 1960 model range in early October 1959, it was able to announce a new high-performance 500 twin, the Meteor Minor Sports. This featured fiercer lift cam profiles, which also gave more overlap on the valve timing. The compression ratio had been bumped up and there were dual rate valve springs with light alloy top collars.

In 1960, a more sporting model, the MMS (Meteor Minor Sports) made its bow. This had more output (33bhp at 6,500rpm), a larger tank and dropped handlebars. It, together with the Meteor Minor, received a new clutch and exhaust. There was also provision for a tacho drive on the timing cover. A 1961 model is shown here.

There was an additional 3bhp, giving a top speed, for the first time on the smaller Enfield twin, of over 90mph (145km/h). The sports model also came with chrome-plated mudguards and fuel tank, the latter painted on its top section. Except for its smaller 17in (43cm) wheel sizes, it could almost be mistaken for the top-of-the-line 700 Constellation model.

The 1961 Range

The 1961 range had two 500 Twins: the Meteor Minor Sports and Meteor Minor de luxe. Of the pair, the de luxe was much as before, apart from the adoption of the 3½gal (16ltr) sports-type tank, but several changes had been made in the make-up of the Sports version. This centred around reducing the cost from the 1960 price of £270 down to £254 the following year (needed because of poor sales).

Enfield's aim was 'to provide a high-performance machine at minimum initial cost'. The result was the higher engine tune, but without the previous chrome-plated, polished aluminium guise of the 1960 machine. Hence the timing cover, primary chaincase and gearbox end-cover were no longer polished – instead having a vapour-blast matt finish. The quickly detachable rear wheel had been deleted and there was a more basic exhaust silencer (still two-into-one). The mudguards and tank were painted instead of the previous highly polished chrome livery.

Sidecar Specification

It was also interesting to note that the Meteor Minor Sports (which replaced the standard and de luxe version for 1961) could (like the 700 Super Meteor Constellation and 500 Bullet) be supplied in sidecar trim at no extra cost. Compared with the solo specification, the modifications comprised lower gear ratios, reduced front fork trail, heavier duty springing at both front and rear – and the addition of a steering damper where one was not already fitted.

7 Dirt Bikes

Even in pre-war days, the Royal Enfield name had been well-known in the feet-up, mud-plugging world of trials. For example, one of the first 346cc enclosed-pushrod Royal Enfield singles took part in the 1926 Scottish Six Days Trial, but broke its crankcases on the rocky Mamore section and was forced to retire.

However, in 1927 Len Welch was back, this time his four-speed machine sporting a steel plate under the sump to protect it and thus avoid the previous year's fate. Although the Royal Enfield name was often seen in the programme, it was not until 1952 that Johnny Brittain, riding one of the factory-entered swinging arm Bullet 350s described below, won this most famous of all British trials. Before that, the nearest Enfield had come to victory in the Scottish was a couple of third places: George Holdsworth in 1938 and Charlie Rogers in 1939.

The Colmore Trial

The Colmore Trial in February 1948 was the scene for an historic Royal Enfield happening, as this was the event that was to see the launch of what was to become the Redditch factory's most famous motorcycle: the swinging arm Bullet single.

A trio of works-prepared prototype 346cc ohv machines, ridden by Charlie Rogers, George Holdsworth and Jack Plowright, were very much the centre of attraction – even though their debut was only modestly successful (Rogers and Plowright each winning first-class awards and Holdsworth a second-class). But in the annals of Royal Enfield history this debut of the swinging arm Bullet is all-important.

The Prototype Machines

Although the development history of the swinging arm Bullet series is related elsewhere, it is nonetheless important to go over the main innovations of the 1948 prototype Works Trials model.

One of its great features, and certainly the main topic of conversation at the Colmore event, was the entirely new, all-welded frame, with swinging arm rear suspension. The main tubes were manufactured of chromium–molybdenum alloy steel. The layout was diamond, that is to say, the crankcase formed part of the frame. When asked why this design was chosen, the answer came back from its creator Tony Wilson-Jones, 'why use a cradle, when the crankcase largely takes the load anyway'. This, in retrospect, was a forward-looking approach, as today most motorcycles use their engine as a stressed member, but not so back in 1948. Yet another case, as can be discovered throughout this book, when Royal Enfield was very much in the forefront of motorcycle design evolution.

For the swinging arm, the rear shock absorbers were of Enfield's own manufacture, the units employing silentbloc bushes top and bottom. As for the swinging arm pivot, this pivoted on a hardened shaft and phosphor-bronze bushes; side thrust was taken care of by shims, and so could be adjusted. The front forks, again of Enfield design and manufacture, came from the existing Model G 350 production roadster.

Displacing 346cc, the new ohv single cylinder engine had a bore and stroke of 70 × 90mm (shared with the Model G). Running on a compression ratio of 6.2:1, it produced 18bhp at 5,750rpm on 'pool' petrol.

Johnny Brittain – Trials Superstar

Johnny Brittain will forever be associated with great Royal Enfield successes in the trials world of the immediate post-war period. When first mounted on the 350 Bullet and later the 250 Crusader, he proceeded to carve for himself and the Redditch-based Royal Enfield factory undreamed of glory from the many victories the pairing gained in both one-day events and the legendary six-day events: the Scottish and the International.

His father Vic began his career during the late 1920s and, until war stopped play in 1939, he become a major force in the trials world. Riding for Norton, he finished runner-up in the 1939 Scottish Six Days and won the British Experts title in 1936. After the conflict was over, Vic Brittain joined Royal Enfield to continue his career. The highlight of this came in the 1948 International Six Days, where he and Charlie Rogers (both riding the new 346cc Bullet) won Gold medals and were part of the victorious British Trophy team.

So it was perhaps a natural progression that son Johnny should have followed in his father's footsteps and joined Enfield; later, younger brother Pat was also associated with the Redditch works.

As he was to reveal in Roy Bacon's *Royal Enfield: The Postwar Models*, published in 1982, Johnny felt 'we were part of a family company and we felt privileged and rather special in fact; my ambitions were to be a good trials rider and an ambassador for the Royal Enfield Company'.

Johnny joined Royal Enfield in 1950. Two years later he won the British Experts title – a month before his twenty-first birthday. This made him the youngest rider to have achieved this in the history of the sport up to that time. Not only this, but it was the first time a father and son had won this prestigious crown.

Also in 1950, he became the first Royal Enfield rider to win the famous Scottish Six Day Trial, beating David Tye (BSA) and Gordon Jackson (AJS).

In 1953 he repeated his Experts success, although Johnny had to be satisfied with third in the Scottish Six Days.

During the early 1950s, Johnny Brittain was also following a twin-track approach by going over to Europe to compete annually in the ISDT, representing his factory and his country – winning, in the process, a clutch of Gold medals and being a member of the British Trophy team on many occasions.

Besides another victory in the Scottish Six Days in 1957, Johnny Brittain also won the Scott Trial in 1955 and 1956.

By the late 1950s, the works Royal Enfield riders, including the Brittain brothers (Pat having joined in the middle of the decade), began campaigning the new 250 Trials, which was based on the Crusader model. But even though both gained several victories in one-day trials, this smaller bike was never so successful in the long distance events.

Then, at the end of June 1965, came news that Johnny Brittain, winner of twelve ISDT Gold medals had retired from the sport, after finding out that he had not been selected to the British Team for the event . He commented, 'I decided I would like to finish at the top of the tree', and went on to say 'the ISDT is the thing I have most interest in. I decided that if I wasn't good enough for the Trophy Team I would retire'. By then he was thirty-four years of age and had been a Royal Enfield works rider for fifteen years and had competed in fourteen ISDTs.

His non-selection, together with an expanding motorcycle business in Bloxwich near Walsall in the West Midlands, sealed his decision. Even so he continued his interest in the sport, and rode occasionally in smaller events, purely for fun.

An Experimental Cylinder Barrel

On these works prototypes, a light alloy cylinder barrel was used experimentally, featuring a cast-in cast-iron liner. But the production roadster never had the aluminium cylinder because the weight-saving due to its design was not worth the additional cost.

The cylinder head, also of aluminium, had cast-in, cast-iron inserts for the valve seats, plug boss and compression release. This compression release was of the two-stroke variety, taking the place of the then conventional exhaust valve lifter, but was designed to lead gases into the exhaust port, so the operation did not create the loud hissing noise usually associated with compression releases.

In order to give improved engine performance, Wilson-Jones had set the valve angle at 80 degrees – considerably wider than usual at that time. Valve springs were of the duplex, helical type, with a stronger tension than on the Model G.

An innovation in the timing gear was that the timing pinion and the worm that drove the oil-pump shaft were not integral on the timing shaft.

The Production Bullet Trials Bike

Royal Enfield first offered the production version of its brand new swinging arm frame Bullet Trials model in time for the 1949 model year. When *The Motor Cycle* tested an example in the 5 May 1949 issue, the tester was impressed enough to say:

> So good is the low-speed torque that anyone with no experience of pre-war competition Royal Enfields would find it astonishing. Even on an estimated gradient of 1 in 2, with the ignition set at near full retard, the engine would chuff-chuff the machine upwards in best gas-engine fashion at 1½ miles per hour. This attribute alone, to my mind, puts the Bullet in No. 1 trials-mount category.

Prior to the arrival of the works prototype Bullet Trials machines at the Colmore in February 1948 – and even for some-times afterwards – many doubted the wisdom of a spring-frame for trials. However, as *The Motor Cycle* tester reported:

> Now that I have had the Royal Enfield for test I am thoroughly convinced that the sooner the stigma attaching to spring-frames for trials is dismissed the better.

He went on to say:

> On rutted, slippery mud, I found the spring frame a valuable asset. Where the rear wheel of a rigid-frame machine would hop, that of the Bullet held to the surface with almost leech-like tenacity. On slithery tree-roots or on adverse cambers I had a better ride (I am convinced) than would have been the case on almost any other trials mount that has been produced. At speed in tracks or lanes, or cross-country, steering, too, was excellent.

It was also discovered that the high standard of comfort provided by the combination of the Terry saddle and the spring frame, made the Bullet an excellent proposition for use in the ISDT or Scottish Six Days events.

Flat out, the 1949 Bullet Trials model would achieve a maximum speed of 65mph (105km/h) and in acceleration stay with many 500 singles of the era. However, this really was not the point, far more important was the Bullet's ability to both 'plonk' and go. At the time this was not a usual combination, with many other so-called trials models either having a brisk engine performance, but little really low down grunt, or excellent low-speed pull, but absolutely no speed; with the Enfield Bullet you could have both in the same motorcycle.

During the early 1950s, the Bullet Trials found a ready market – and factory riders headed by Johnny Brittain succeeded in scoring victory after victory in trials events both in Great Britain and abroad. Then from 1955 onward, demand dwindled, until a new updated version was launched in August 1958. This was the 'Works Replica' and as the name implied, incorporated many of the features successfully proved in major trials by Brittain and Peter Stirland.

Heart of the Works Replica was a power unit based on that of the 346cc Bullet but suitably modified for the purpose. Both cylinder head and barrel were aluminium castings.

Ignition was by a wading-type Lucas magneto with manual control. No dynamo or lighting equipment was provided. The carburettor, a $^{15}/_{16}$in (2.4cm) Amal Monobloc, was equipped with a Vokes lightweight air filter.

Gear ratios, as used by the works-entered machines, were 7.56:1, 10.58:1, 16.25:1 and 22.68:1, these being used in conjunction with a 17-tooth gearbox sprocket. Alternative sets of gear pinions could be supplied to order, with 15, 16, 18 and 19 tooth sprockets available as options.

A short, hi-level exhaust header pipe was fitted on the offside of the bike, terminating in a small, oval muffler mounted inside the rear frame loop – where it was most out of the way – and thus clear of the rider's leg.

Light but strong, the frame was manufactured in chrome–molybdenum steel tubing and was a part-brazed and part-welded construction. Although based on the production roadster Bullet, the Trials frame differed in several details. An undershield (bash-plate) was provided beneath the engine; this being vital as otherwise there were no cradles under the engine, and even as early as 1927 the Enfield factory had fitted under-engine protection, after experiencing broken crankcases in the 1926 Scottish Six Days.

A horizontal sub-frame loop provided support for the rear mudguard, the rigidity of which was increased by a steel strengthening section, which passed over the top of the guard; both it and the front guard were of aluminium construction. The footrests were set well back to give good control when the rider assumed a poised riding position. To clear the offside footrest, the long chromed-steel kickstart lever was cranked and given a folding foot-section.

The front wheel was equipped with a 2.75 × 21 tyre, with a 4.00 × 19 at the rear. Both hubs were of the full-width aluminium type, the rear incorporating the famous Royal Enfield cush drive. Brake drum diameters were: 6in (15cm) front and 7in (18cm) rear, with 1in (2.5cm) linings. Other measurements of interest included ground clearance of 6½in (16.5cm), a seat height of 31in (78.7cm) and a wheelbase of 53in (135cm); the weight (dry) was 314lb (142kg).

Finished in metallic silver grey, including the frame, with the 2.5gal (11ltr) fuel tank in matt-chromium plate (with plastic Royal Enfield badges), the revised Bullet Trials cost £242 7s 9d when released in the summer of 1958.

The Works Replica Bullet Trials continued to be listed until the end of 1961, when it was superseded by the new 248cc Trials Crusader. However, a few of the Bullet Trials were still constructed after this time to special order.

The magneto was a genuine racing one, but there was room for a magdyno if needed (the latter being needed both for the upcoming street bike and also for the Bullet built by the factory for the ISDT later in 1948).

Semi-Unit Construction

A form of unit construction was used, in that the gearbox (made by Albion) was bolted directly to the rear of the engine. Thus most of the advantages of a full unit design were gained, without the disadvantage of having to split the crankcase in order to dismantle the gearbox. With the Royal Enfield arrangement, separate oil was used for the gearbox. Ratios employed for the Colmore Trial were: 7:1, 10:1, 14:1 and 19.75:1.

Clutch operation was by a quick-thread three-start worm instead of the usual Enfield long lever used previously. A ⅜in (1cm) pitch duplex primary chain was specified, running in a new type of cast alloy oil-bath chaincase.

Brakes were single-sided SLS 6in (15cm) assemblies, front and rear. The forward end of the rear brake rod was pivoted at approximately the pivot point of the swinging arm. This position ensured that the action of the spring frame did not prevent the rear brake from being applied evenly. Tyres fitted on these prototypes were 2.75 × 21 front, 4.00 × 18 rear.

Rear Chain Adjustment

Rear chain adjustment was of the serrated 'snail' cam variety. Depending upon the way the cam was turned, the wheel spindle was either pushed to the rear or allowed to move forward. Notches or serrations in the cam engaged with a stop-peg for locking purposes. Provided the corresponding notches on each cam were used, the wheel was kept in alignment.

A new type of mounting was employed for the fuel tank, which was carried on a pair of horizontal bolts passing through the tank's 'ears' and frame lugs. The front mounting carried a rubber bush.

Finish of the Colmore Cup bikes was in chromium (front forks, tank and rear shocks) and chromatic green. The mudguards were polished aluminium (as were the primary chain case and rear chain guard).

Ground clearance, when the machine was unladen, was 6¾in (17cm) under the gearbox and 7¼in (18cm) under the front skid plate, which protected the engine's crankcases. With a 10-stone (63.5kg) rider in the saddle, the clearance on the level was 6in (15cm).

Testing the Prototype

In March 1948, one of the few non-Enfield personnel who tested an example of the Works Trials prototypes commented: 'The spring frame seemed to contribute to rear wheel adhesion on all types of going. Slow-speed pulling was excellent and the power would mount with the revs in a vibrationless and very healthy manner.' And there is no doubt that these features gave the Redditch-built model a definitive advantage over rival manufacturers' products.

A First Victory

In June 1948, Charlie Rogers won the ultra-demanding Allan Jefferies Trial. Organized by the Bradford MC, this event took place over the upper reaches of the Yorkshire Dales, rather on the lines of the original out-and-home Scott Trials of the same area.

In putting up the best solo performance, Charlie Rogers lost only twelve marks. Royal Enfield also won the Team award (Charlie Rogers and T.U. Ellis on Bullets, G.E. Broadbent on the 249cc model). The class field included the likes of Billy Nicholson (499cc BSA) and Geoff Duke (348cc Norton), so this was no hollow victory.

In *The Motor Cycle* report of the event, was the following statement:

The most wonderful effort on High Tension was the feat of Charlie Rogers (346 Royal Enfield) who avoided the rocks after taking a faulty line and pulled out of what appeared an utterly impossible position without a sign of footing, to the astonishment of all who saw him.

ISDT Glory

In September 1948, the new Bullet covered itself with glory in the International Six Days Trial, held that year in Italy, with San Remo on the Italian Riviera as its base. This was the second post-War ISDT, the first having been run with a smaller than usual entry in Czechoslovakia the previous year.

In the British Trophy team there were two Bullet 350s, ridden by Charlie Rogers and Vic Brittain, whilst Jack Stocker rode a 500 Enfield in the Vase contest. This latter bike was one developed from a Model J – as 'Jolly Jack' preferred a larger displacement and had earlier declined a Bullet ride – featuring a cast-iron head and barrel and a rigid frame. The engine was pepped using a hotter inlet camshaft, high-compression piston and modified porting.

Rogers and Brittain ended up part of the victorious British Trophy squad, whilst Stocker helped his fellow Brits collect the Silver Vase. It was a valiant effort too, as for the final two days, including the speed test, Stocker had to struggle on after his front forks had fractured.

1937 saw the introduction of a special trials model, that was not only campaigned by the factory but also sold to private owners.

The Twin in Competition

Much of the prototype testing of the Royal Enfield 500 Twin (*see* Chapter 6) had been carried out in the Swiss Alps, before production got underway in 1948. This seems appropriate, given that in the not too distant future, a specially prepared version of the model would be upholding British honour in similarly mountainous terrain.

Catalogued as a gentleman's touring mount, it was, in production guise, hardly a tearaway, but with considerable pulling power in any gear, to belie its humble 25bhp power output.

Its first off-road adventure came in 1951, when much to everyone's surprise, and not least Royal Enfield, an invitation came from the British Team selectors to prepare a trio of the 500 Twins to take part in the tests to be held in mid-Wales, for possible selection for that year's ISDT.

These tests were successful, and when the teams were announced it was seen that Jack Stocker, on one of the twins, was included in Britain's official Trophy squad, to be held in the mountains of northern Italy, around the lakeside town of Varese, situated on the shores of Lake Como, some 40 miles (64km) north of Milan.

In the event, not only did Stocker help Great Britain gain the much coveted International Trophy, but the Enfield works team, which besides Stocker, comprised Johnny Brittain and Stan Holmes on two more twins, collected the manufacturer's team prize – with no marks lost.

Royal Enfield also prepared three other 500 Twin models for the Swedish Silver Vase squad. So all-in-all the Redditch company were well represented in Italy that year. *The Motor Cycle's* Midland Editor, George Wilson, also made good use of one of the Enfield 500 twins in covering the event for his journal, affectionately known as the 'Blue 'Un'.

True, there had been a few missed heart beats during the final day's speed test when Stan Holmes' model blew a cylinder-head gasket, but because the design made use of separate heads, he was able to continue and retain his hard-earned gold medal – and help his team mates with the team prize.

The ISDT bikes pioneered a series of features, which were subsequently transferred to the following year's production model. For a start there were the lighter and stronger die-cast crankcases, forged front fork ends and new front mudguards, which rose and fell with the wheel.

The following May, Stocker arrived at the Welsh selection tests with a new 692cc twin prototype. As related in Chapter 8, this was virtually a pair of 346cc Bullet single cylinders on a 500 Twin bottom end.

The 1952 ISDT was located in the Bad Aussee area of Austria, and two of the bigger Twins had been prepared for Jack Stocker and for the one-legged sidecar star, Harold Taylor. The smaller 496cc twin was not forgotten, and a pair of those were given to Don Evans and Johnny Brittain for the Vase A and Vase B teams, respectively.

In an awfully wet, muddy and ultra-demanding event, Evans crashed heavily on the third day, suffering concussion, which led to his retirement the following day, whilst Brittain was destined to drop out on the fifth day with engine failure.

On a more positive note, many valuable lessons were learned, particularly as regards the new, larger engine. These were subsequently incorporated when production began later that year, including die-casting for the cylinder heads, a redesigned crankcase breather and new low-expansion pistons.

All-in-all, the twin-cylinder Enfield's brief foray into the world of long-distance trials not only gained the Redditch marque considerable publicity and prestige, but also, perhaps most importantly, played a vital role in machine development.

Determination Counts

Such determination was in many ways what the ISDT was all about, so it came as no surprise when Stocker was retained the next year for the Vase Team, which Great Britain won again. Enfield returned home with the manufacturer's team prize, together with no less than five gold medals to prove the capabilities of its machinery.

In 1950, when the Six Days was staged in Wales, it was yet again Great Britain and Royal Enfield who walked off with the silverware and the gold medals.

Charlie Rogers retired from riding and was put in charge of machine preparation at the Redditch works; a post he was to hold for the next decade and a half. Now promoted to the Trophy squad, Jack Stocker rode a 350 Bullet.

A Fourth Trophy Victory

Great Britain won the coveted Trophy for the fourth year in succession in 1951, its fourteenth success since the event began in 1913 and, as recounted elsewhere, several riders used the new 500 Twin. From then on a mixture of singles and twins of various engine sizes were campaigned in the ISDT until well into the 1960s, Enfield's outstanding rider during the period being Johnny Brittain. The last Royal Enfield ISDT gold medal, at factory level, was Johnny Brittain in 1964.

Other notable Royal Enfield ISDT riders included Tom Ellis, Don Evans, Peter Stirland and Terry Cheshire, but none of these matched the overall performances of Johnny Brittain, both for the number of starts (fourteen) and gold medals (twelve). This figure tied with the record then held by George Rowley (AJS) who had won twelve golds from thirteen ISDT. Strangely, both men had been born in the West Midland's town of Wolverhampton.

Other Trials

Besides the International, Royal Enfield also succeeded in countless other trials ranging from one to six days in duration. Just prior to the outbreak of the Second World War, in early September 1939, the Redditch works experienced a rich vein of form; perhaps the highlight being Charlie Rogers British Experts victory, and also the couple of third places gained in the Scottish Six Days in 1938 and 1939. It was that man Rogers who headed the RE trials squad in the immediate post-War period; Charlie's first competition event being the 1946 Exmoor Trial, which he won without dropping a mark. He also won the John Douglas Trial, with excellent back-up from other Enfield teamsters. It is also important to mention Bullet-mounted N. Holmes, who finished runner-up in the 1949 Scottish Six Days.

A New Star

After Charlie Rogers hung up his helmet, his replacement, J.V. (Johnny) Brittain emerged as one of the greatest trial riders the world has ever seen. His ISDT success has already been mentioned, but Johnny's record in the Scottish Six Days was equally impressive, with victories in 1952 and 1957, runner-up in 1956 and third in 1953.

In fact Johnny Brittain was in many ways Mr Royal Enfield, with his unique combination of success in both one-day and long-distance trials. His abilities in one-day trials were there right from his debut in the Enfield team in 1950. In 1952, at the tender age of twenty, he became the youngest ever runner of the British Experts title. That year he also won the Scottish Six Days and was third in the ACU Trials Star (the British Championship).

In 1953 he repeated his success in the Experts and his third place in the Trials Star. This, combined with his numerous wins in one-day events, made him and Royal Enfield a feared combination.

Johnny Brittain continued this level of success throughout the remainder of the decade. He was also joined in the Enfield team by his younger brother, Pat, another highly competent rider.

These victories no doubt helped sell the various trials replicas turned out by Enfield during his period, but also influenced buyers of the production roadsters, by keeping the name in the headlines.

Johnny Brittain finally retired in the mid-1960s. Although not really connected with Enfield's own failing fortunes as a motorcycle manufacturer, nonetheless the works trials squad would probably have been axed anyway due to the parlous state of the firm's finances at this time.

Scrambles

Although for several years in the 1950s Royal Enfield offered a scrambles version of its popular Bullet model to the general public, it did not enter a works team. However, things changed in 1963 when a works machine, based on the Crusader ohv 250, made its debut in the high-profile TV *Scrambles* series, ridden by Peter Fletcher.

One of the original trio of Bullet Trials models that made their debut at the Colmore Trial in February 1948.

Close-up of the 1950 Bullet Trials engine.

The 1952 version of the production 350 Bullet Trials mount; besides the roadster there were also scrambles and road-racing versions listed that year.

Successes gained by the likes of Johnny Brittain and Peter Stirland ensured that Royal Enfield sold production versions of its Bullet Trials model for over a decade; this is the 1959 version.

ABOVE: *Nearside view of the 1959 Bullet Trials engine, showing aluminium head and barrel, aluminium primary chaincase and racing-type magneto.*

LEFT: *Johnny Brittain was Enfield's top trials star. Here he is making good progress in the 1960 Scottish Six Days aboard his works 346cc Bullet. He was destined to finish fifth, after twice having won the event in the 1950s.*

A 1959-type Bullet showing features such as the tucked-in hi-level exhaust, alloy mudguards and single saddle. Together with the Ariel HT5, BSA Gold Star and Norton 500T, the Bullet was one of the truly great British heavyweight mud pluggers before the arrival of the lightweight two-stroke in the mid-1960s.

The engine had been specially tuned and ran a 10:1 compression ratio, energy transfer ignition and a straight-through exhaust pipe. To cope with the stress of off-road racing, the frame had been strengthened by beefing up the area around the swinging arm pivot. The most noticeable feature of the whole machine was its leading link forks, controlled by Armstrong-made spring and damper units. But it was soon found that this machine was not competitive, so a brand new two-stroke machine was designed.

The Starmaker Engine

Even before Royal Enfield came up with its GP5 road racer, the Redditch firm had built a two-stroke scrambles prototype, which appeared late in 1963. This machine used a bought-in 247cc (66 × 72mm) Villiers Starmaker piston-port, single-cylinder engine. There was a traditional diamond-shape frame, with leading link forks (similar to those used on the Crusader-engined bike), a full-width aluminium front hub and a single-sided steel rear hub. Ridden by Bill Gwynne it was not able to challenge the established marques, such a Greeves or Cotton.

Production Begins

But this did not stop the company putting a production model on sale at the end of 1964. Unlike the production GP5 racer, the scrambler retained the Villiers engine, this being kitted out with a four-speed gearbox and an Amal Monobloc carburettor. Running on a compression ratio of 12:1, it put out a claimed 22bhp. Although it was an attractive machine, very few examples were actually sold. Even a factory-backed model ridden by Mick Bowers did not enjoy too much success.

Even so, Royal Enfield can be justifiably proud of its dirt bikes thanks to its great success gained in the trials arena, rather than off-road racing, with that man Johnny Brittain as the really big name. But many others helped to build the legend, none more so than Charlie Rogers, who was not only a most able rider, but a top-class mechanic.

Others from the pre-war days of the 1930s, right up to the Redditch works' final closure in the mid-1960s, achieved a level of success that put the company on a par with the really great names of the trials world including BSA, AJS, Greeves, Bultaco and Montesa.

Besides the Bullet, Royal Enfield built a trials version of the 250 ohv Crusader, but it never achieved the success of its elder brother.

Probably the ultimate Trials Crusader, this machine has been extensively modified with many lightweight components, including Bultaco-style bodywork, conical brake hubs, alloy wheel rims, modern suspension and Amal Concentric carburettor.

ABOVE: *American Bruce Argetsinger with this Bullet dirt track racer, constructed to compete in Dinosaur and Classic classes. Built to 1951 specifications, the machine has a reproduction of the rigid dirt track frame, which Royal Enfield offered to USA dirt racers in the late 1950s.*

Royal Enfield built a small number of Villiers Starmaker-powered motocrossers in the period 1963–65; it only achieved minimal success.

8   Meteor

Excitement reigned on stand 31 of the 1952 London Show at Earls Court – the reason why? Well, the Redditch-based Royal Enfield concern had just launched a new big Twin, and in doing so had created Britain's largest model with vertical cylinders and two pots – the Meteor 700 (marketed in the USA as the Indian Trailblazer).

Three Wheels

The show bike was displayed fitted to a Watsonian sidecar, the factory believing that its new machine would have a particular appeal to the sidecarist, whether he was keen on taking the whole family out for a sedate tour, or for fast road work. Remember, Great Britain had not yet embraced the small affordable car as it did later in the decade, with the arrival of the Mini. So at the time of the Meteor's launch there was still a considerable demand for what could best be described as a 'sidecar tug'.

So the show Meteor was fitted as standard with a specially robust rear fork, designed to ensure the spring-frame was entirely suitable to withstand the stresses imposed by high-speed sidecar work. This applied equally to either a single-seat sports chair or one of the large double adult sidecars, which were still very much in vogue at the time.

This December 1952 advertisement for the newly released 700 Meteor proclaimed the virtues of the big parallel Twins: 'Fast! Powerful! Reliable!'

Solo Trim

In solo trim, the Meteor was, for its day, an extremely fleet sports-tourer. Heavier than the well-proven 500 Twin by a mere 10lb (4.5kg) or so, the 692cc engine had plenty of flexible muscle, hence its equal appeal as a sidecar machine. *Motorcycling* achieved a maximum speed of 94mph (151km/h) in an early test. The Meteor's top end was based on the 70 × 90mm of the Bullet 350 single. The '700' size was not just arrived at by doubling up the capacity of the single, but from designer Red Pardoe's wish to conform to the Royal Enfield modular policy. This saw the use of the crankcase casting of the 500 Twin. The physical dimensions, strength and rigidity of these allowed the design team to go past the 650cc limit of rivals BSA (A10 Golden Flash) and Triumph (Thunderbird). So the Meteor was an excellent example of modular planning, using as it did the bore and stroke of the Bullet and the crankcase layout of the 500 Twin. Like the latter, the Meteor was also noteworthy for its use of entirely separate cylinder heads and barrels.

Extra Finning

Even so there were notable differences. Externally the cylinder head had an extra fin and all the fins on the head were longer. Internally, the restriction of the crankcase size prevented the big-end cap from being assembled as it was on the 500. The connecting rod was still in RR56 aluminium, but fitted with shell bearings, and the cap was retained thanks to the use of special socket-head cap screws (in 85-ton tensile steel);

This Meteor was specially prepared by the Redditch works as a 'show' model, with cutaway internals …

… not just the engine, but other components including even the magdyno and battery.

1952 Meteor	
Engine	Air-cooled, overhead-valve parallel twin semi-unit construction, with separate cylinder and heads
Bore	70mm
Stroke	90mm
Displacement	692cc
Compression ratio	6.5:1
Lubrication	Dry sump, twin oil pumps
Ignition	Battery/coil
Carburettor	Amal 276 1⅟₁₆in (2.7cm)
Primary drive	Duplex chain
Final drive	Chain
Gearbox	Albion, four-speed foot-change
Frame	All steel, tubular construction
Front suspension	Royal Enfield telescopic fork
Rear suspension	Swinging arm, twin Armstrong hydraulic units
Front brake	Drum 6in (15cm)
Rear brake	Drum 7in (18cm)
Tyres	Front 3.25 × 19; Rear 3.50 × 19
General Specifications	
Wheel base	54in (1372mm)
Seat height	29½in (749mm)
Ground clearance	5½in (140mm)
Dry weight	405lb (183.7kg)
Maximum power	36bhp @ 6,000rpm
Top speed	106mph (171km/h)

Enfield ground these to locate the cap to the con-rod and screwed directed up into it. But at the small ends, the gudgeon pins still ran directly in the eye of the rods.

Running on a compression ration of 6.5:1, the Meteor put out 36bhp at 6,000rpm. This extra power over the smaller Twin meant that an extra plate had to be added to the clutch, which was also deemed necessary because of the additional load imposed by sidecar use. In its 20 January 1955 issue, *The Motor Cycle* tested a Meteor to sidecar specification hitched to a Canterbury Victor child–adult chair. The 69mph (111km/h) they achieved in both third and top suggests a degree of over-gearing, but with the ignition retarded (it should be noted that the original Meteor had coil ignition, but from the 1955 model year, magneto) and careful use of the throttle, the engine would pull as low as 12mph (19km/h) in top gear. This more than probably

any other example proves just how flexible the original Meteor power plant really was. The journalist and author Bob Currie once described the Meteor 700 as 'woofly rather than sporting and intended principally for sidecar haulage'.

The Development Process

In creating their bigger Twin, the Royal Enfield design team did not leave things to chance by simply assuming that the marriage of the 500 Twin and 350 Bullet would be a success. Besides extensive bench and road testing, they also subjected it to competition usage. Much interest (and speculation!) had been created, when in May 1952 an entry by W.J. (Jolly Jack) Stocker had been made for one of the prototypes in Wales for the British Team selection. The machine was in semi-ISDT trim. Much valuable data was gained after Stocker and others rode these

A 1926 ohv Royal Enfield twin-port single 'flat tank'; typical of the Redditch factory's products of the period.

Originating in pre-First World War days, the big Enfield V-Twin (this is a 1926 996cc side-valve model) was to run until the outbreak of the Second World War and proved an excellent sidecar machine.

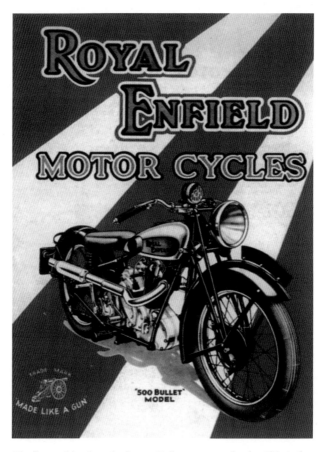

The first model to bear the famous Bullet name was the ohv 500 single with sloping cylinder and hi-level exhaust, circa 1933.

Some 35,000 Royal Enfield motorcycles were built for military use during the Second World War. The machine illustrated is a Model CO with a 348cc ohv engine.

A late 1930s 1,000cc V-Twin with non-standard front forks, but otherwise largely as it left the Redditch works.

Very original and unrestored 1949 350 Bullet, only the dual seat and silencer are non-standard.

The Ted Pardoe-designed 495cc 500 Twin made its debut in 1949. The model shown dates from 1950 and is entirely stock.

Launched at the Earls Court Show in London during November 1952, the 692cc Meteor was an excellent machine for both solo and sidecar use. Features included dual drum front brake and swinging arm frame.

When it appeared in August 1956, the 246cc unit construction single marked a modern approach for Enfield. It was the work of the young draughtsman Reg Thomas and was to sire a whole range of models over the next decade.

Café racer-styled 250 Continental GT. Note the crankshaft-mounted rev counter and the clean lines of the engine assembly.

This is the final version of the Crusader Sports, circa 1965. A lively little mount, it was overshadowed by the recently launched Continental GT.

A true classic, the Bullet ohv single remains in production, a testament to its advanced design when it was launched over half a century ago.

The 500 Bullet Army is a military specification motorcycle that is also available on the civilian market.

The 500 Bullet is also fully capable, with the appropriate lower gearing, for sidecar use. This model is seen here with a Watsonian 'chair'.

Classic 1960s-style Clubman S. Specification includes drop handlebars, alloy tank, swept-back pipe and Gold Star-type silencer.

Clubman S at rest. The nearest one can get to a Gold Star Clubman or Velocette Thruxton.

Clubman S power unit; probably the prettiest Bullet ever, with loads of polished aluminium and bright chromium plate.

American dirt-track action with a specially prepared Bullet single. During the 1950s, Royal Enfields were sold in the USA as Indians.

Bullet single-cylinder engine with pushrod-operated valves, coil ignition, four-speed gearbox and aluminium cylinder head.

BELOW: The existing British Royal Enfield importers Watsonian—Squire built this 350 Bullet 'Trials' prototype in 2001; it is now in limited production.

machines in competition that summer, ensuring that when the 700 Meteor was launched, it really was ready for service.

Gear Ratios

In solo guise, the Meteor's gear ratios were 4.47, 5.81, 8.05 and 12.45:1; whilst for sidecar use Enfield offered 5.03, 6.55, 9.07 and 14:1. When supplied for chair use, besides the alternative gearing, the front forks were also modified, including heavier springs and a steering damper fitted.

Beefing up the Chassis

To accommodate the extra power of the 700 engine, the chassis was given attention. This was largely achieved by a combination of frame strengthening, modifying the internals of the damping and stiffening up both the front and rear suspension, compared to the 500.

To cope with the combination of increased performance and higher weight, attention was also given to the braking. Enfield engineers thus saw fit to provide the 6in (15cm) dual front brake (first seen on a machine ridden in the 1950 ISDT) with its handlebar-mounted compensator, together with a 7in (18cm) rear stopper (equipped with a conventional Royal Enfield cush-drive assembly). It has to be said that the double front stopper was not really up to the job, made worse by its more than often poor set-up; both brakes needed to work in unison – something that most owners failed to achieve.

The Meteor's touring credentials were helped by the factory's excellent optional pannier set, complete with a sturdy steel frame.

General Equipment

The general equipment of the 700 Meteor was much as for the 500 Twin, with deeply valanced mudguards, similar tyre sizes and many of the cycle component parts. However, at 4gal (18ltr), the tank was larger – as well the carburettor size, up from $^{15}/_{16}$in (2.4cm) to $1^{1}/_{16}$in (2.7cm).

So Smooth

For such a large capacity vertical twin, the 700 Meteor in its original low state of tune proved exceptionally smooth. Not only this but it was also very responsive at low engine revolutions. This meant that there was little point in hanging on to the gears and screaming the engine. Far better to change-up early and let the engine's torque pull the bike along. Cruising speeds were up in the 70–80mph (113–129km/h) region with the engine feeling completely unstressed. However, the bolt-up Albion gearbox and clutch seemed under far more pressure than on the smaller twin, the former being rather stiff in action, whilst the latter, although light, was prone to problems; more so when used to haul a sidecar.

Minor Changes

The first set of changes, although relatively minor, came in October 1953, with the announcement of the 1954 Royal Enfield range.

The Meteor engine saw the adoption of light alloy pushrods instead of the original steel components. The main reason for this change was that thermal expansion of the aluminium rods was substantially the same as that of the light alloy cylinder head, hence valve clearances were less affected at working temperatures – another benefit was a slight reduction in mechanical noise. The modification brought the 700 Meteor engine into line with other Royal Enfield four-strokes employing alloy heads.

Another modification (also on the 500 Bullet single) was brazed-on malleable lugs on the lower members of the sub-frame carrying the pivoted rear fork (swinging arm); this form of construction replaced the bracing tubes and welded-in steel gusset plates hitherto employed.

The most noticeable change for 1954 (shared with several other models) concerned the adoption of a one-piece aluminium fork-crown casting, which embraced the headlight and formed an instrument console. Referred to as a casquette, it incorporated twin pilot lights (one each side).

The 1954 brochure for the Royal Enfield spring-frame models had a Meteor with a country scene as its setting.

Each of these twin pilot lights took a 6V, 3W bayonet-fitting bulb, and was equipped with a rubber-mounted chromium-plated rim.

A 30/24W double-filament bulb was employed for the 8in (20cm) diameter, pre-focus headlamp unit. Vertical adjustment of the light beam could be obtained by merely slackening the locking screw in the headlamp rim catch; operating in the slot, the screw allowed the whole assembly to pivot slightly from the two lower retaining screws.

The double-sided front brake, fitted as standard to the Meteor. The idea was born thanks to racer Bill Lomas welding up a pair of Enfield brakes on his very special 250 racer (see Chapter 9).

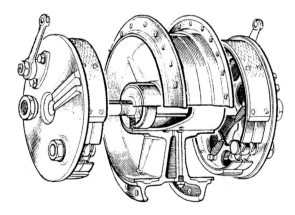

The working components of the dual front stopper. This used a full-width aluminium drum with iron liners and a pair of brake plates, as shown.

Magdyno

For the 1955 model year, both twin-cylinder models – the 500 Twin and the 700 Meteor – were fitted with Lucas magdyno ignition and lighting sets, in place of the coil ignition and dynamo lighting previously employed. In each case the magdyno was fitted at the top rear of the crankcase and was driven by duplex chain, from a sprocket on the inlet camshaft.

Like the Bullet singles, both the Twins were given redesigned cams embodying quietening ramps, which resulted in a marked decrease of mechanical noise. Also, like the Bullet range, the Twins benefited from a neater gearbox end cover. Though the footchange selector mechanism was fundamentally unaltered, the footchange pedal and the kickstart level were now mounted on coaxial shafts, thus ensuring superior placement of the gear lever in relation to the offside rider's footrest. The former worm-gear operation of the clutch thrust rod was superseded by an orthodox clutch fulcrum lever fully enclosed within the end cover.

Finally, to take advantage of the superior premium grade fuel by then available, new high compression pistons with a ratio of 7.25:1 were specified for the 700 Meteor.

High Performance Version

In September 1955, a new higher performance 700 was announced; known as the Super Meteor, this was a considerably modified version of the Meteor, which it replaced.

Plastic tank badge used from 1956 onwards.

Development of the 692cc engine had resulted in an increase of both power and torque – with the added advantage of a slight reduction of the engine speed at which peak power was generated.

The new unit put out 40bhp at 5,500rpm; this compared with the Meteor's 39bhp for the 1955 model and 36bhp previously – both at 6,000rpm. This gave the 700 Enfield a 100mph (161km/h) potential for the first time. Because of the engine's altered power characteristics, overall gearing had been raised by some 3 per cent, solo top gear ratio now being 4.33:1.

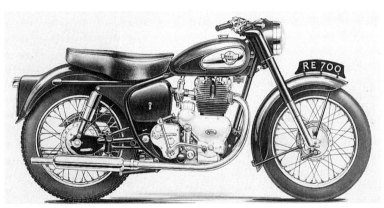

For the 1956 model year, Enfield introduced the new Super Meteor. Based on the Meteor, this had increased power output, alternator, magneto, new frame, new tank mounting, folding kickstarter and chrome tank panels. A 1957 model is shown.

Stiffened Crankshaft

To cope with the extra power, the one-piece crankshaft had been stiffened by an increase in crankpin diameter from 1⅜in (3.5cm) to 1¾in (4.4cm). To compensate for the increased crankpin weight, the crankshaft outer webs, which were previously circular, were cut away adjacent to each crankpin.

Increased Finning

The finning of the cast-iron cylinder barrels and their aluminium heads had also been considerably increased to provide greater heat dissipation. Spigot location of the heads on the barrels was superseded by the use of two hollow dowels for each joint, the dowels surrounding the outer head/retaining bolts. Elimination of the spigot permitted an increase in width of the cylinder-head gasket at the points adjacent to the pushrod tunnels and enabled the tunnels to be straightened.

Valve Gear Improvements

Without enlargement of the valve seats in the cylinder head, the diameter of the inlet valve head had been upped from 1½in (3.8cm) to 1⁹⁄₁₆in (4cm). Gas flow at part valve lift had been improved by radiasing the valve seat into the port and blending the throat of the valve into its seating. This practice had been first introduced on the 499cc Bullet single a year earlier.

The compression ratio of 7.25:1 remained unchanged from the final version of the Meteor.

The oil circulation rate had been doubled by the simple expedient of changing the oil-pump driving worm (which was integral with the timing sprocket retaining nut on the crankshaft) from single-start to two-start thread. The felt oil-filter was now no longer in the oil return to the oil compartment; instead it had been relocated between the feed pump and the big-end bearings, as on the Redditch company's single-cylinder four-stroke models including the famous Bullet.

Auto-Advance Mechanism

Control of the Lucas SR2 magneto was now by automatic advance, whilst the rotor of the AC generator (alternator) was carried on an extension of the crankshaft. Since the rotor was mounted on the inner half of the primary chaincase, the alternator was thus undisturbed by removal of the outer half of the case. The rectifier was located under the nose of the fuel tank.

The Amal carburettor size remained unchanged at 1¹⁄₁₆in (2.7cm) (although the instrument was now of the Monobloc type), whilst the air filter shared the nearside compartment of the pressed-steel box with the tool kit. The battery was contained in the offside of this box. The end of the box was retained by a thumb screw. Built into the tool compartment lid was a useful pocket – suitable for stowing the likes of spare bulbs, fuses or spark plugs.

A New Frame

Only one malleable lug was employed on the new frame of the Super Meteor, at the steering head; the remainder of the frame's construction was by welding. Two tubular loops were attached to the rear section of the 1½in (3.8cm) diameter top tube and were cross-braced to its rear extremity. The loops then swept behind the pressed-steel box, already described, and the gearbox before terminating together at a point below the engine and gearbox assembly.

The lower end of the tapered front down-tube picked up to the front of the crankcase. Box-section rearward extensions from the top of the loops provided an anchorage for the dual seat and the top mounting point of the Armstrong rear shocks. Two short cross-tubes were welded into each extension, providing sidecar and pannier attachment points. Gusset plates welded to the front of the loops supported the swinging arm pivot.

Detail Refinement

Detail refinements on the Super Meteor included a folding kickstart (previous fixed) and a new mounting for the fuel tank, which relieved it from frame stresses (i.e. vibration) and simplified its removal. Tank attachment at the front was by means of a horizontal bolt, which passed through a rubber-bonded steel sleeve on the frame. At the rear, a spring steel clip secured the tank to the frame top tube, from which it was insulated by rubber packing.

A new style plastic motif was a feature of the fuel tank (this also being found on the majority of other 1956 model year Enfields, excluding the Clipper and two-strokes).

Quickly Detachable Rear Wheel

Announced the previous year as an optional extra on the Bullet and twin-cylinder ranges, the QD (quickly detachable) rear wheel incorporating a full-width light alloy hub was adopted for the above models for 1957, including the Super Meteor, together with chromium-plated tank side panels, as standard equipment. The 1957 Super Meteor was listed at £260 18s.

Coil Ignition – Again

When details of the 1958 Royal Enfield range were announced towards the end of 1957, it was seen that, like the smaller Twin, which had adopted coil ignition twelve months earlier, it was now to be fitted to the Super Meteor. The only other change was, like the Bullet range and the smaller Twin, the fitment of a new-shape silencer (claimed to be more efficient) and made by specialists Burgess, to Royal Enfield specifications.

1958 was to see the introduction of the Airflow fairing and front mudguard. This substantial device was developed in co-operation with the Bristol Aviation Company and their wind tunnel facilities. This was proof, if any was needed, of Royal Enfield's forward-looking approach during this period, catering for all riders, from committed enthusiasts to commuters. Early Airflow mouldings were made by Enfield; later these were manufactured by the Bristol company.

Around the same time, Enfield loaned a Super Meteor to the Road Research Laboratory for development work on anti-lock brakes, based on the Maxaret system, which had been proved on the Ferguson racing car. Sadly, Tony Wilson-Jones, Royal Enfield's chief development engineer, could not see much of a future for this device, and the project was quietly allowed to lapse. However, as quite often in its history, Enfield was very much at the forefront of technology; this was another example of Wilson-Jones' judgement being less than perfect.

With the arrival of the even more highly tuned Constellation, in the spring of 1958, the Super Meteor was to fade into the background, even though production was to continue until as late as 1962. As events described in Chapter 11 reveal, both the factory and its customers would have been better off sticking to the Meteor.

1958 Super Meteor with chrome tank panel, plastic badge and twin exhaust systems.

The Super Meteor engine, unlike the Constellation, had a single carb head. This had the advantage of being much easier to set up for the home mechanic.

As on the other Enfield Twins, the vertical split between the pots means ease of maintenance and less cost if replacements are needed, but less rigidity than one-piece barrels and heads.

Siamezed Exhaust

For the 1959 season, the Super Meteor was fitted with a siamezed exhaust system similar to the incoming Constellation. Bosses were now provided on the steering head lugs so that the Airflow fairing might be readily attached, as on the other models.

As before, the Super Meteor (together with the Constellation and Bullet single) could be supplied in sidecar specification at no extra cost.

For the 1960 model year, the Super Meteor (and Constellation) were given longer lasting neolangite-bonded clutch plates and a new style casquette. Then, a year later, it gained (again with the Constellation) a new wider rear mudguard moulded in fibre-glass. For the convenience of rear wheel maintenance, the complete assembly – mudguard,

seat, inner guard and sub-frame – was quickly detachable; at the front, two clips welded to the sub-frame engaged with a cross-member on the main frame beneath the seat nose, whilst slotted lugs picked up on the spring-unit upper mounting bolts. Attached to lugs on the sub-frame, a chromium-plated lifting handle was provided at each side. The handle passed through rubber grommets in the mudguard moulding. The sub-frame was a complete loop and, at the rear, it had a lug to which the boxed-in rear number plate was bolted.

Another 1961 change was the introduction of the larger 4¼gal (19ltr) fuel tank from the Constellation. However, as with this latter model, there was a modified method of mounting. But unlike the Constellation, the tank on the Super Meteor was painted, rather than chromium plated.

A 1960 Super Meteor and single-seat Watsonian Sports sidecar.

The Super Meteor provided a comfortable riding stance, thanks in no small part to the sensible handlebar layout. Note the large aluminium steering damper knob.

For both 700s, there was a new Lucas battery (coded MLZ9E) with a clear body. There was also a new silencer, torpedo in shape, with a polished, cast aluminium tailpiece decorated on its upper face by a narrow fin. Also new was the clutch, featuring a star-shaped outer plate, conventional pushrod, six pressure and five friction plates, including sprocket.

Silentbloc Swinging Arm Bushes

From January 1961 all Super Meteors (and Constellations) leaving the Royal Enfield plant used silentbloc instead of bronze bushes for the swinging arm (this move did nothing for the handling). Another modification was the semi-faired rear mudguard, initially of fibre-glass, now a steel pressing; the appearance remaining identical – the change being necessitated by stress fractures of the fibre-glass version in service caused by vibration.

When the 736cc Interceptor was launched for the 1963 season, the Constellation and Super Meteor merged (using the Constellation name), with a specification more akin to the Super Meteor: low compression, single Amal carburettor and 40bhp at 5,500rpm. This machine was clearly

This highly unusual Meteor has been 'chopped' into a prize-winning custom bike. Only the engine remains from the original bike, and even this has been extensively worked on with reversed cylinder head, SU carburettor and engraving of the outer engine casings. The owner is Dino Kingsford; venue Kent Custom Show, circa mid-1980s.

intended as a sidecar machine, with features such as lowered gearing, reduced fork trail, stiffer suspension front and rear, steering damper and, in addition, fitted with the same size tyres front and rear, both with square section for sidecar use. It could also be ordered specially, in solo guise.

Due to declining sidecar sales, and the introduction of the bigger capacity Interceptor, the final 692cc Royal Enfield Twin departed the factory in early 1963. It was the end of a model that had first appeared just over a decade earlier with the launch of the Meteor at the London Show in late 1952.

American Sales

During the decade spanning the 1950s, Royal Enfield sales, together with other British manufacturers including AJS, Matchless, Norton and Vincent, were all handled by the Indian company.

Indian, together with Harley-Davidson were – and still are – the most famous of all the American motorcycle marques. Founded in 1901 by George M. Hendee and Carl Oscar Hedstrom, they built up an enviable reputation in the first half of the twentieth century. Their most famous models were the Scout 600cc V-twin (1919), Chief 1,000cc V-twin (1922) and Big Chief 1,200cc (1923). But, like Harley-Davidson, Indian was hard hit by the Great Depression, caused by the Wall Street crash of October 1929. This saw Indian acquired by the industrialist E.P. DuPont in 1930.

For the remainder of the 1930s Indian slugged it out with HD for sales on the home market. During the Second World War both firms were major suppliers to the military. Then in 1949, a cash injection was made by British entrepreneur

John Brockhouse, and soon Brockhouse assumed control of the American company; but this failed to transfer into increased sales of Indian's traditional V-twins. The result was that Brockhouse marketed the British marques referred to above – plus Royal Enfield. In fact, unlike the others, Royal Enfields were re-badged as Indians for the American market, with sales beginning in 1951. Eventually a whole host of models arrived in the USA. These included the following:

- Fire Arrow (350 Bullet);
- Chief (700 Meteor);
- Trail Blazer (700 Meteor);
- Fire Arrow (250 Crusader);
- Hounds Arrow (250 Crusader).

The machines were suitably modified and restyled for the American market; for example: more deeply valenced mudguards and, in the case of the Chief (700 Meteor), 16in (41cm) wheels. The Chief was also sold for police duties, a notable user being the NYPD (New York Police Department). The Brockhouse Indian operation finally ended in 1960.

Later there were to be many attempts to relaunch the Indian name, notably by the well-known publisher and motorcycle enthusiast Floyd Clymer. But none of these involved Royal Enfield, except for Interceptor engines.

As for Royal Enfield motorcycles, these continued to be sold in the States during the 1960s by various smaller distributors. Today the Indian Madras-made Enfields have, as in Europe, a loyal and enthusiastic customer base.

Other Interests – and an Inside View

Royal Enfield has never received true credit for its wide range of motorcycles – and certainly

Indian Chief (basically an Americanized 692cc Meteor) circa mid-1950s. The spec included crashbars, 16-inch wheels and police equipment.

never for its other interests. In fact, in many ways Enfield was a major force – not only did it have its well-known Redditch facilities, which covered no less than 35 acres (14ha), but at various times there were other plants including satellite factories at Bradford on Avon, Westwood, Wiltshire and Feckenham, plus a Scottish shadow factory.

The truth is that, compared with the likes of Norton, Velocette, Vincent, James and the like, Royal Enfield was huge, and for quality matched the likes of BSA and Triumph.

Besides motorcycles, it produced bicycles in vast quantities during the same period. It was a major components supplier to both the wider motorcycle and bicycle industries. Unlike many, Enfield was not simply an assembler, but designed and manufactured most of its component parts.

Enfield Industrial Engines designed and produced a range of diesel engines comprising 100mm and 85mm single and twins – both vertical and horizontal, and a 350cc vertical, both marine and industrial versions, together with transmission systems with diverse applications. To quote former employee Bob Humphries: 'Reliability was proven by applications such as the Antarctic expedition with Enfield's Ray Watton accompanying the expedition to supervise continuous operations throughout the Arctic winter.'

Enfield engines were also used by other manufacturers. These included the Berkeley three-wheel sports car (using the 692cc Constellation) the Floyd Clymer American Indian and Rickman (both of which used the 736cc Interceptor). Other applications included hovercraft.

The Bradford on Avon works shared an old mill by the river with the Spencer-Moulton rubber company. Alex Moulton was the inventor of the Hydralastic suspension, first used on the BMC Mini by Alec Issigonis. Royal Enfield and Spencer-Moulton co-operated on a unique suspension system for a little-known prototype scooter – a brilliant idea that, sadly, was not proceeded with. The Moulton cycle with rubber suspension was produced by Enfield (and Rayleigh) before Moulton and Enfield went their own ways.

Finally, it is worth pointing out that during the reign of Major Smith, Enfield was not ruled, as was much of the rest of the British industry, by cost accountants with little knowledge or interest in motorcycles, but Major Smith was an autocrat – even if he was a fair one. Probably his biggest failing was that in his later years, he did not authorize enough investment. However, as a fully qualified and experienced engineer, at least what investment there was, was usually money well spent.

Enfield through the years also had some excellent designers – Ted Pardoe and Tony Wilson-Jones are names that immediately spring to mind, but potentially the greatest was Reg Thomas. He not only created the Crusader, but also a superb 175cc overhead cam single (which remained a prototype only), plus a Streamliner (the latter now on show in a Japanese museum).

Reg Thomas in fact designed a vast array of machinery – not only connected with two wheels, but also such diverse projects as drawings for an outboard motor, a lawn mower, a massive road-sweeper and even a machine to climb up the big steel cables of a gold mine in South Africa to clean them!

To quote Bob Humphries again:

> The problem with a family firm like Enfield is that very often, there is no-one in the wings waiting to take over when the Manager retires or passes away. E & HP Smith (no relation to Major Smith) bought the Enfield company for a very small sum. They were an insignificant company without any idea how to run an enterprise of the size and calibre of Royal Enfield. What's worse, they were asset-strippers. This soon become obvious as assets went out of the door. They acquired a sizeable integrated plant with every facility, broke it up and sold if off! Industrial sabotage!

Yes, the end of the British Royal Enfield company is sad indeed – and it only goes to prove that all good things can fail, just as a plant will fail without care, attention and water. But at least, unlike most British marques, the name survives in the present day.

9 Road Racing

Many enthusiasts may recall the much publicized, but ultimately largely unsuccessful GP5 two-stroke single of the mid-1960s, whilst some may remember the sight of the 'Flying Scot', Bob McIntyre, aboard the 700 Super Meteor and Constellation Twins in the Thruxton 500-Miler in the late 1950s. Even fewer know about the exploits of future world champion, Bill Lomas, on his home-brewed dohc Enfield 250 single in the late 1940s, but it is a near certainty that most readers will not know the rest of Royal Enfield's long racing career; a career that actually began at the turn of the twentieth century and continues to the present time – almost since the dawn of the internal combustion engine.

Early Efforts

As related in Chapter 1, Enfield's first 'motorcycle' was a crude affair, with its single-cylinder engine mounted on a bracket attached to a pair of rigid front forks and driving the rear wheel by way of a crossed belt. From this exceedingly humble beginning in 1901 was to come a long line of machines that, as often as not, at least during the company's first half-century, were true pioneers in innovative engineering progress.

Typical of this pioneering spirit was dry sump lubrication, Royal Enfield being the first to produce a motorcycle featuring such a system, while, in 1912, the Redditch-based marque had begun constructing engines of its own design, instead of buying in units from outside suppliers.

Tourist Trophy

Enfield's first appearance in the Isle of Man TT came in 1911, and coincided with major changes to this annual speed feast that had begun in 1907. For starters, the Snaefell 'Mountain' Course,

Future World Champion Bill Lomas winning at Brough, East Yorkshire on his home-brewed 248cc dohc Enfield, 7 April 1950.

pioneered by the cars, was used by motorcyclists for the first time. This presented a formidable challenge to riders and machines alike, with suspensions as primitive as the largely unsurfaced roads. In fact, only from Douglas to Ballacraine was tarred, whilst the Mountain section was little more than a cart track, riders having to select a vacant wheel rut when attempting a passing manoeuvre.

The move to the 37.73 mile (61km) mountain circuit was accompanied by the introduction of a race for the popular 2½hp machines. Known as the Junior TT, it was as that time for either 300cc singles or 340 twins.

A pair of Royal Enfield V-Twins were entered: one retired, and the other, ridden by H. Greaves, came home a magnificent fifth out of thirty-four starters in the four-lap, 151 mile (243km) race. Greaves' machine used a 339cc (60 × 61mm) JAP-made V-Twin engine, with Enfield's own two-speed transmission and all-chain drive.

A Wonderful Showing

After relatively poor showings in the 1912 and 1913 TTs, the Junior of 1914 provided Royal Enfield and its supporters with a wonderful demonstration of speed and reliability, with eight

of the nine machines finishing. Not only this, but with third, eighth, fifteenth, twentieth, twenty-first, twenty-third and twenty-sixth from the forty-eight starters, it was an impressive display. As for the race itself, this was staged in wet, misty conditions and proved a tussle between the Enfield V-Twins (using their own 340cc 54 × 74mm power units), the AJS singles and Douglas flat twins. The leading Royal Enfield rider was F.J. Walker, who initially led the race before falling. Even so, he battled back to a gallant third at the finish, only to crash a few yards after taking the flag – due to a wooden barrier being placed across the road to prevent slower riders going for another lap. Sadly, his injuries were such that Walker died some five days later, never regaining consciousness.

Brooklands

Besides its TT success, Enfield also competed at the Brooklands track in Surrey in the pre-First World War period. Probably the best results were a second and third place in the 350cc category of the 1913 Brooklands Six-Hour race. Again the trusty 340cc V-Twin was used. This competition was benefiting the standard production line that employed developments of this power plant.

The 340cc ioe V-Twin of the type used by F.J. Walker to gain third in the 1914 Junior TT. It featured dry sump lubrication, forward-mounted magneto and chain final drive.

More TT Success

Two riders achieved considerable success with Enfield during the inter-war years: J.G. (John Gordon) Burney (later to become the great Stanley Wood's brother-in-law) and C.S. (Cecil) Barrow.

Burney rode Enfields in six TT races from 1925 until 1928; his best placings were sixth in the 1926 Junior and tenth the same year in the Senior. Barrow achieved runner-up in the 1928 Lightweight, seventh in the 1927 Junior and finally, a magnificent eighth in the 1935 Senior. This latter result, riding a specially tuned four-valve Bullet single with inclined cylinder, was a fabulous result considering Barrow was aboard what amounted to a race-kitted roadster, and was ranged against an impressive array of specialist factory racers from the likes of Norton, Moto Guzzi, Velocette and Husqvarna, and riders such as Jimmy Guthrie, J.H. (Crasher) White, Stanley Woods, Walter Rusk and many other stars.

Team Award

Besides Barrow and Burney, another regular Royal Enfield TT competitor was G.L. (George) Reynard who came home fourth in the 1927 Junior, and was also placed sixth in the 1928 Senior. Not only this, but the trio of Barrow, Burney and Reynard also won the Manufacturer's Team Award for the company in the 1927 Junior TT. It is also worth mentioning that the legendary Stanley Woods raced an Enfield in the 1925 Junior TT, and George Burney gave the Redditch marque its first Grand Prix victory when he won the 350cc Ulster GP in 1925, at an average speed of 65.5mph (105km/h).

Technical Developments

From 1925 until 1929 Royal Enfield used bought-in JAP engines for its machinery. In addition, during 1926 an over-the-counter customer racer powered by a twin-port 344cc JAP single was marketed, but by 1930 Enfield was again relying on engines designed and built by itself for both racing and its production roadsters. The former were essentially specially tuned versions of the series production ohv singles.

An important Royal Enfield development was that of plain big-end bearings, when most rivals relied on the roller bearing variety. First trials were carried out on factory-entered models in the 1934 and 1935 TT series. Essentially the plain big-end

A leading Enfield racer of the inter-war years was J.G. (John Gordon) Burney. Married to Stanley Wood's sister Violet, Burney's best placing in six TTs was sixth in the 1926 Junior. He is pictured here with his 1927 TT mount.

bearing consisted of a floating duralinium bush running on a hardened crankpin, with a hardened ring pressed into the big-end eye of the connecting rod.

The results proved good enough for racing purposes, but needed more development before it could be introduced into the series production roadsters. For racing, the combination of large clearance and a good supply of Castrol R vegetable oil was acceptable, but the excess of mechanical noise when used with a mineral oil and effective silencing proved more than customers were prepared to accept. However, the Enfield engineering team of Ted Pardoe and Tony Wilson-Jones worked away at the problem, and a solution was found by replacing the duralinium bush with a steel component, this latter item being faced on both sides with white metal. This arrangement provided an excellent compromise, by allowing reduced running tolerances and making less exacting demands upon the quantity and grade of lubricant required. So this really was a case of racing improving the breed in the truest sense.

Record Breaking

During the 1928 TT, the Swedish rider E. Magner had taken part in the Lightweight and Junior races on Royal Enfield machinery. Although he was a retirement in the Junior, the Swede came home sixteenth in the Lightweight and Cecil Barrow brought his Enfield home runner-up behind race winner F.A. (Frank) Longman's OK Supreme. This was a real test of endurance, both for man and machine, as these 250cc class machines had to take in no less than seven laps of the fearsome Mountain Circuit, a distance of 264.11 miles (425km).

Although Magner never returned to race in the Island, his Royal Enfield association certainly did not end there. In 1930, driving a 1,000cc JAP V-Twin-engined machine and sidecar, he captured the world sidecar speed record by covering the flying mile at an average two-way speed of 117.76mph (189km) on a frozen lake in his native Sweden.

Post-War

After the mid-1930s, Royal Enfield had disappeared from the racing scene, instead contenting itself with participation in the 'feet-up' trials game (*see* Chapter 7). Although several Royal Enfield entries were made in the 125cc class (including the TT: fourteenth in 1951 and a retirement in 1952), it was really one man who put the Redditch company back on the racing map during the immediate post-Second World War period: Bill Lomas.

Bill Lomas

Bill Lomas, who was later to become world champion with the Italian Moto Guzzi marque, began his association with Royal Enfield after he was demobbed from active service. This came about after a young Lomas visited the Redditch factory to collect some spares one day, where he met Jack Booker, the pre-war trials and racing rider who was, at that time, Enfield's Competition boss. Booker offered Lomas a job at Enfield's in the Competition Department. Bill went on to reveal that not only did he 'settle in a hostel in Redditch with Charlie Rogers [works trials rider and development man] as my neighbour', but also that 'design chief Mr Tony Wilson-Jones was very good to me and allowed me to work on my race bikes and use the dyno to test the engines'.

In addition, Bill Lomas was given the task 'to build all the trials engines and, most importantly, those to be used in the International Six Days Trial'. He was closely involved with the success garnered by the Enfield team riders in the 1948 ISDT.

RE 125 Two-Strokes

Lomas also played around with the RE 125 two-stroke engine (*see* Chapter 5), experimenting with various port changes and exhaust modifications. He even tried a high-compression head with a methanol mixture. With a double reverse cone exhaust and by brazing an additional exhaust port, maximum speed was raised to 75mph (121km/h), with particularly impressive acceleration.

Bill Lomas cresting the mountain at Cadwell Park on his 500 Enfield JAP, 1949.

After fluffing his start at Cadwell Park, Bill Lomas stormed through the field to finish runner-up on its debut. However, upon his return to the works with the 'racerized' RE 125, his boss Jack Booker commandeered the tiny bike, fitted knobbly tyres and took it scrambling. Unfortunately, this meant the end of another potentially successful Enfield racing project.

Clubman's Bullet

Besides his very successful ventures with both pushrod and dohc-based Enfield 250 specials (*see box on page 112*), Bill Lomas also rode one of the new swinging arm 350 Bullet models in the 1949 Clubman's TT in the Isle of Man. Jack Booker was keen enough to offer Lomas a Bullet, to see if it could be made competitive. After a session of tuning, the results were very encouraging, with the engine putting out 25.6bhp at 7,400rpm, and a maximum speed of around 105mph (169km/h) was possible thanks to the following specifications:

- modified valves;
- high compression piston;
- Lomas cams;
- straight-through exhaust (pipe rather than megaphone);

- Amal 1⅛in (3cm) TT carburettor.

All the factory had to do was to get it homologated by the ACU – by offering these components as a 'sports kit' in its sales brochure.

Unfortunately, this was not done, so instead Lomas had to use his Bullet in the Clubman's TT with a totally standard spec. In this form the best output was 21.8bhp at 6,800rpm and a top speed of some 90mph (145km/h). But it was still decided to go ahead. In the race, when lying in the first half-dozen, Lomas was forced out through a broken tappet. Even so, it had been an excellent showing, with the main opposition being Norton, BSA and Velocette. Besides Bill Lomas, other competitors aboard Bullets in the 1949 350cc Junior Clubman's TT were L. Bertorelli, C.M. Hopwood, W. Lishman, S.T. Seston and K.G. Adcock.

The first Enfield home (out of fifty-nine finishers) was Bertorelli in twenty-eighth position, at an average speed of 67.56mph (109km/h). As for Bill Lomas, his early Royal Enfield performances had marked him down as a star of the future and he went on to ride for factories such as NSU, MV Agusta and finally Moto Guzzi winning Grands Prix, TTs and world titles along the way, before finally retiring (when Guzzi quit) at the end of 1957.

Lomas-Enfield 250 Special

As explained in the main text, the Bill Lomas 250 Royal Enfield began life as a 1938 production roadster. Bill first raced it in 1947, with the original rigid frame, telescopic front forks and a home-tuned engine (using the production type ohv cylinder head). For the 1948 season it gained rear springing, by removing the rear portion of the frame and by bolting a pair of ⁵⁄₁₆in aluminium plates onto the rear frame mountings. As Bill describes in his excellent book *Bill Lomas World Champion Road Racer*:

> Between these, I put in an Enfield swinging arm, the dampers being set at an angle with several holes on the top mounting plates, rather in the way of the swinging-arm Velocettes. This made it possible to vary the spring and damper strength.

Bill Lomas proved his potential as both a rider and tuner by winning the Cadwell Park circuit championship three years in a row on his home-brewed Enfield Special. Jack Booker had given him the alloy cylinder he had used in his pre-war ISDT 250 and, as Bill recalled, 'you could still see the small hole drilled in one of the fins where the official sealing wire had been'.

The only real engine failure on the ohv Lomas-Enfield was when a con-rod let go at Scarborough, punching a hole through the crankcase. However, once one of the new, stronger 350 Bullet rods was put in, there was no repeat performance.

By the end of the 1948 season, it had become apparent that the push-rod set-up had reached the limit of its development. A maximum of around 7,800rpm was possible before valve bounce set in, the power output of the 1949 ohv 250 engine being around 23bhp on petrol.

DOHC

For a considerable time Bill Lomas had had the idea of a double overhead camshaft (dohc) conversion; he saw this as the way to more revs and thus more power. His father Harry thought it would be time wasted as by this time Bill had a factory Velocette ride and had left Enfield's employ, but Bill still decided to go ahead. His aero-modelling experience came in useful in producing some accurate drawings and wooden patterns for the timing cases and, thanks to his contacts (including fellow special builder Dennis Jones), he went ahead with the dohc conversion, which took him from August 1949 until February 1950.

The bottom half of the engine was virtually as before and a conventional cast-iron cylinder was used. The real work and innovation was in the head and cam-box. The former was an aluminium-bronze product, originally of Enfield manufacture, but extensively modified for its new role. Alterations to the internals of the engine included the provision of a positive oil-feed to the big-end bearing and the discarding of the conventional Royal Enfield oil sump. Instead, a controlled quantity of oil was returned to a separate tank by a second pump formed by the two idler gears of the magneto drive. The exact amount returned was limited by the extremely small oilways, which were of 30/1000in diameter.

Gears and Chain

The innovative gear-cum-chain camshaft drive was carried in an aluminium casing. A pinion on the crankshaft mated with an idler pinion that drove a combined gear and sprocket. The drive was then taken by a ⅜in chain to the camshafts, a pair of jockey sprockets being interposed to provide the necessary right-angle changes in direction of the drive. One of the aforementioned sprockets was mounted on an eccentric to provide for chain adjustment, whilst a slipper-type tensioner took up the adjustment on the rear run. All pinions and sprocket shafts featured fully floating bearings, while each camshaft was carried on a trio of ball-race bearings. A constant supply of lubricant was fed to the camboxes by external oil pipes. The Amal TT-type carburettor was mounted on an alloy distance piece, that was finned.

As *The Motor Cycle* once remarked:

> The whole ensemble of the power unit is somewhat reminiscent of the famous TT-winning (1939) Benelli of the same capacity, but which of course employed gear drive to camshaft.

Perhaps this was to be expected because, as Bill Lomas was to say later:

For a long time I'd had an idea for a dohc conversion, being spurred on by the performance and looks of the fantastic 250 Benelli.

A Brilliant Debut
Bill Lomas and his 250 double-knocker special certainly made a brilliant start to the 1950 racing season. In its first three meetings it came second at Anstey, first at Brough and first again at Cadwell Park, stamping its authority on the British 250cc short circuit racing class.

The 1950 model employed the modified frame with twin-shock rear suspension and Enfield telescopic front forks, an Albion 4-speed close-ratio gearbox and a clutch from the same source. Besides the engine, the most significant feature of the Lomas-Enfield was the double-sided 6in front stopper, formed by joining together back-to-back a couple of standard production Royal Enfield hubs. This identical set-up was later used on the twins and some Bullet models; which, in its own way, is a lasting tribute to the largely self-funded Lomas racing efforts.

Key features of the 1950 Lomas-Enfield 250 dohc engine were as follows:

1. Each camshaft and tappet had a direct oil feed. The lubricant ran back through the cam bearings into the drive casing, lubricating everything on its way. This was then pumped from the timing case into an alloy tank by the two timing case gears originally used to pump the engine oil back into the sump tank. The oil in the separate oil tank was fed through an oil pipe back into the sump tank. This helped cool the oil. The big-end bearing was a Velocette KTT type, with a special crankpin to suit the Enfield crank flywheels.
2. 29mm Amal GP Carburettor with 4in manifold.
3. Petrol compression ratio 9.61, giving 23bhp at 8,200rpm. Methanol compression ratio 11.51, giving 24.2bhp at 8,500rpm.
4. Valve timing: inlet open 55° BTDC, closing 78° ATDC;
   exhaust open 80° BBDC, closing 50° ATDC.
5. Valve lift 0.335in.
6. Ignition timing 48° BTDC
7. Tappets used were flat-base Enfield components, shortened and hard-chromed. Tappet clearance was by valve stem caps of various thicknesses.
8. It was also projected to use oversquare 70 × 64mm bore and stroke measurements with an aluminium Alfin cylinder barrel.

Syd Lawton

The next Royal Enfield involvement with racing came in 1956, when the former Norton works rider Syd Lawton, co-owner of Southampton dealers Lawton and Wilson, entered one of his Redditch concern's 692cc Super Meteors (*see* Chapter 8) in the 1956 Thruxton Nine Hours (the race winner covering over 650 miles (1,045km)). After two hours, the 750cc class was led by the Lawton Super Meteor, ridden by Dennis Christian and Eddie Crookes. However, it was eventually sidelined due to a bent valve – caused by rider error in changing down instead of up!

A return was made by the Lawton equipé the next year, 1957, when another of the Redditch-built twins piloted by Derek Powell and Brian Newman finished third, averaging 71.69mph (115km/h). Actually, as *The Motor Cycle* race report recorded: 'The Royal Enfield Super Meteor with Derek Powell aboard led comfortably on an eased throttle. Given a reasonable run it was obviously so fast, and so well ridden, as to seem a certain winner.' However, tank trouble (a split seam) reared its head, eventually forcing the team back into third place, but this was still a good result – it was the only Enfield of any description in the race and it came home in the top three. This was in contrast to makes such as BSA and Triumph who suffered many retirements.

Bob McIntyre on the Syd Lawton-entered Super Meteor (converted to Constellation spec) during the 1958 Thruxton 500-Miler. Together with co-rider Derek Powell, the team finished runners-up to the Triumph Tiger 110 teamsters of Mike Hailwood and Dan Shorey.

Thruxton 500-Miler

For 1958, the Nine Hours became the 500-Miler. Three Royal Enfields (all 692cc twins) took part, two finishing (second and third), the other retiring (with a broken crankcase). The race centred on a duel for the lead between the Super Meteor (converted to Constellation specification) of Bob McIntyre and Derek Powell (entered by Syd Lawton) and the Triumph Tiger 110 of Mike Hailwood and Dan Shorey. Once again the Enfield proved the fastest bike out on the track, and again it suffered tank problems that eventually cost it victory. The third place Enfield (a new 1958 Constellation) was ridden by Ken James and Brian Newman.

The reason that Lawton's machine of McIntyre/Powell was a Super Meteor instead of one of the new Constellations, was that Lawton did not have too much confidence in some of the changes incorporated by Enfield's designer Tony Wilson-Jones (*see* Chapter 11). This was the Lawton's number one bike (he also entered the James/Newman machine), and sported Norton Roadholder front fork tubes (needed because of McIntyre's hard riding).

McIntyre again rode for Lawton in the 1959 event, but first suffered clutch gremlins after leading in the early stages then, when trying to make up for lost time, he crashed and subsequently retired. A crash (caused through the primary chain breaking) also put McIntyre (partnered by Alan Rutherford) out of the 1960 race.

The late Syd Lawton, talking to the author about his Thruxton experiences in the long distance production races of the 1950s and 1960s, had this to say about the big Enfield twins he campaigned in various guises from 1956 through to 1961:

> I really felt that of all the big British vertical twins the Royal Enfield had the most potential. Not only was it the biggest [at the time], but also the fastest. But unfortunately Tony Wilson-Jones did not do a particularly good job with the Constellation and, of a list of some thirty items that needed attention, only a few were ever acted upon. I just could not get through to him [Wilson-Jones] and I got the impression he resented my input.

In fact, as Syd also revealed, the final year of his involvement was typical of the Wilson-Jones influence. The Enfield development engineer 'taking it into his head to introduce new big-end bolts, which were supposed to be stronger'. Unfortunately, soon after the start of the 1961 500-Miler, a big-end bolt broke, the result being a locked engine, and rider Bob McIntyre coming into contact with the Thruxton tarmac at well over 100mph (161km/h).

Single-carb Super Meteor-engined racing sidecar out of J.E. Marchant photographed in the paddock at Crystal Palace, 2 July 1960.

Syd Lawton then switched his allegiance to Nortons, winning three Thruxton marathons in successive years (1962, 1963 and 1964) with one of the excellent 650SS models. Even so, right up to the end of his life, Syd stuck to his belief that the Enfield twin could have been a winner at Thruxton. Also, it is probably worth mentioning that brilliant rider though he was, Bob McIntyre was not really best suited to endurance racing. A point Lawton conceded to me – and why, from 1962 onwards, he switched to the combination of Phil Read and Brian Setchell.

Two-Fifty Success

The introduction of the Crusader Sports had also signalled the use of Enfield's unit 250 single in production class events such as the Thruxton classic. Probably the best year was 1963, when John Hartle and Monty Buxton shared a works-

Racer/journalist Ray Knight with his 500 Royal Enfield twin-engined special; the balance of the machine was an early AJS 7R, circa 1962.

Besides the big twins, Royal Enfield also achieved considerable success in long-distance races during the early and mid-1960s with its various unit construction ohv 250 singles. Dave Simmonds is shown here during the 1966 Brands Hatch 500-Miler. The bike is a Super 5.

supported Super 5 to gain a brilliant runner-up position in a hotly contested event. When one considers that there were works or semi-works entries from the likes of Bultaco, Montesa, Honda, Ariel and DKW, this was an impressive display by the Redditch factory. Sad to say, that year the only big twin Enfield (a Constellation), ridden by Ray Knight and Peter Walker, went out with a broken connecting rod.

The GP5 Project

The GP5 project lasted some two years and was probably the most serious attempt by Royal Enfield to build a purpose-built racing motorcycle in its entire history, rather than one developed from an existing production roadster.

Its origins can be traced to late 1962 and the launch of the new Villiers Starmaker single-cylinder 247cc (68 × 68mm) piston port two-stroke engine (in both road racing and scrambles forms) and the subsequent arrival of the Greeves Silverstone, Cotton Telstar and DMW Hornet over-the-counter customer racers. The Greeves in particular proved a real star – literally – by winning the coveted ACU (Auto Cycle Union) 250cc Star British Championship series in 1963, with Tom Phillips aboard, at its first attempt.

In late 1962, Royal Enfield had accepted one of a number of take-over bids (this following, in April 1962, the death of the much respected managing director and major shareholder, Major Frank Smith), by the E. and H.P. Smith Group of companies (no relation).

From the Smith Group came a new joint managing director (together with Enfield's existing Major Vic Mountford), Leo Davenport, to oversee the Redditch operation. Davenport certainly had a motorcycling background, having been a former racer himself of no mean talent. In his career he had won no less an event than the 1932 Isle of Man Lightweight (250cc) TT, on a New Imperial.

Davenport Takes Control

Besides his role as joint MD, Davenport also became the Enfield Competitions Manager. He could see the success that Greeves in particular had achieved – not just road racing, but also scrambling. So he set about authorizing the development of both tarmac and dirt racers. Initially developed by Charlie Rogers, the first result was the debut of a prototype scrambler, which, ridden by Bill Gwynne, was powered by a bought-in Villiers Starmaker engine. Like the road racer that followed, the dirt iron sported a set of Reynolds

Geoff Duke was recruited by the then joint managing director and race boss, Leo Davenport, to publicize the marque and advise on racing matters. Geoff is seen here outside the Redditch works with the prototype of the GP5 racer, spring 1964.

leading link forks, whilst both front and rear brake hubs were full width aluminium assemblies from Enfield's own foundry.

The Prototype Arrives

By the time the first prototype road racer arrived in early 1964, Davenport had hired Geoff Duke to help develop its new road racer and its production roadsters. At that time Duke had only been retired from racing himself a relatively short while, and had also run the Scuderia Duke Gilera squad in the 1963 World Championship series. So in many ways he was an ideal choice, both from expertise and the publicity standpoint.

Davenport realized that as Enfield was coming onto the scene a year later than the others, and with the Greeves Silverstone already very much a household name, the GP5 simply had to be a superior bike. Even though the Redditch-built newcomer was intended, like the Cotton, DMW and Greeves, primarily as a customer racer, a limited programme of competing as a factory (works) was envisaged.

Hartle Tests at Oulton Park

In mid-March 1964, ex-Norton, MV and Gilera works rider John Hartle gave the Enfield racer its first track test at Oulton Park, Cheshire. As *Motorcycle News* reported: 'If looks are anything to go by, the 250 Enfield is a winner already. It is beautifully styled and looks like a miniature MV with all cycle parts finished in silver and red fittings.'

A Stop-Gap

What many did not realize at the time, was that the bike Hartle used was to be a stop-gap – the later production models (and those used by the works) were considerably different, as is detailed later.

The frame was of Royal Enfield's own design, but built by Reynolds Tubes Ltd and, as already stated, was kitted out with the same company's front fork, full-width hubs and a Villiers Starmaker engine. The carburettor was a 1½in (3.8cm) Amal GP with remote float chamber, bolted very close to the head. The bodywork, tank, seat and fairing were fibreglass and made for Enfield by the Mitchenhall Brothers. At the time *Motor Cycle News* reported

Except for a slight pattering at the front end, caused by oversprung fork springs, John Hartle gave full marks to the new Royal Enfield 250 racer when he tried it at Oulton Park last week. There certainly couldn't have been much adrift with it, for at this first try-out, John lapped the Cheshire circuit at 82.5mph [133km/h].

John Hartle testing the original Starmaker-powered GP5 prototype at Oulton Park in March 1964.

But in the very same story, MCN were asking, 'Was this Hartle's first and last ride on the Enfield racer?' – saying that, although he had been entered by Geoff Duke (that is, the factory) at the International Hutchinson 100 meeting at Silverstone on 4 April, it now seemed likely that there would be a change of rider. Considering that the reason given was that Hartle's oil company commitments were different from those of Royal Enfield, and that Hartle and Duke had been together with Gilera the previous year, this seems a strange excuse.

However, a few days later everything appeared to have been sorted out, with *Motor Cycle News* reporting that agreement had been made between Hartle's oil company (Castrol) and Royal Enfield, who as a factory were contracted to Shell Mex and BP (Shell and BP then being a combined operation). Other names mentioned were the Canadian Mike Duff and Tony Godfrey. Leo Davenport was also said to be 'Pleased with progress made so far' and was confident that the use of electronic ignition would be the next step towards speed and reliability. This was the first public confession that neither of these was up to standard!

A record crowd of 55,000 saw the GP5's race debut at Oulton Park on Easter Monday 1964. John Hartle was lying eighth when he struck ignition trouble and was forced to retire. The first six finishers were: Alan Shepherd (MZ), Ralph Bryans (Honda), Tommy Robb (Honda), Dan Shorey (Surtees Ducati), Ken Martin (Bultaco) and Bruce Beale (Honda). So, even though Hartle had posted a retirement, lying eighth against this level of competition was quite impressive.

Meier Arrives

Behind the scenes, approaches had been made to acquire the services of the top two-stroke tuner, the German Hermann Meier. Then working in Spain with the Lube concern, Meier's record was impressive. He was well known to British race fans thanks to the Ariel Arrow for which he had been responsible, that finished seventh in the 1960 Lightweight TT – with only fully-fledged works entries from Honda, MV Agusta and Morini in front of Meier's rider Michael O'Rourke.

Meier's task was twofold: to develop the existing Starmaker-powered engine and to design a brand new unit. However, it was in the latter area where what happened and what should have happened did not match up. Hermann Meier claims that his brief upon joining Enfield was 'to be given a clean sheet of paper and use my talents to create a competitive engine'. But what actually took place, after he had already taken up the role of Enfield engineer, 'was to utilize as many components from the Smith Group of companies as possible'. So Meier was forced (against his wishes) to fit the Albion five-speed gearbox and barrel-cam clutch and an Alpha-made bottom end with its pressed-in crankshaft and crankpins. The latter, hated by Meier, meant that instead of using even the existing Starmaker's 'square' 68 × 68mm dimensions, he was stuck with the Alpha's old-fashioned long-stroke 66 × 72mm bore and stroke, when he would have preferred to use either square or slightly short-stroke measurements. So instead of the all-new unit that Meier had envisaged, he could only use his undoubted skill in the top end of the motor. This he did to considerable effect in the design of the top-hat-shaped combustion chamber, and the use of a cylinder barrel with no less than four transfer ports.

Hartle Injured, Duff Takes Over

Something of a problem occurred at the beginning of April, when Hartle was injured whilst practising on a Norton for the Silverstone meeting. This meant that Mike Duff took over the prototype GP5. The *Motor Cycle News* race report stated:

> An interesting dice in the 250 race was between Dave Chester and Bill Ivy on production racer Yamahas (TDIAs) and Mike Duff on the Royal Enfield racer. These machines seemed fairly evenly matched on performance but Duff's ride into ninth place was particularly creditable, having been very slow starting and last-but-one to get away.

Geoff Duke then made an arrangement for John Cooper to test race the new Enfield (still in Starmaker guise) later in April at Snetterton, but this was soon rescheduled for 3 May at John's local Mallory Park circuit. Cooper's Mallory outing ended with an excellent fourth place, behind Alan Shepherd (MZ), Derek Minter (Cotton)

With the arrival of German two-stroke engineer and tuning wizard, Hermann Meier, in late spring 1964, a new engine was designed and built to replace the original Villiers unit on the GP5. Unfortunately, Meier was saddled with an Alpha bottom-end, so he was restricted in what he could achieve.

and Tom Phillips (Aermacchi), and in front of fifth place man Bill Ivy (Yamaha). All-in-all an excellent result for the bike that was now referred to as the 'works development' machine.

Testing Rather than Racing

At this time it was very much a case of testing rather than racing – trying not just new riders, but new ideas and settings, some of which worked and some of which did not. Up to now it had been a reasonably successful start, but as events were to prove there was still a lot of work to be done. During May 1964 it was announced that the Villiers concern had built three six-speed gearboxes. These were designed by John Flavill, and were to be supplied to Cotton, DMW and Royal Enfield (Villiers not knowing at this time that a new machine, which would not be using its engine, was under development).

TT Debut

In mid-May, when the largest TT entry ever was announced, Royal Enfield had three entries: John Cooper, John Hartle and Griff Jenkins (the latter riding for Chas Mortimer Senior). When TT practising began, only two Enfields were now listed, Cooper and Jenkins, but in the race itself both machines failed to complete a lap. Cooper was alleged to have gear trouble (most probably more serious) and Jenkins' race ended in a high-speed crash at Glen Vine, that effectively destroyed the recently completed bike. Actually a mere eight riders completed this gruelling race from sixty-three starters!

Following the TT debacle, nothing was heard from the Royal Enfield race squad for some weeks until, at the end of June, yet another rider – this time racer and Triumph tester Percy Tait – gave the Redditch company its best result yet, with a third in the 250cc race at Scarborough's annual Cock o' the North meeting. This was also the debut of a non-Starmaker-engined bike. Geoff Duke was at the meeting, keeping a watchful eye over both bikes. Tait was teamed up with Johnny Simmonds (who rode the newest machine). Both

bikes qualified for the final, but Simmonds' bike refused to start immediately prior to the race, and thus had to be loaded back into the van. Tait (on the original Starmaker prototype) held second for much of the race, but eventually was relegated to third by John Swannack on a 1963 production Greeves RAS Silverstone. *Motor Cycle News* said: 'He [Swannack] rode superbly and try as he might, Tait could not hold the Greeves rider from Worksop.' Swannack also set the fastest lap of the race.

Tait then travelled with the Enfield squad to the Ulster GP, where he came home twelfth, a lap adrift of the race winner, Phil Read (Yamaha RD56).

Manx Grand Prix

After Ulster, it was then on to the Isle of Man for the Manx Grand Prix. 1964 marked the return of the Lightweight (250cc) race at the September races, and it was here that the Redditch marque believed they could succeed. Even so this was supposed to be a race for non-works machinery. Enfield got by, by describing their bikes as prototypes.

There were in fact two GP5 entries. One, the Starmaker-engined machine ridden by Manx-man Neil Kelly, turned in the fastest practice lap so far that year by a 250, when it was wheeled out for the Wednesday evening session, at 82.39mph (133km/h).

Kelly's team-mate Dennis Craine (also an Isle of Man resident) was aboard the new 'Mark 2', with the non-Villiers engine and five-speed Albion gearbox. *Motor Cycle News* described it as 'probably the smartest-looking machine in the Manx'. Unfortunately, smart did not mean fully sorted, and it was the last bike to get underway, Craine having trouble first in getting the right rear chain adjustment, and then in getting started. He eventually got out, did a lap, but due to 'over-gearing' and thus much extra clutch slipping, had the clutch give out. But Craine still 'felt I have a very good chance of winning the first 250 Manx since 1948'. He claimed that the handling of his machine had 'been improved considerably, by the fitting of a fork-to-frame steering damper'. All through the remainder of the practice sessions both Enfield's showed up well, although the Villiers-powered bike fared best.

Two First Lap Retirements Once Again

Both Enfields were to retire early in the race, but Geoff Duke was quoted as saying: 'The factory are far from downhearted about the way things went, although after heading the practice leader boards, naturally there was great hope that one of the bikes – more probably the Starmaker-engined version – would do quite well.' Geoff also went on to comment, 'The Enfield-engined bike was very much a prototype', and 'but from what we saw of it in practice and in the race until Dennis Craine went out with gearbox trouble, we were very pleased'.

At least the handling of the 'Mark 2' was much improved, Dennis Craine saying that his Enfield handled 'better than a Norton'.

Earls Court

The Earls Court Show in November 1964 saw the official launch of the production GP5, which the factory said would 'cost £350 and put out 34bhp at 8,000rpm'. But once again fate was not on Enfield's side as almost immediately the ACU banned the GP5's transparent nose cone of the Mitchenhall Bros Avon fairing (also specified for Cotton and Greeves). It was also announced at the Show that Enfield had signed the Rhodesian racing star Gordon Keith to race works GP5s in 1965.

Gordon Keith's Try Out

In February 1965, the 1964 Lightweight Manx GP winner, Gordon Keith, tested the latest GP5. These tests, which were staged at Mallory Park, were concerned not so much with the engine, but more with a new five-speed Albion gearbox, open primary chaincase and clutch, improved braking and a new design of tank and seat unit. (the latter devised by Geoff Duke). Suffice to say, the original 1964-type Albion five-speed box had

A 1½in (3.8cm) Amal GP carb dominated the Meier GP5 engine. The contact breakers are housed behind the small crankcase cover. Experiments were also carried out with an early form of electronic ignition.

1965 GP5 (Production)

Engine
Layout   Air-cooled two-stroke single cylinder with alloy head and barrel
Bore and stroke   66 × 72mm
Displacement   246cc
Compression ratio   12.5:1
Lubrication   Petroil
Ignition   Battery/coil
Carburettor   Amal 1½in GP2
Fuel tank capacity   7gal (32ltr)

Transmission
Primary drive   Duplex chain
Final drive   Chain
Gearbox   Albion, 5-speed
Frame   Duplex, all steel, tubular construction

Suspension
Front   Reynolds leading link fork
Rear   Swinging arm, Girling hydraulic units

Brakes
Front   Full width drum 7in
Rear   Full width drum 6in
Tyres   Front 2.75 × 18; rear 3.25 × 18

Performance
Maximum power   34bhp @ 8,000rpm
Top speed   120mph (193km/h)

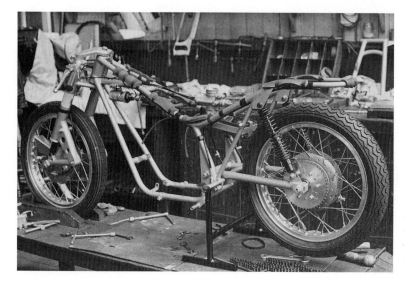

The chassis of the definitive GP5 was a truly excellent design. The full duplex affair was made in Reynolds 531 tubing; suspension was taken care of by Reynold's leading link front forks and Girling rear shocks.

Geoff Duke's rider choice, Percy Tait, really came on strong during the Hutchinson 100 international meeting at Silverstone on 17 August 1965. In terribly wet conditions, Tait finished a magnificent third behind the Yamaha works pairing of Phil Read and Mike Duff.

been appallingly poor. For example, my brother-in-law Tony Plumridge's Greeves RCS, purchased new in mid-1965, had so many gearbox problems that in the end the Greeves factory fitted a four-speed Albion as the only way of solving this – the original five-speed HJ5 units fitted to the GP5 were just as bad. So Albion had responded by redesigning the offending assembly; although better, it was still far from perfect.

Of all the riders who rode the GP5 at works level, Gordon Keith must have wished several times that he had not been signed up, as he suffered many setbacks. Even from the first meeting at Mallory Park in early March, things did not go according to plan, when Keith's bike jerked to a halt on the starting grid. It had apparently locked solid – probably once again due to the ongoing transmission problems.

Rare Successes

At Brands Hatch in late March, Keith brought his Works GP5 home in sixth place, behind Derek Minter (Cotton), Dave Degens (Aermacchi), John Blanchard (Aermacchi), Bill Ivy (Cotton) and John Cooper (Greeves). But it was in Castle Combe in late April that the combination of Keith and GP5 gained its first real success, beating

Derek Minter (Cotton) to finish runner-up in the 250cc race behind Dave Simmonds' Honda CR72 twin. But once again the GP5 failed its Isle of Man test, with Keith and Percy Tait both going out during the race. However, at the International Mallory Park Post TT meeting, Gordon Keith finished fifth. This was an excellent result, bearing in mind the high level of competition, with only Read and Duff (works Yamahas), Dave Simmonds' fast CR Honda and Gilberto Milani's factory Aermacchi in front of the flying Enfield.

John Rudge Gives the GP5 its First Victory

The GP5's first victory finally came at the beginning of July 1965, when Tamworth rider John Rudge dominated proceedings at the Midland Racing Club's meeting at Perton, near Wolverhampton, when he not only demoralized the opposition by winning the 250cc final by half a lap, but then showed the 500s the way home too. Rudge proved he was good at national level, too, on his production GP5 by finishing third at Castle Combe a week later against the 'big boys'.

Neil Kelly rode a GP5 in the Isle of Man Southern 100 races, finishing third. By now it seemed that the Redditch two-stroke was becoming more race-worthy. This was confirmed when first Gordon Keith came in third at the national Thruxton races in late July, a result repeated by Percy Tait at the international meeting at Silverstone in mid-August. Of all these results, Tait's performance has to be seen as the best. Not only did he finish (albeit in terribly wet conditions) with only the Yamahas of Mike Duff and Phil Read in front, but now with a twin spark transistorized ignition, the GP5 proved it was at long last fast and reliable.

At Silverstone, Tait's machine was timed at 132mph (212km/h) during the 50-mile (80km) race, and John Rudge was proving the best of the riders to have purchased a GP5, again doing well at Castle Combe in early September (fourth in a star-studded field).

The Manx Signals the End

During practice for the 1965 Manx Grand Prix, Neil Kelly took his works-supplied RE5 round at 86.44mph (139km/h) and was consistently on the practice leader board. The Manxman was thus a strong favourite for a top three position in the race. However, when lying third in the final lap, Kelly was forced out with clutch trouble only a few miles off the finish, at Guthrie Memorial on the Mountain climb – a heartbreaking experience for both the rider and Enfield's race team.

The Manx result, or lack of it, was to prove the straw that broke the camel's back, and after almost two seasons of development and racing, it was announced by Leo Davenport (now sole MD, as Major Vic Mountford had died towards the end of the previous year) that the factory 'had decided to withdraw from road racing' and that the contract with Gordon Keith 'had been amicably terminated'. Davenport went on to say that 'the position will be reviewed during the winter'. But in the author's opinion, this latter statement had more to do with attempting to sell existing stocks of the production GP5 than ever making a return. Geoff Duke had purchased one of the works development machines, which it was reported 'Percy Tait will continue to race'. This also confirms the author's views.

The Real Reason

Actually, the real reason for Davenport's 'quit' notice was more about money than results. The latter had not been as successful as everyone had hoped, but as the above story shows things were beginning to improve, both the performance of the bikes and their reliability. In fact, as often as not the retirements had not been caused through engine or chassis problems, but instead by transmission weaknesses due to Hermann Meier and

James (George) Ward during the 1966 Lightweight Manx GP on his GP5. He finished 17th, gaining a Silver Replica; note the Honda CB72 front brake.

These fairing-off views of a pristine example of the production GP5 give an indication of the machine's main features. Notice how low and purposeful the bike is.

RIGHT: Meier-designed top-end saw aluminium for both the head and barrel, with extensive finning. Note also the aluminium primary chaincase, Amal GP carb with its 'matchbox' float chamber, and springs to retain the exhaust header pipe into the cylinder.

his development team being saddled with inferior Albion-made gearboxes and clutches. Also, considering what his instructions and parameters had been, Meier had largely delivered the goods. As Rudge's production bike had proved, the GP5 was capable of beating the other, over-the-counter, British-made production racers from rival factories.

Sadly, the fact was that the whole GP5 project came too late. By the mid-1960s, Royal Enfield was in big financial trouble and the advent of the Yamaha twins (in TD1B form from 1965) was a reality. With a year's extra development, in other words, starting at the same time as Greeves, Cotton and DMW in 1963, the author is positive that Enfield would have come out on top. Remember, it had a superior performance and superior handling in its final guise over anything else that the British industry could offer at that time.

Full-width alloy hub, Reynolds forks with Armstrong shock absorber, alloy wheel rim and Dunlop KR76 racing tyre.

Money was thus the reason why it all came to a halt at just the wrong time. Estimates put a figure of £150,000 on the cost to design, develop and build the GP5, and it appears as if only twenty-odd bikes were actually sold. After Major Mountford's death in November 1964, Davenport lost a valuable and enthusiastic supporter for his racing programme. From then onwards he was under increasing pressure to deliver – or else. The 'else' side of the argument eventually won!

The entire stock of what remained of machines and spares from the race shop was later sold off to the Sunderland dealer Tom Cowie for a sum of £4,000. Most of the bits ended up being snapped up by special builders, all of whom at least appreciated the excellent handling endowed by the fine chassis of the definitive model.

Tom Cowie later became the massive Cowie Group of car dealerships throughout Britain during the late 1970s onwards. Later still, in the early 1990s it became the Arriva brand name and today, beside its many car dealerships, it also runs Arriva buses and trains.

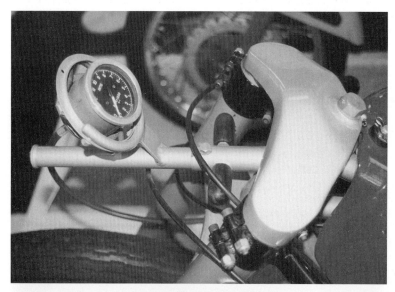

Steering head, Smiths rev counter and front fairing support; the latter being adjustable.

The combined seat and tank unit was a feature of the Meier GP5. The idea came from Geoff Duke.

GP5 – An Inside View by Bill Woolnough

During the early sixties, my friend James 'George' Ward raced a G50 Matchless. My employers, North Anglian Autos of Kings Lynn, gave him some assistance and I spannered for him. The highlight of our racing year was the Manx Grand Prix on the Isle of Man. George's best result on the G50 was 13th place in the 1964 Senior. However, the availability of spares became critical and the G50 was sold. As we were Royal Enfield dealers, events led to George purchasing a GP5 in 1965. The sales manager and I went to the factory to collect the bike as George was otherwise engaged on his day job, driving trains out of Kings Cross. We looked forward to meeting Hermann Meier and hoped to be shown around the race shop. On our arrival at Redditch we found that we were in the way somewhat. A contingent from the Indian factory was there, and we were told that the 350 Bullet was made under licence in Madras.

Eventually we were greeted by Hermann Meier who seemed very nice, but when we asked if we could see the race shop he said no, that would not be possible. We later learned that there wasn't one! The assembly shop foreman, Charlie Rogers, built the bikes in his spare time and Meier built the engines. We were handed a typewritten card with the bike's data on it and taken into the yard to find that the bike had been wheeled out of the assembly shop and leant against a wall. It was a case of 'There it is, thank you very much, goodbye.'

First time out at a Snetterton BMCRC club meeting, and the rear torque arm broke cleanly across the front bolt hole. It ripped out the cable and broke the brake plate in two. End of play for that day. I made my own torque arm and it gave no further trouble. Once that was cured, we turned our attention to a much more persistent problem. From cold the bike would fire up first time on a soft plug, and once warmed up a hard plug was put in for the start. On being bump-started it would fire up, start to rev, and then almost die in clouds of smoke as the engine bogged down with excess fuel. Eventually it would clear and take off like a scalded cat after the rapidly disappearing opposition. The factory told us what to do to cure it, but it did not work. It improved, but was never fully reliable.

Add to this that at the end of every meeting the bottom of the primary chaincase was full of rollers from the two-row chain. We soon realized that there were improvements to make. In the midst of all this, George announced that he had entered for the Manx Grand Prix! I told him that it was a waste of time to take the GP5 to the Isle of Man, but he was undeterred.

Quarterbridge – first corner, first lap of practice – and the front wheel tucks under and George is on his ear. Mystified, he examines the bike to discover that the front wheel is soaked in petrol/oil mixture. The problem was caused by the petrol tank breather mounted in front of the one-piece tank and seat unit, which had no baffles. Under braking there was nothing to stop fuel from escaping down a plastic pipe that was tucked out of the way inside the lower half of the fairing. On the initial plunge down Bray Hill, the pipe became dislodged from inside the fairing to hang beside the front wheel, discharging fuel onto the tyre. A simple non-return valve cured the problem, letting air in but preventing fuel from coming out. The breather pipe was secured out of the way.

Of greater concern was the primary chain that needed replacing after every practice session. We resorted to a cheaper standard chain in place of the racing chain that lasted no longer, and we used them up at a frightening rate. Every time the bike stopped we put on a new chain. I tried fitting a slipper tensioner from a BSA A65, which the Enfield reduced to powdered metal in one lap. It was found later that the problem stemmed from the enormously heavy Interceptor clutch, which coped with the brute force of the big twin but, for some reason, when coupled to a 250 2-stroke, destroyed chains in no time at all. The single leading shoe front brake also gave problems in that, by the time the bottom of Bray Hill was reached, there was no brake. It became enormously hot and boiled the grease out of the front wheel bearings. Thereafter, the bike was fitted with a twin leading shoe hub from a Japanese Honda CB72 road bike fitted with racing linings, which coped quite well.

Another problem shown up by the early morning practice sessions on the Isle of Man was the position of the HT coil. This was hung from the frame just below and behind the steering head. The first blast of cold, damp Manx air would condense on the coil and cause misfiring, and eventually the engine would stop. Brought down to Douglas, away from the fog on the mountain, it would fire up first time. After a lot of head-scratching, we mounted the coil in front of the fairing and the problem was solved.

However, I was seriously worried by the primary chain problem, and I was convinced that the GP5 would never complete a four-lap race over the 37¾-mile mountain circuit, often described as the toughest test of man and machine in motorcycle racing. In spite of all these problems, we went on to campaign the bike in short circuit club racing for five years. Our results were as follows. In 1966 we finished 17th; in 1967 again 17th, this time winning a silver replica. In 1968 we retired; in 1969 stopped on first lap, got going again to finish 52nd, and in 1970 retired.

I was later told by Roger Boss, the Royal Enfield sales director, that Hermann Meier was opposed to the GP5 being sold when we took delivery. He was of the opinion that the bike was not sufficiently developed. However, the 'Top Brass' overruled him. I think our experiences show that Meier was correct. The bike was fast, handled well, but was very fragile.

10 Unit Singles

When Royal Enfield announced its new Crusader 250 in August 1956, it had the distinction of being the first unit construction design of the capacity to be launched by a major British manufacturer in the post-war era. Furthermore, with a claimed power output of 13bhp at 5,750rpm, it was also the most powerful. Yes, the Enfield concern stole a march on its rivals and in doing so created a model range that ran for a decade.

In the 30 August 1956 issue, *The Motor Cycle* described 'the Crusader – a sleek, de luxe, modernistic, eye-catching two-fifty'. These words, at the time, were entirely true, as the model abounded in interesting technical detail.

A Complete Departure

The Crusader's overhead valve engine and gearbox was contained in a single unit – and not bolted up as on the Bullet or the Twin; this marked a complete departure from existing Royal Enfield four-stroke practice.

A notable feature of the design was that the entire engine and gearbox, except for the crankshaft and connecting rod, could be dismantled without removing the unit from the frame. On the original Crusader, the rear chain was totally enclosed. The wheels were of 17in (43cm) diameter – a feature now virtually standardized at the beginning of the twenty-first

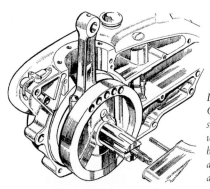

Details of the Crusader unit single crankshaft with plain bearing big-end and split con-rod arrangement.

Announced in a wave of publicity in August 1956, the 250 Crusader, with its ohv unit construction engine, was the first really modern British production model in its class, pre-dating other notable entries such as the Ariel Arrow, BSA C15 and AMC unit singles. This example with an Airflow fairing dates from 1958.

century, but almost unheard of in the mid-1950s. The use of a 17in diameter was a factor that contributed greatly to the seemingly compact nature of the bike.

A Lively Roadster

The original Crusader was conceived very much as a lively roadster, rather than an out-and-out sports model – something many enthusiasts of the marque will probably find difficult to believe considering the hotter versions that were to follow later, such as the Crusader Sports, Super 5 and Continental GT.

A definite modern feature, and again very much against previous Enfield practice, was the use of the short-stroke 70 × 64.5mm bore and stroke dimensions, giving a displacement of 248cc.

What made the Redditch factory choose this layout? Actually the choice of an ohv unit single was made by Major Frank W. Smith, then chairman and managing director of the company. From an interview he gave in February 1957, Major Smith considered that this offered:

> the best possibilities for combining a brisk road potential, economical running, even firing and the ease of development from known data. Unit construction of engine and gearbox was an obvious requirement for a de luxe model of up-to-date conception, with the proviso that accessibility of engine and gear mechanism for servicing must not be inferior to that obtainable with separate units.

So these were the considerations when Enfield draughtsman Reg Thomas was instructed to lay out the power unit for the first time on paper in 1954. For Thomas, at that time one of Enfield's younger employees, it was his first opportunity for original design – and thus provided an exciting and stimulating challenge, which he subsequently proved he was capable of meeting.

Completing the key staff who were responsible for the Crusader's birth was Tony Wilson-Jones, chief engineer at Enfield by that time, who was responsible for transforming Thomas's drawings into metal.

Cast-Iron One-Piece Crankshaft

The Crusader, like the Enfield parallel twin, employed a cast-iron one-piece crankshaft – the material used being a high-grade commercial iron. The H-section connecting rod was of RR56 light alloy (exceeding 7,000rpm risks con-rod breakage) and incorporated a split big-end with a plain bearing of white metal, steel-backed pattern. The gudgeon pin for the small-end ran directly on the con-rod, without any form of bushing. The piston was a full skirt type of aluminium construction, featuring three rings.

The crankshaft mainshafts featured a roller bearing on the offside and a ball race on the nearside. The outer race of the ball bearing was retained in the crankcase by a circlip, whilst the inner race was pressed on the crank mainshaft up to the flywheel and kept in the correct position by means of distance pieces and the engine sprocket. To accommodate differential expansion between the crankshaft and crankcase, the other end of the shaft was not located.

Primary and Camshaft Drives

Primary and camshaft drives on the Crusader engine were both on the nearside (left). The reason behind this layout was because the Enfield design team felt that it was logical to divorce the generator from the drives, to eliminate the possibility of damage from a chain failure.

Primary drive was by a ⅜in (1cm) pitch simplex chain. Outboard of the engine sprocket was another sprocket from which an 8mm pitch duplex chain carried the drive to the single camshaft mounted high up in the casing. Both chains were adjusted by slipper tensioners, accessible when the side cover was removed.

The camshaft was supported by a pair of ⁹⁄₁₆in (1.4cm) bronze bushes. Its drive sprocket was keyed to the shaft and located outboard of the outer bearing, housed in a cast-alloy outrigger plate bolted to the crankcase and forming the outer wall of the cam chamber. The inner bearing was a press fit in the crankcase.

Oil Pump

Between the camshaft and the outer bearing was a spur pinion that drove the oil pump at half engine speed through an idler gear. The oil pump drive shaft extended transversely through the upper portion of the crankcase ahead of the cylinder barrel; the ignition contact breaker assembly was on the offside end and accessible through a circular, detachable plate secured by a couple of screws.

Cylinder Barrel and Head

When first launched, the Enfield ohv unit engine had a cast-iron cylinder barrel and head (the latter was later of aluminium). The head featured a part-spherical combustion chamber. Both the head and the barrel were secured by five long through studs screwed into the crankcase. An included valve angle between the valves, at 65 degrees, was quite small – this was needed to obtain a well-shaped combustion chamber and to enable a relatively flat-top piston to be used. This again clearly illustrates that the original Crusader was a decidedly touring oriented machine, and was to effectively limit the design's more sporting intentions later on.

The compression ratio was 7.3:1. The valve head diameters were, at the time, considered quite large at 1⁷⁄₁₆in (3.7cm) inlet and 1⅜in (3.5cm) exhaust; both valves were a semi-tulip shape, with the inlet being manufactured in silicon-chromium steel, the exhaust in nickel-chromium-tungsten steel.

Conventional Enfield Valve Gear Layout

Valve gear layout followed conventional Enfield practice, with both rockers carried directly in pedestal split bearings of sintered iron, each retained to the head by four studs. The steel pushrods were operated by rocker-type radiused followers that ran directly on a common spindle supported in the crankcase wall and the outrigger plate already mentioned. The deep one-piece aluminium casting that acted as the valve-gear cover was retained by a single, shouldered hexagon-headed stud. Valve clearance adjustment was made at the top of the pushrods, not at the top of the valves.

The Lubrication System

Oil was contained in a 3-pint tank, cast between the crankcase and gearbox components. A notable feature, at least for British motorcycles at the time of its inception, was that the primary chain was lubricated by the engine oiling system (unlike on the Bullet or the twins).

The lubricant was drawn from the oil compartment by one of the two oscillating plunger-type pumps and delivered via a felt filter to a passage in the offside cover. Running in an oil seal in the cover was an extension of the mainshaft, and oil flowed from the cover into the shaft where drillways transferred it to the big-end. In the top of the filter there was a release valve that directed oil back into the top of the container.

From the big-end, the oil was fed to the main bearings, small-ends and the cylinder walls by splash – the oil was then collected in a small sump at the base of the crankcase. It was then picked up by the scavenge pump and some of it was diverted via a spring-loaded ball valve and a neatly disposed external pipe to the rocker pedestals.

From the valve gear the lubricant drained down the pushrod tunnel to the cams and followers, building up in the cam chamber. Since the oil pump and its gear train were also housed here, the oil build-up served to lubricate the train of gears and to submerge the pumps, thus avoiding the possibility of excessive aeration of the oil. From the cam chamber the oil overflowed into the primary drive compartment, lubricating the camshaft drive chain on its way. In the bottom of the case it again built up, to lubricate the primary chain, and overflowed back into the sump.

Since the crankcase and chain compartment were interconnected, the resultant large volume simplified venting.

During 1955, Royal Enfield had introduced a breather system on its four-stroke models. This consisted of a short piece of plastic tubing flattened at the end remote from the crankcase – a very simple arrangement and one they also specified for the unit 250 engine.

The Transmission

An unusual feature of the gearbox was that the layshaft was behind the mainshaft, instead of below it. This layout was chosen because there was no length restriction – the new unit engine being 4in (10cm) shorter than the old Clipper motor and its separate gearbox. Another reason was because this layout enabled the foot change mechanism to be more conveniently located for connection to the rider's gear pedal by internal linkage.

Identical to that employed in the Clipper, the gear cluster was of Albion manufacture. However, the positive stop and selector mechanisms for the new unit engine were of Royal Enfield's own design and manufacture. Overall gear ratios were: 5.8:1, 7.83:1, 10.44:1 and 16.96:1. To permit dismantling of the engine-gear unit (except the crankshaft assembly), without removal from the frame, the offside ends of the gear shafts were carried in a bolted-on bulkhead under the main side cover. (If the gearbox bearings had been located in the main offside engine castings, the crankcase would have needed splitting before the gears could be withdrawn.) Not quite the super-quick cassette gearbox of the twenty-first century, but well along that concept. A three-plate clutch featured a mixture of cork and fabric friction material.

The Frame

Of all-welded construction, the Crusader's frame had no seat tube and was of the non-cradle type (that is, the engine-gear unit formed the lower section and acted as a stressed member). There was a single front down-tube.

The rear swinging arm and telescopic forks provided an excellent combination of good handling and comfort. The rear shocks were more steeply angled than on the Bullet or Twins, but this did not seem to have any adverse effects. The front forks carried the familiar Enfield cast alloy

casquette fitted with a Lucas headlamp and twin pilot lights. Also housed in the top of this assembly was a Smiths speedometer, light switch and ammeter.

Full-Width Aluminium Hubs

Full-width hubs, cast in aluminium and incorporating 6in (15cm) single leading-shoe drum brakes, were fitted to both wheels, the rear being QD (quickly detachable) and featuring the famous Enfield rubber vane cush drive. Both were shod with 17in (43cm) chrome-steel rims and Dunlop tyres – a ribbed front, studded rear.

Both mudguards of the original Crusader were deeply valanced and very heavy, the front being unsprung with a single rear loop stay. The rear mudguard also acted as the support for the dual seat and was strengthened by a further loop stay that ran along each side of the machine for the final two-thirds of the seat length.

Combined with the small wheel size (at the time bikes usually had 18in or 19in) and the substantial mudguarding, the original Crusader looked an extremely solid piece of kit, giving a distinct air of quality. It also looked very modern when compared with the majority of its British lightweight rivals. For example, at the time of its launch, no other British maker offered a four-stroke unit 250, and in fact BSA, then the largest concern, were still offering the public two exceedingly outdated and poor performing machines – the side-valve C10L or the overhead-valve C12, whereas the likes of AJS, Matchless, Norton and Triumph had no 250s (if one discounts the 200 Cub) at all in this class!

Full Chain Enclosure

The final drive chain was fully enclosed. Set against the original bike's touring credentials this was an outstanding feature. No lubrication was provided, because previous Enfield experience with models such as the Bullet had shown that the most important thing was keeping the final drive chain clean, which gave an enormous improvement in the service life.

The chain case was of the twin-tunnel type and comprised four components: the conduit portion, the tail-piece and two gaiters. The first was constructed of steel pressings and comprised a pair of rectangular section tunnels, linked ahead of the rear-wheel sprocket. In the upper tunnel was an orifice, normally filled by a rubber plug, for chain-tension checking. Both the conduit portion and the semi-circular channel-section tailpiece were held to the brake shoe plate by screws. Each tunnel, too, was bolted to the nearside arm of the swinging rear fork by a slotted lug permitting chain adjustment. By means of corrugated plastic gaiters, that were a push-in fit, the forward ends of the tunnels were coupled to stubs cast into the left-hand crankcase half next to the gearbox sprocket.

Amal Monobloc Carb

Carburation was taken care of by an Amal 375/16 Monobloc-type ⅞in (2.2cm) carburettor. Under the offside engine outer cover was a Lucas RM/3 AC generator (alternator), the rotor of which was keyed to the crank mainshaft and the stator bolted to the crankcase. The contact breakers, condenser backplate and advance/retard unit were mounted in the outer cover forward of the generator.

A New Silencer

Together with the majority of its other four-stroke models, when the 1958 Royal Enfield model range updates were announced in October 1957, the Crusader had been given a more rounded silencer, made specially by the Burgess company to Royal Enfield specification. On the technical front, minor changes had been made to the gearchange mechanism and the lubrication system. The compression ratio was also raised from 7.3:1 to 8:1.

At the beginning of 1958 it was announced, at the Royal Enfield Annual General Meeting, that 'a form of streamlining and weather protection' had been developed for the Crusader model. But no other details were forthcoming. However, a few weeks later, at the end of February all was revealed in the shape of the new Crusader Airflow model.

This was no simple factory fitted fairing, but a full integration job, which also involved certain departures in frame and front fork specification. It was noted that the shielding could not be fitted directly to the standard Crusader model, and there was no intention by the Enfield factory of marketing the kit as an after-market accessory (although a kit was later made available for fitting to customers' existing machines).

Fibreglass was chosen for the main bodywork and also for the new streamlined front mudguard. Compared to the standard model, which then cost £212 1s 6d, the Airflow version came out at an additional £44. At £256 1s 6d (including UK purchase tax) it was the most expensive British 250 in the market.

Even though the Airflow option was later given to other models in the Enfield range (Bullet and Super Meteor, for example) its extra cost sorely limited sales. If one discounts specialist, limited-production machines, such as Vincent's Black Knight, the Crusader Airflow was the first production motorcycle (as opposed to scooter-type machines) to offer real weather protection, so much a feature of twenty-first century motorcycling. Today we take it for granted; but back in the late 1950s it was revolutionary – and Royal Enfield were the pioneers of the fully faired street bike. Also in March 1958 came an economy version of the Crusader, the Series 2 Clipper. This had more skimpy mudguards, a lack of chrome, no chaincase (only a top guard), a non-full-width rear hub and unpolished outer engine casings.

Crusader Sports

When the 1959 model range was announced in early October 1958, the big news from Royal Enfield was the debut of the Crusader Sports, for which the Redditch company claimed a maximum speed of 80mph (129km/h). Contributing to the increased power output of 18bhp at 6,250rpm were high-lift cam profiles featuring a

For 1959 Royal Enfield introduced the more sporting, and ultimately more popular Crusader Sports. It had a more highly tuned engine and a more radical riding stance, plus an abundance of bright chromework.

1960 Crusader Sports

Engine	Air-cooled overhead-valve unit construction, single cylinder with vertical cylinder, alloy head, cast-iron barrel
Bore	70mm
Stroke	64.5mm
Displacement	248cc
Compression ratio	8.5:1
Lubrication	Dry sump, twin oil pumps
Ignition	Battery/coil 6V
Carburettor	Amal $^{15}\!/_{16}$in (2.4cm) Monobloc 376
Primary drive	Chain
Final drive	Chain
Gearbox	Four-speed, foot-operated
Frame	All-steel, tubular construction
Front suspension	Royal Enfield telescopic fork
Rear suspension	Swinging arm, with Girling hydraulic units
Front brake	Drum 7in (18cm)
Rear brake	Drum 6in (15cm)
Tyres	3.25 × 17 front and rear

General Specifications

Wheelbase	52in (1321mm)
Ground clearance	6½in (165mm)
Seat height	29in (737mm)
Fuel tank capacity	3¾gal (17ltr)
Dry weight	313lb (142kg) with oil and 1gal (4.5ltr) petrol
Maximum power	18bhp @ 6,250rpm
Top speed	85mph (137km/h)

greater degree of overlap than those fitted to the standard version. In addition, crankshaft flywheel weight had been reduced, providing a zippier level of acceleration. The compression ratio had been upped from 8:1 to 8.5:1.

Although similar to the existing Crusader, the cylinder head was now an aluminium component, and modified to accommodate a larger 1⁹⁄₁₆in (4cm) diameter inlet valve (1⁷⁄₁₆in (3.7cm) standard). For longer life, the tips of both inlet and exhaust valve had been hardened.

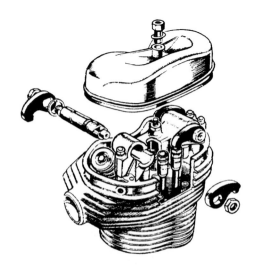

A New Front Fork

Although the Crusader Sports retained the original Crusader frame, the front forks had been replaced for the heavier duty ones found on the Meteor Minor twin-cylinder model, and embodied two-way hydraulic damping. The front brake diameter had been increased from 6 to 7in (18cm). The carburettor had been changed to a larger 376 ¹⁵⁄₁₆in (2.4cm) Amal. Cosmetically the Sports version came with a larger, chromed fuel tank, rear set footrests, sports handlebars and new sports mudguards (chromed). On the standard Crusader, the cylinder head was changed from cast iron to aluminium, although it retained the original valve and carb sizes.

Valve Gear Modified

In the spring of 1960, modifications to the valve gear for both the Crusader Sports and standard Crusader were announced. These had been necessary following problems experienced with the introduction of the aluminium head for both models a few months before; and, said the factory, to improve engine oil-tightness.

Hitherto the Crusader valve gear had followed traditional Royal Enfield practice, with the rocker

ABOVE LEFT: Revised valve gear of the Crusader unit engine, introduced into production from spring 1960. The modifications were designed to achieve quieter operation and longer service life.

Peter Padgett (the founder of the well-known Padgetts of Batley dealership and racing entrants) hustling a Crusader Sports through its paces at Cadwell Park race circuit during the early 1960s.

spindles integral with their operating arms and carried in split bearings, each secured to the cylinder head by four studs and nuts. For the revised design, the two studs at the front and rear were retained, but these now carried a single cast aluminium block, hollowed on the underside and bored to accept the rocker spindles. A stud passed vertically through the middle of the block, which also served to retain the rocker cover. Internal drillings provided an oil supply to the rocker spindle bosses.

Built-Up Rockers

The new rockers were built-up assemblies, with separate operating arms pressed from ¼in-thick (0.6cm) steel, each located against its appropriate spindle shoulder by a flat milled on the spigot, and secured by a nut. A spring washer between each valve rocker arm and the bearing block prevented end float and so provided quieter running; with the earlier, one-piece rocker design there was no provision for a spring washer.

Wider bearings than before were employed – a further factor in quietening the mechanism and also lengthening working life – and in consequence the arms were mounted at right-angles to the spindle, so improving the operating geometry and obviating side-thrust on the valve guides.

With the original pattern of Crusader rocker cover, any over-tightening of the retaining stud could distort the joint flange and thus cause oil leaks. To counter this the Enfield design team reinforced the cover, by providing three ribs that radiated from the stud boss and helped to spread the load more evenly. The remaining design change, also adopted in the interest of oil-tightness, was the use of socket head screws fore and aft of the pushrod tunnel, in place of the original single stud and nut. This alteration called for modification to the shape of the cylinder head and barrel castings in this area.

The 85mph (137km/h) 250

In a July 1960 road test, *The Motor Cycle* recorded a maximum speed of 85mph (137km/h) and, even though this was a highest one-way speed with a moderate tail wind, it was still highly impressive. Not only this, but the engine was also exceedingly flexible for a sports model. Road holding, braking and ease of starting were all given full marks.

However, there were aspects of the Crusader Sports that the tester did not find to his liking, notably:

- the riding position, with the low handlebars putting too much weight on the rider's arms and wrists, particularly at low speeds;
- limited steering lock;
- a tendency for bottom gear to occasionally refuse to engage until the machine was eased backward or forward a short distance.

Making History

In September 1961, Royal Enfield launched the Super 5, which made history by becoming the first British production motorcycle with a five-speed gearbox. It was also the first Enfield model to sport leading link front forks, but, of course, it was the fact that the newcomer had five-speeds that really made the headlines.

However, the Albion-made gearbox had to fit into the space normally used to house four-ratios, and this led to unreliability (a fact suffered by all the other 250 Enfields using the five-speed cluster).

Essentially the new gearbox was based on the old four-speeder, but had three close-spaced pairs of gears, which moved together along the shafts to engage with the driving dogs. Overall top gear ratio was higher than the Crusader Sports, leading the journalists of the day to claim a '90 mph potential' for the Super 5. But 'as delivered' this speed was only possible riding downhill.

The Leading Link Fork

The Super 5 engine was fitted into the Crusader Sports frame and swinging arm, but at the front were new leading link forks. Actually they were not really new at all, but had been tested out in 1957 on one of the twin-cylinder models.

Topping the leading link front fork assembly was a headlamp casquette, which, unlike that of other Enfield models, was of pressed-steel construction and did not embody the twin pilot lights. Concealed within the fork tubes were long and slim Armstrong-made hydraulic damped spring units. The links that carried the wheel spindle of the Super 5 were steel forgings pivoting on phosphor-bronze bushes; the cover plates were vacuum-formed from self-coloured black pvc. Anchored to the nearside fork leg through parallelogram linkages (which allowed firm and progressive braking without locking

the front suspension), the front brake was a 7in (18cm) assembly with a full-width hub. The quickly detachable rear wheel was equipped with a 6in (15cm) diameter full-width brake drum.

The front mudguard of the Super 5 was of static pattern, with deep valences – these being needed as the wheel came upwards under braking, whilst the guard stayed stationary. The rear mudguard was modelled on that already in use on the 700 Constellation Twin, though smaller in size. This embraced the rear sub-frame structure and thus formed a base for the dual seat.

The 1961 Clipper. Based on the standard Crusader it used a famous Enfield name that had always been applied to the economy model within the range.

The 1962 Super 5 with five-speed gearbox and leading link forks; otherwise it was closely related to the Crusader Sports model.

Five-speed gear cluster. First used in the Super 5 model, it was to prove troublesome for its entire existence.

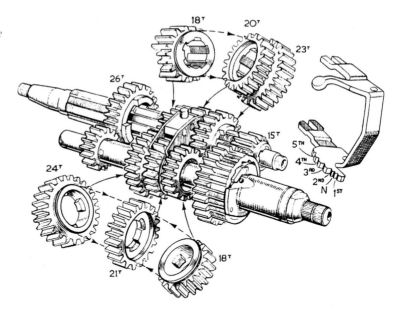

BELOW: Rhodesian Gordon Keith with his factory entered Super 5 during the 1965 Thruxton 500-Miler – held that year at Castle Combe, Wiltshire.

Fashion Over Function

It was very much a case of fashion winning over function regarding the fate of the excellent leading link front forks, with Armstrong spring-and-hydraulic struts concealed in the stanchion, that Royal Enfield had introduced on the Super 5 in the early 1960s. These were never accepted by the buying public, even though on the street and on the vicious pavé circuit at MIRA, it was shown to be the Redditch marque's best fork ever.

To give as good a ride on the road, a telescopic fork at that time had to have such soft springing as to be hopelessly lively (like a pogo stick!) on the pavé. To match the leading link fork's pavé performance, the teles required sidecar-strength springs that ruined its road behaviour. Moreover, in spite of its superiority, the link fork needed less wheel travel than the telescopics required. Did the customers flock to buy the new fork? Not a hope! It just would not sell, so the works was forced to revert to its ageing teles. So much for fashion.

The Super 5 first appeared in 1962 – basically a Crusader Sports with the new forks and a five-speed gearbox. On the first model, RE thought it was the deeply valanced front mudguard that was putting off potential buyers. So for the 1963 season they offered the machine with a Crusader-type chrome mudguard. However, this still did not do the trick – the result being the Continental with an orthodox telescopic fork. And, of course, its performance was not up to that of the link type. In 1964 the leading link was an optional extra; by 1966 it had been dropped altogether. This was even though the GP5 racer had adopted the leading link fork from the outset – and was highly acclaimed for its road-holding and handling, if not always for its mechanical robustness.

An engine from the Continental, with rev counter drive pick-up on the clutch side (furthest away from the camera). The neat lines of the Crusader-based motor are evident in this view.

The Continental of 1963 with its Italian-style fuel tank, chromed mudguards, racing pattern rear shocks, 'Ace' bars, flyscreen and chequered tape on the upper fork legs, styled very much to appeal to the café racer cult.

The final version of the Crusader Sports as it was offered in 1965 and 1966.

Crusader Sports Remains the Favourite

Even though the Super 5 boasted an extra gear and the latest suspension technology, it was the Crusader Sports that remained Enfield's best selling 250. And because of this, it became a popular model with 1960s British youth, many being customized as café racers.

One of the neatest conversions was offered by dealers Deeprose Brothers of Catford, London. Deeprose offering a kit of extras (items could also be purchased individually) for around £50.

Chief among the engine modifications was a piston that raised the compression ratio from 8.5:1 to 9.75:1, a special cam giving higher and quieter lift and a larger carburettor (1⅛in/2.9cm) In addition, the ports of the cylinder head were modified to improve gas flow.

A new Clubman Gold Star-type exhaust pipe swept around the engine, with a Gold Star Silencer. The Deeprose engine and exhaust modifications were claimed to increase performance by 10 per cent. For those wishing to race their 250 Enfield a megaphone (unbaffled) was available.

A crouched racing position was offered by rearset footrests, with reversed gear lever and special brake pedal, and short clip-on handle bars; a racing type saddle allowed room for a pillion passenger, at least for those enjoying a close relationship.

The Deeprose package was completed by sports pattern lightweight alloy mudguards, plastic gaiters for the front forks, a large diameter chrome-plated headlamp and chrome-plated rear suspension springs. And the crowning glory was the choice of either a TT 5gal (23ltr) or 3gal (17ltr) short circuit-racing type petrol tank.

As one journalist of the time described the Deeprose Crusader, 'Not intended for serious ride-to-work use; the open road is its playground'.

Enfield's Sportflow

It was not just the likes of Deeprose who were cashing in on the café racer boom of the early 1960s, Enfield themselves got into the act, eventually creating the Continental GT to meet demand for such a bike direct from the factory. But before this, in 1962, came the Sportflow fairing.

One August day in 1962, Mick Bowers and Charlie Rogers from Royal Enfield and Vic Willoughby (himself a former racer of no mean ability) from *The Motor Cycle* met up at MIRA (Motor Industry Research Association) test track near Nuneaton to carry our a series of tests with the new Super 5 model with and without an Airflow fairing and both five- and four-speed gearboxes. Surprisingly, the results were not so far apart as the interested parties had expected – the maximum speeds being the same for the naked bike/rider flat on the tank as with the faired bike/rider hiding behind the fairing. In the end, Willoughby had this to say in his report:

- The fairing gives you 10 mph (if the rider in both cases is sitting upright).
- It also (the fairing) give your an extra 10 mpg.
- Five speeds are fun.
- They aid performance most in adverse conditions.
- The 'overdrive' [five-speed gearbox] top gear needs a fairing to pay-off in speed.

Continental

The big news, at least for lovers of the 250 unit Enfield, came towards the end of 1962 with the announcement of the Continental. Like the Super 5, this was a five-speeder, but housed in a frame equipped with an orthodox telescopic front fork. The most eye-catching feature was its Italian style 'jelly-mould' fuel tank complete with quick action filler cap.

But there was a whole lot more – for example, a neat light alloy casting atop the fork, housing the matching Smiths speedometer and tachometer and lighting switch. A chromium-plated headlamp was carried on brackets from the fork and there was an air scoop for the 7in (18cm) front stopper, ball-ended handlebar control levers, chromium-plating on the shortened front mudguard and rear mudguard, plus covers and springs on the rear shocks. A fly screen was standard; there was even chequered tape at the top of each fork leg!

An Alloy Head is Standardized

All four of the road-going 250s now had an alloy cylinder head and a 9:1 compression ratio but, whereas the Clipper employed standard cams and a carburettor size of ⅞in (2cm), sports cams were used in the Crusader Sports, Super 5 and Continental. Carburettor size of the Crusader Sports was ¹⁵⁄₁₆in (2.4cm), and that of the Super 5 and Continental (1⅛in/2.9cm).

For 1963 the Crusader Sports reverted to chrome-plated conventional mudguards at front and rear, and a five-speed gear cluster was available for a princely sum of £7 10s.

New for the Super 5 was a front mudguard of which the stays were attached to the brake plate (on the rearside) and a special distance piece (on the offside), the guard therefore rising and falling with the wheel.

GT – the Ultimate

To the eyes of many younger enthusiasts in the mid-1960s, the Continental GT rated very highly when it was first revealed to the public in November 1964, catalogued as a new model for the following season. With its bright red fibre-glass racing-style tank, sweptback exhaust header pipe, clip-ons, fly-screen, bolt-on discs on the front hub (bacon slicers), rear sets and bum-stop seat, the newcomer was quite a surprise package – even though the Enfield design team had already come up with such attractive bikes as the Crusader Sport, Super 5 and Continental in the previous few years.

As has already been related, at the time it was fashionable to strip machines of superfluous equipment and fit various 'go-faster' accessories. With the arrival of the Continental GT, young riders could at last buy a factory-built café racer (at least from a British manufacturer), and could thus save themselves the expense and trouble of tuning and customizing a more sedate bike. Compared with the existing Continental, the GT came with a larger 1⅛in (3.0cm) carb, with a long bellmouth; it also had a higher (9.5:1) compression piston. Compared with the Continental, the GT put out 21.5bhp (an extra 1.5bhp) at 7,500rpm. Another feature, where the GT differed from the Continental (or for that matter the other 250s), was the use of a 3.00 × 18 rear tyre to give increased ground clearance. Dunlop Gold Seal tyres were the normal original equipment factory choice for the GT.

Both mudguards were finished in red to match the fuel tank.

Factory drawings showing details of the ohv unit single-cylinder engine.

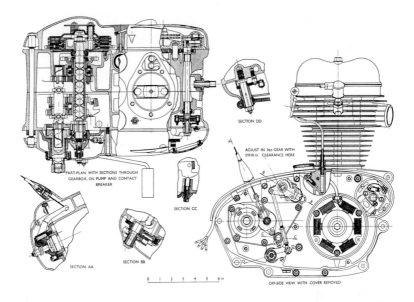

The sweptback exhaust header pipe, open bell mouth for Amal Monobloc carburettor and racing-style tank of the Continental GT. This is a 1966 example.

The angled rear shock with exposed chrome-plated spring, rear-wheel speedo drive and Lucas rear light and number plate support are all evident in this view.

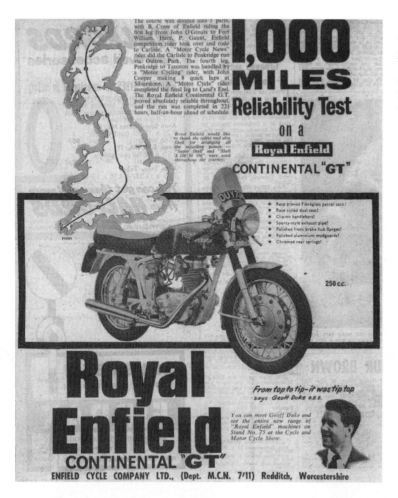

The course was divided into 5 parts, with B. Crow of Enfield riding the first leg from John O'Groats to Fort William. Here, P. Gaunt, Enfield competition rider took over and rode to Carlisle. A "Motor Cycle News" rider did the Carlisle to Penkridge run via Oulton Park. The fourth leg, Penkridge to Taunton was handled by a "Motor Cycling" rider, with John Cooper making 8 quick laps at Silverstone. A "Motor Cycle" rider completed the final leg to Land's End. The Royal Enfield Continental GT proved absolutely reliable throughout, and the run was completed in 22½ hours, half-an-hour ahead of schedule.

1,000 MILES
Reliability Test
on a
Royal Enfield
CONTINENTAL "GT"

Royal Enfield would like to thank the riders and also Shell for arranging all the refueling points—"Super Shell" and "Shell X 100/30 Oil" were used throughout the journey.

* Race proved Fibreglass petrol tank!
* Race styled dual seat!
* Clip-on handlebars!
* Sporty-style exhaust pipe!
* Polished front brake hub flanges!
* Polished aluminium mudguards!
* Chromed rear springs!

250 c.c.

Royal Enfield
CONTINENTAL "GT"

From top to tip – it was tip top
says Geoff Duke O.B.E.

You can meet Geoff Duke and see the entire new range of "Royal Enfield" machines on Stand No. 75 at the Cycle and Motor Cycle Show.

ENFIELD CYCLE COMPANY LTD., (Dept. M.C.N. 7/11) **Redditch, Worcestershire**

This advertisement appeared in Motor Cycle News *on 11 November 1964, publicizing the successful 1,000-mile John O'Groats to Land's End marathon undertaken by a team of riders on the newly introduced Continental GT, a few days previously.*

Rakish café racer lines of the Continental GT. Geoff Duke described it thus: 'This is a really super version of the Continental, which will delight the young enthusiast with its sporty looks and traditional Continental performance'.

The bolted-on aluminium brake 'bacon slicers' of the Continental GT. Very much a case of style over function.

John O'Groats to Land's End

Royal Enfield certainly made a big attempt to ensure that the launch of the GT was noticed – by putting one example through a highly publicized John O'Groats to Land's End run. The 'run' took place in late October 1964 with the bike's launch a few weeks later.

The plan was for the bike (registration number DUY 734B) to complete over 1,000 miles in less then twenty-four hours – going from the very north of Britain to the very southern extremity, and taking in sessions at the Oulton Park and Silverstone race circuits.

Pat Braithwaite (of *Motor Cycle News*) was the first official pressman to ride, when he took over from factory rider Peter Fletcher at Carlisle (there were no motorways such as the M6 then, only the M1 north of London and a short stretch around Manchester).

Although Geoff Duke had been scheduled to test the GT over five laps of the Oulton Park circuit in Cheshire, Pat Braithwaite handed over to fellow journalist Bruce Main-Smith (*Motor Cycling*). He rode it to Silverstone, where John Cooper really put the little Enfield through its paces, averaging over 70mph (113km/h) around

An unusual view of the top end of the Continental GT engine and Amal Monobloc carburettor.

the Northamptonshire circuit – with a fastest lap at nearly 73mph (117km/h). There had been some concern, just before Cooper took over, as the GT had developed a slight misfire, but this turned out to be a loose wire in the ignition switch that was shorting out; a by-pass wire-up direct to the battery solved the problem.

After Silverstone, with Bruce Main-Smith back in the saddle, the GT headed south again, this time across the testing hills of the Cotswolds.

At Chippenham in Wiltshire came the last change of rider, when David Dixon (*The Motor Cycle*) took over for the final run down to Land's End. When interviewed in the late 1980s, he was still enthusiastic about the memory of 150 miles (241km) of bend-swinging. 'I loved it. It was quick and would pull on to well over 70mph. Beautiful little bike.' Dixon averaged around 50 mph (80km/h) – which was not all on main roads – and there were no motorways in the west then. When Dixon arrived at Land's End, the only people there to welcome him, apart from *The Motor Cycle*'s photographer, were the factory chief Leo Davenport (a former TT winner in

BMF Concours d'Elegance at Woburn Abbey, circa early 1970s. Left to right: Honda C77, Royal Enfield Continental GT and Suzuki K10.

pre-war days) and joint managing director Major Vic Mountford.

The epic journey had been completed with time to spare in twenty-two hours, twenty minutes. The publicity this generated was considerable – a well-remembered press advertisement showed John Cooper flat out on the little Enfield around Abbey Curve, Silverstone.

Go-Faster Goodies

Two enterprising London Royal Enfield dealers, Gander and Gray and Deeprose Brothers, both produced some go-faster goodies. Gander and Gray even produced a special version of the Continental GT. Christened the Gannet, this featured a ported cylinder head with larger inlet tract, a lumpy 10:1 piston, lead-bronze big-end shells, alloy wheel rims and a full race fairing.

American Spec

In 1967 an American specification Continental GT, almost identical to the UK model with the exception of braced motorcross handlebars, was exported in small numbers.

Sad to say that 1967 was also the final year of Royal Enfield 250's production. The long-established concern had finally hit the financial rocks. Why is discussed elsewhere in this book, but suffice to say that the various stock and manufacturing, along with the famous Redditch site in Worcestershire, were sold to the local development corporation and now forms part of an industrial estate.

The Royal Enfield big twin design was acquired by Manganese Bronze, who owned the Norton Villiers Group. Production of the 750 Interceptor Twin was transferred to the Westwood Works at Bradford-on-Avon, but the 250 unit range ended with the Redditch closure. A sad day.

11 Constellation

With the arrival of the Constellation in spring 1958, Royal Enfield's reputation was to suffer badly, thanks to listening to a clamour of demands from various agents and importers for 'the biggest cubes and the maximum horsepower'. But, as Laverda were to learn to their cost during the early 1970s with the Italian company's original 1000 3C triple, having the largest engine and the most power can be a recipe for disaster. And so it panned out for the Redditch-based marque, whose slogan had been 'Made Like A Gun'. The Constellation invented a new calling card: 'Blow Up Like a Bomb'.

Origins

The origins of Enfield's folly had begun back in 1948, when it had made the decision to build an unglamorous bike – the 500 Twin – for an unglamorous era. Its 496cc ohv vertical twin-cylinder engine was designed as a soft touring bike to appeal to riders used to austerity and only just recovering from six years of war. With a lowly compression ratio of 6.5:1, the long-stroke 64 × 77mm engine produced 25bhp at 5,750rpm. Its main priorities were minimum production costs (hence its modular concept that saw it use the pre-war Model S Enfield's bore and stroke), an ability to run on low-grade 'pool' petrol, ease of maintenance (hence the design having separate cylinder barrels and heads) and fuel economy; this made it ideal for commuting to work during the week, whilst touring at the weekend. Performance did not come into the equation.

Geoffrey Brown with the 692cc Constellation he and Ray Knight shared during the 1962 Thruxton 500-mile endurance race in late June that year.

Later, when in 1952 it upped the engine size to 692cc (using the 350 Bullet singles with long-stroke bore dimensions of 70 × 90mm) to create the Meteor, the emphasis was still very much on the old priorities with the power output (36bhp at 6,000rpm) remaining less a priority than easy starting, low down pulling power and ease of maintenance. Even when the higher performance Super Meteor arrived at the end of 1955, its extra go was limited to 40bhp and a reduction in engine revolutions to 5,500rpm.

Out-and-Out Sportster

Then came the Constellation (known to many by its shortened name 'Connie') with maximum power comfortably exceeding 50bhp and engine revolutions soaring to 6,250rpm, the by-now ten-year-old Enfield parallel twin engine was being asked to run harder than it ever had been envisaged it would need to. For example, the separate barrels and heads, that had been such a boon for owners in earlier days, were now a definite nuisance, giving as they did far less rigidity than the single block layout adopted by the Constellation's chief rivals – the Triumph Bonneville, BSA Super Rocket and Norton Dominator.

Production Begins

In April 1958, Royal Enfield introduced no less than three new Twins: a pair of short-stroke 500s and the Constellation. However, the engine at least had been in production for some months, but only for export.

Like that of the Super Meteor on which it was based, the Constellation featured a one-piece crankshaft supported in a ball race bearing on the driveside and a roller bearing on the timing side. To cope with the increased power output, the material for the shaft was high-tensile nodular iron. The pistons giving an 8.5:1 compression ratio were higher than those of the Super Meteor (7.25:1), and unlike the latest those of Super Meteor, the Constellation came with a Lucas K2F magneto with manual control – even though it had a crankshaft-mounted Lucas RM14 alternator of 70W output that fed the battery via a conventional rectifier. In this instance, however, the current generated was only used for the lights and horn.

On the original Constellation models, a single Amal TT9 racing carburettor of 1 3⁄16in (3cm) bore was fitted (later replaced by a pair of Monoblocs) higher lift camshafts, and a siamezed exhaust system.

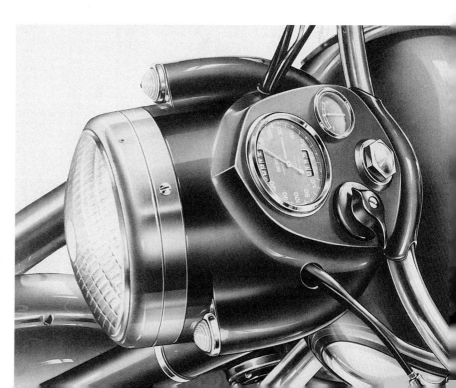

A feature of several Royal Enfield models, including the Constellation, was the casquette fork head, that embodied headlamp, pilot lights, speedometer, ammeter and light switch in one unit.

A New Frame

As on the latest 500 twin, a new frame was employed, based on the existing one but strengthened to accommodate the additional power (but missing out on uprating the engine mounts!). The chassis remained similar to the Super Meteor and included an air filter; there was also a new 4¼gal (19ltr) fuel tank, and a steering damper came as standard. The tank was fully chrome plated, but to lessen the glare there was a top section finished in Burgundy red to match the tool/air cleaner box assembly and the chainguard. Frame and forks were enamelled in black and the mudguards polished alloy (the latter later changed to chromed-steel components).

115mph (185km/h)

Motor Cycling took one of the new Constellations to Belgium and electronically timed it at 115mph (185km/h); the same journal averaged over 80mph (129km/h) from Brussels to Ostend. The test bike also recorded an average of 51mpg (5.55ltr/100km) while in *Motor Cycling*'s care – a very impressive figure with all this speed testing. However, even then the unreliability when ridden hard, which was to dog much of the Constellation's career, showed its

The café racer cult hit its peak in the 1960s. This 1967 photograph shows left to right, Tom Thompson, sister Jackie – later to become a well-known model – and a friend with Tom's 1962 Constellation. The other bike is a Velocette Viper single.

head; when approaching Ostend at around 110mph (177km/h), the *Motor Cycling* tester experienced problems when one of the rocker oil feed pipes parted from its union and deposited oil over the engine. Other problems noted by *Motor Cycling* concerned oil around the engine breather, flooding of the carburettor if the prop stand was used, and placing the bike in too upright a position when this stand was in place. The centre stand was the usual Enfield cast aluminium component.

Twin Carburettors

When the 1960 range was announced in early October 1959, it was seen that the Constellation had received a number of power unit developments aimed at combating some of the gremlins that had occurred in service. Most noticeable was the adoption of the twin Amal 389 Monobloc 1³⁄₁₆in (3cm) carburettors in place of the single racing TT instrument. The Enfield design team did this because, although high-speed performance was unaffected, starting was improved and there was enhanced pulling power in the low and mid ranges. To promote smoother running, the balance of factor of the crankshaft had been revised, lighter pistons (still 8.5:1 compression ratio) and a more substantial cylinder head steady comprising a pair of steel plates attached to a lug on the underside of the frame top tube. The tank mounting was also modified; a considerable amount of sponge rubber had been added under the tank in an attempt to stop fuel tank fracture, caused by a tank suffering excessive vibration. A new crankcase system had been adopted (for all the Twins), with a flap valve being embodied in the driveside end of the crankshaft, crankcase pressure being relieved by discharge into the primary chaincase. An outlet was provided in the top face of the chaincase and from there a pipe led excess oil mist to the rear chain. A small baffle integral with the case prevented oil thrown up by the primary chain from finding its way through the breather outlet – at least that was the theory. Unfortunately, some Constellation engines actually exploded due to gas build-up.

New, too, was a drain pipe leading from the base of the cylinder block on the left (nearside). This pipe conveyed excess oil from the camshaft tunnels and cylinder walls to the oil container; the drain connecting with annular cavities at the base of the cylinders. These latter measures were in response to the poor record of oil-tightness compared to the earlier, less stressed versions of Enfield's parallel-twin series. In truth, the Constellation was never completely oil tight – quite simply this was the cost for over-extending an engine originally designed to put out over half the power output of the Constellation.

Another problem highlighted by the Constellation centred around the oil-container design, which, as on all the Royal Enfield four-strokes up to that time, at least of the post-war era, was cast integrally with the crankcase, behind the crankshaft compartment and above the gearbox. Although this had the advantage of giving a fast warm-up from cold, it also allowed the highly tuned Constellation to overheat far too easily.

A Lower Compression Ratio

The following year, 1961, brought more changes. The first of these was an admission that the Constellation engine specification had been wrong from the outset, as the compression ratio was reduced to 8:1 – again, in an attempt to improve the still less than perfect reliability. There was also another attempt at improving the mounting of the fuel tank, as tanks were a continual source of problems, particularly from seams suffering under stress at high speeds, causing leakages.

As on the latest Super Meteor there was a new, wider rear mudguard; at first this was manufactured in fibreglass, but soon this material was replaced by pressed steel. The front mudguard was now chrome-plated steel. Also for 1961 there was a new Lucas battery with a translucent plastic outer case, plus a new silencer, and (as described in Chapter 8) the Constellation and Super Meteor featured a new clutch.

Early in 1961 silentbloc bushes replaced the phosphor-bronze type for the swinging arm pivot.

1961 Constellation	
Engine	Air-cooled, overhead-valve parallel twin semi-unit construction, with separate cylinders and heads
Bore	70mm
Stroke	90mm
Displacement	692cc
Compression ratio	8:1
Lubrication	Dry sump, twin oil pumps
Ignition	Lucas magneto, with manual control
Carburettor	Two Amal 1³⁄₁₆in (3cm) Monoblocs
Primary drive	Duplex chain
Final drive	Chain
Gearbox	Albion, four-speed, foot-change
Frame	All steel, tubular construction
Front suspension	Royal Enfield telescopic fork
Rear suspension	Swinging arm, twin Armstrong hydraulic units
Front brake	Dual 6in (15cm) drum
Rear brake	Drum 7in (18cm)
Tyres	3.25 × 19 front; 3.50 × 19 rear
General Specifications	
Wheelbase	54in (1372mm)
Ground clearance	6in (152mm)
Seat height	31in (787mm)
Fuel tank capacity	4¼gal (19ltr)
Dry weight	427lb (194kg) with oil and 1gal (4.55ltr) petrol
Maximum power	51bhp @ 6,250rpm
Top speed	112mph (180km/h)

The Problems Continue

Even though some of the problems that had affected the Constellation had been laid to rest by this time, others most certainly had not. One of the most problematic was blown head gaskets – hence the drop in compression ratio to attempt a cure, which was only partially successful.

Another was the clutch. When the Constellation had made its debut it introduced a new clutch, also used on the short-stroke 500 series. Known as the scissors-action type, this worked well on the smaller Twin, but was marginal in the Constellation. Another problem could be difficult starting – not helped by the kickstart gearing and aggravated by the machine's higher compression than its softer brother, the Super Meteor. When the TT9 carb was fitted, things were even worse – the instrument also leaked and flooded – something the switch to twin Monoblocs largely cured.

Yet another Constellation problem was that crankcases went out of shape – caused through lack of rigidity due to the separate cylinder layout – again the extra stress caused by the added power output only highlighted a problem that had been there, at least potentially, since the very first 500 Twin back in 1948. Unfortunately, Tony Wilson-Jones, when interviewed in 1960 concerning the Constellation could only make the

OPPOSITE: The Constellation was an attractive motorcycle; it is just a pity that its looks and performance were not matched by improved reliability.

comment: 'The chap who has the misfortune to score one barrel has a much lighter bill to pay than had he to renew the complete block.' What he did not explain fully was that this layout might have been acceptable on the less potent models, but in the 50bhp-plus Constellation, some owners might be faced with having to fork out for a new set of crankcases! And it is worth noting that the Constellation needed the heavy chrome-steel front mudguard; as without it the Enfield-made forks were not really capable of performing their task on such a powerful bike. Again, this was probably why the lightweight alloy guards of the early Constellation were soon ditched in favour of the later steel type. The front guard actually carried out a vital task, doubling up as it did as a

LEFT: *Constellation with optional Airflow fitted. This kit could be purchased either ex-factory fitted to a new machine, or as an after-market dealer-fit accessory. Essentially the Airflow comprised the fairing and front mudguard assemblies.*

fork brace. The dual 6in (15cm) fork brake, mentioned elsewhere in this book, was another component that was found wanting on the Constellation. Vibration problems were not helped by the frame's tendency for the engine plates to become elongated in service.

In the end, Royal Enfield solved many of the problems, but not with the Constellation; instead, it was detuned back to the Super Meteor's level of tune and given a single Amal 376 1⅟₁₆in (1cm) for 1962 and 1963. The majority of the failings were solved with the launch of the even larger capacity 736cc Interceptor for the 1963 model year (*see* Chapter 12).

The Constellation name was not continued on the new bike, it having been tarnished beyond repair.

All in all a sad chapter in Royal Enfield's history, but at least the engineering team got things right, even if it took longer than it should have.

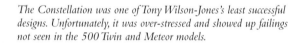

The rider's-eye view of the Airflow fitted to a Constellation.

The Airflow fairing and front mudguard provided an integrated approach to rider protection. Unfortunately, as with many true advances, it was ahead of its time and subsequently found few takers.

The Constellation was one of Tony Wilson-Jones's least successful designs. Unfortunately, it was over-stressed and showed up failings not seen in the 500 Twin and Meteor models.

12   Interceptor Series 1

When the Interceptor arrived on the British market – after being available in the United States for several months – it represented a genuine and largely successful attempt to put right the wrong meted out by the infamous Constellation. The extra engine size was a result of American pressure on Enfield in response to Norton's newly released Atlas 750.

This American Cycle World *advertisement from June 1960 shows that the name Interceptor was already in use across the Atlantic.*

A Major Redesign

Although at first glance the two models looked essentially the same motorcycle but with different engine capacities, the Interceptor was a major redesign.

To achieve its larger 736cc engine size both the bore (up from 70 to 71mm) and the stroke (from 90 to 93mm) had been altered.

In an attempt to subdue the problems of engine vibrations, the crankshaft balance factor had been changed. This came in conjunction with a modified frame in which the engine was now more securely mounted, since in the Constellation movement of the engine and gearbox in the frame had often resulted in oval holes appearing in the mounting plates. The Interceptor's rear engine plates were considerably more substantial that the earlier Enfield twins, whilst at the lower rear of the Albion gearbox there was now a substantial aluminium block additional to the conventional mounting points attached to the frame just below the swinging arm pivot, and acting as a bracket retaining the gearbox; this can be retro-fitted to any of the earlier Enfield twins.

Because of the change of stroke there was a new nodular-iron crankshaft. This ran in a redesigned crankcase. Again, the crankcase had proved a problem area with the Constellation,

RIGHT: *At the time of its UK launch, the 736cc (71 × 93mm) Interceptor was the largest British motorcycle in production. It was a good performer too, being capable of around 115mph (185km/h).*

BACKGROUND TO A WORLD FAMOUS NAME

The Enfield Cycle Company's works complex in the West Midlands town of Redditch. It was of considerable size and not the small operation that many have seen fit to wrongly describe it in recent years.

A special sidecar version of the Interceptor was available with revised gearing and suspension.

even distorting in the most serious cases. New, too, were the cylinder heads (still separate castings), with the pair of Amal 389 Monobloc 1³⁄₁₆in (3cm) carburettors now flange-mounted on parallel induction stubs (not splayed as on the Constellation), and head to cylinder barrel bolt size was upped from ⁵⁄₁₆in (0.8cm) to ³⁄₈in (1cm).

To combat the problem of blown head gaskets, this method of sealing the head–barrel joint was axed in favour of cross triangular-section steel rings (like a piston ring in fact). Sealing of the pushrod tunnels was achieved by the use of steel thimbles to which were bonded heat- and oil-resistant rubber sealing rings.

A Revised Lubrication System

Though retaining the familiar double-acting Royal Enfield oil pump, the lubrication had been considerably revised. Breaking away from past practice, together with the cylinder-block sealing methods, the development team had given the new engine a higher degree of oil-tightness than before. From one side of the delivery pump an oil supply fed the big-end bearings through a filter. From the other, the oil went through a release valve (which directed any surplus to the crankcase oil container) and then to the inlet and exhaust rocker gear assemblies.

Draining through the pushrod tunnels, oil accumulated in the inlet and exhaust camshaft tunnels, that were now completely sealed from the bore of the crankcase mouth. From the inlet cam tunnel, oil was fed back to the tank; from the corresponding exhaust tunnel, the overflow was directed into the timing gear, from which a drilling led directly back to the sump, this being considerably larger than in Enfield's previous twin-cylinder designs (again addressing a problem, experienced in the Constellation, of the lubricant becoming too hot). Another change was the switch to flexible oil pipes to the rockers (again targeting a former weakness).

The Magneto is Retained

Magneto ignition with its manual advance and retard, as on the Constellation, was retained. The power output had risen to 52.5bhp (a 1.5bhp increase over the Constellation) at 6,000 instead of 6,250rpm. But the biggest gain was in usable power, the rev band being so wide that, on a top gear ratio of 4.20:1, useful urge was available from speeds as low as a mere 18mph (29km/h)!

The interceptor was very much a return to the easy cruising characteristics of the original 692cc Meteor, but with much improved acceleration and a higher top speed.

Cycle parts-wise, there were no real changes except those already listed, plus a return to a conventional (chrome plated) rear mudguard and the addition of a new (non-spike) prop stand as a cost option extra. Finally, a change was made back to phosphor-bronze swinging arm pivot-pin bushes, thus giving the rear end a more solid feel than with the flex-prone silentbloc type.

Testing the Interceptor

When *The Motor Cycle* tested an early example of the Interceptor in December 1962, they found it would show 105mph (169km/h) on the speedometer with the rider sitting upright, and that it would cruise indefinitely at between 90 and 95mph (153km/h), but also make it seem easy.

Tester Vic Willoughby described the characteristics of the bike in the following manner:

> A machine that, at the twist of a grip, gobbles distance with the utmost deception. That gets off the mark on a 1 in 3 climb as smartly as many machines would do facing the other way. Yet it is tractable enough on full retard for the rider to hop off and walk alongside without a trace of snatch from the silk-smooth transmission. In bottom gear, of course. Yes, the Interceptor is a road burner of the aristocratic type – disdaining noise and fuss. However exuberantly the machine was ridden the baritone exhaust was never obtrusive. Nor was there much mechanical noise.

Gearing Gripes

Even though the Interceptor had a hugely torquey power delivery, a combination of gradient

ABOVE LEFT: *The Interceptor 1 put right several of the problems that had afflicted the Constellation. These improvements centred around decreasing the high levels of vibration by mounting the engine more securely in the frame and revising the crankshaft balance. The lubrication system was also altered which, together with improved oil-tightness, added up to a much superior motorcycle.*

LEFT: *One-piece crankshaft and main bearings from the Interceptor engine. A British 50 pence coin gives a size comparison.*

and stiff head wind could pull the cruising speed down below 90mph (145km/h). When this occurred, it exposed a failing of the third gear ratio, at 36 per cent the drop from top gear was way above average.

In fact the transmission area was now the Enfield big Twin's biggest gripe. The gear change still had that short, stiffish movement typical of all Enfield's using the bolt-on Albion-made gearbox. But more worrying was that *The Motor Cycle* reported 'metal had to be filed from the underside of the pedal and the top of the footrest hanger before the pedal could be set low enough for operation without lifting the foot from the rest'.

Clutch Improvements

On the Constellation the clutch was found to be wanting, being not only prone to give problems after even mild abuse, but also difficult to adjust. That on the Interceptor was a definite improvement, being reasonably light to operate, would engage drive smoothly and stood up well to being abused.

Adjustment had been improved now that three of the six springs could be adjusted independently, thus allowing the pressure plate to withdraw squarely. Other changes to the clutch for the Interceptor were the clutch sprocket's anti-friction bearing was changed from the Constellation's fifty-four balls to a ring of low friction material and the clutch's two inner driving plates were changed from inserts of friction material to bonded-on facings of J17 synthetic cork-based material, as on the two outer drive plates.

Inconsistent Starting

Like the Constellation, the Interceptor had magneto ignition – with manual advance and retard. This meant that the rider had to retard the ignition (by a handlebar-mounted lever) for idling. Auto-advance would also have benefited cold starting – which was often a hit and miss affair, particularly when the temperature was around freezing or below. Then thick oil and the low gearing

of the kick starter made it difficult to spin the Interceptor's engine fast enough to get a really fat spark with the ignition retarded far enough to prevent a kick-back. Auto-advance would have provided optimum spark strength for all purposes.

Some help could be gained by moving the kickstart lever forward a couple of serrations on its shaft, thus helping to lengthen the swing. The best starting drill (from cold) was found to entail moderate flooding, half retard of the ignition lever, no air and about one-eighth throttle. Even this did not always work. For no apparent reason, the engine would either fire up first or second kick – or prove obstinate, when the rider had to resort to over-flooding/full throttle as the only way to get it going.

Camshaft Problems

A particular problem was, and still is, the camshafts. This was for two reasons. First, the tooling for shaping the cams was by now so old and worn that it had to be constantly reset. This resulted in cams having many variations, thus resulting in problems when trying to set the valve timing. Not only this, but batches of hot cams were made in America; these were also being imported into Britain at that time. All this needs to be taken on board for anyone contemplating either an engine overhaul or restoration of an Interceptor (or Constellation).

Varied Compression Rate

Officially the UK model Interceptor (Series 1) compression ratio was given at 8:1 for all engines built from 1962 to 1968. However, as with the cam profile, not everything is that clearcut. Actually, several bikes ended up with the American market's higher 8.5:1 ratio and, confusingly, some machines were fitted with lower 7.5:1 examples. It should be noted that the 8.5:1 piston does not have any compression plates, the 8:1 has one and the 7.5:1 two. Failure to observe this will mean the risk of piston damage, caused by the crown of the piston/s hitting the cylinder-head sealing ring.

Oil Comments

The 1962 *The Motor Cycle* tester stated that whilst oil consumption was 'moderate' at cruising speeds, it rose to 'about 250 miles a pint when the machine was cruised in the nineties'. Of course, this latter figure could well have been simply because the magazine was using a virtually new machine that had not yet bedded down. What it most certainly was not though, was through external loss. 'Not a smear of oil blemished the outside of the engine, gearbox or primary chaincase at the end of the test – and only a little was flying on the rear wheel rim by the driving chain.'

During the *Motor Cycle* test, a maximum one-way speed of 108mph (174km/h) (conditions: moderate three-quarter wind) was obtained. UK price, including taxes, was £310, cost extras being prop stand, pillion footrests and stop light.

Attention to Detail

There is no doubt that in designing the Interceptor much attention was given to getting rid of the many and various weaknesses that had been evident in the Constellation. As a further example of this policy were two other features that, although small, were nevertheless important. The first concerned the oil seal at the rear of the engine sprocket that now had its steel washer supplemented by a second, thinner steel washer. The other was that the steel washer originally fitted to the timing side outer roller race was replaced by a better-sealing steel and rubber oil seal.

More Development

Mid-1963 saw more changes introduced. The alternator was changed from a Lucas RM15 to an RM19. At the same time the Amal Monobloc

1963 Interceptor	
Engine	Air-cooled, overhead-valve parallel twin semi-unit construction, with separate cylinders and heads
Bore	71mm
Stroke	93mm
Displacement	736cc
Compression ratio	8.5:1
Lubrication	Dry sump, twin oil pumps
Ignition	Lucas magneto, with automatic advance and retard
Carburettor	Two Amal 389 Monobloc 1⅛in (3cm)
Primary drive	Duplex chain
Final drive	Chain
Gearbox	Albion four-speed, foot-change
Frame	All steel, tubular construction
Front suspension	Royal Enfield telescopic fork
Rear suspension	Swinging arm, twin Armstrong hydraulic units
Front brake	Dual 6in (15cm) drum
Rear brake	Drum 7in (17cm)
Tyres	Front 3.25 × 19; rear 3.50 × 19
General Specifications	
Wheelbase	54in (1372mm)
Ground clearance	6in (152mm)
Seat height	31in (787mm)
Dry weight	410lb (186kg)
Maximum power	52.5bhp @ 6,000rpm
Top speed	115mph (185km/h)

carburettors were given right as well as left float chambers. Late in 1963, from engine number YA15411, a minor alteration was made to the primary chaincase cover.

For the 1964 model year not one, but two Interceptors were offered: de luxe and standard. The former featured 12V electrics – running a pair of Lucas MKZE-2 6V batteries in series and a zenor diode. The de luxe version retained the chrome-plated tank and mudguard, whereas the standard model was given painted components, whilst retaining the 6V electrics. A few sidecar specification models were sold, with different gearing and stiffer suspension.

To improve cold weather running the magneto ignition was modified with a K2F magneto (42369B) incorporating an automatic advance unit (LU540 44111). A year on, when the 1965 model range was announced, the standard version had been axed.

The long-running casquette had been abandoned in favour of a separate headlamp shell (QD for the American market) with an aluminium instrument-mounting console.

Extending the Wheelbase

Attention had also been given to the chassis by means of a lengthened and cross-braced swinging arm, and lengthened top mounting brackets for the rear shock, which were now of Girling manufacture rather than Armstrong. The wheelbase was now 57in (145cm) instead of 54 (137cm) – and the swinging bushes were now silentbloc again.

As an option, high motocross-style braced handlebars were now offered. The USA model, known as the TT, was fitted with separate exhausts, smaller tank and an 18in rear wheel.

Late in 1965, from engine number YB16319, a modified oil filter neck extension and filler cap (with a dipstick) were introduced. Then, from engine number YB16573, came the removal of a detachable camshaft bearing housing.

So even though Enfield was in trouble, improvements were still made to the Interceptor.

Fork Differences

At this time there were a number of differences concerning the front forks. On the British market machines the original shrouded covers continued, whereas the American bikes sported rubber gaiters. Confusingly, some of the Interceptor's fork legs had chrome molybdenum alloy steel in 12 or 14 gauge, others carbon steel in 8 gauge. The latter had the same outside diameter (and of at least the same strength), but were never used on American export bikes. Although all these types had the same external diameter, owing to the different wall thicknesses, different springs and internal components were to be found.

The 8-gauge variety were never fitted to Stateside-bound machines or for sidecar use, and for the latter use the special fork ends with reduced trail were no longer available.

Export Only

Towards the end of 1965, Royal Enfield's Redditch operation began to come under considerable financial constraint, imposed by the board of the parent E. & H.P. Smith Group. This had the effect of severely limiting production and, in the case of the Interceptor, meant the big Twin's withdrawal from the home market – all bikes now going for export, notably to North America.

For the American market these were now known as the Road Sports and Road Scrambler. But changes were afoot, both to the motorcycle and its manufacturing location. The end had come for the Interceptor 1, after some 1,800 examples had been built over a five-year period.

The Mark 1A

By the middle of 1967 it was revealed that Redditch-built motorcycles, including the Interceptor, had come to an end. A new model, the 1A, was now being built at the Westwood, Bradford-on-Avon factory of Enfield Precision Engineers (also owned by the E. & H.P. Smith Group).

A Velocette-Made Frame

Little known at the time was that the frame for the new Interceptor was now being produced by the Birmingham-based Velocette concern. Although the 1A was to be sold in Britain, it was entirely tailored for the USA market with its tiny 'peanut' shaped tank holding a shade over 2gal

(9ltr). The Road Sports version was painted with chrome panels and rubber knee pads; the Road Scrambler had an all-chrome finish, except for a couple of Royal Enfield logos.

The front forks continued with the previous heavy duty, rubber gaiters, there were high and wide (braced) handlebars, a chromed headlamp (including the shell), a new aluminium fork yoke (known as the triple clamp Stateside), matching Smith's speedometer and tachometer, whilst the front brake used the 'bacon slicer' bolted-on discs in the style of the 250 Continental GT ohv single. The twin mufflers were flat on the Road Sports and upswept on the Road Scrambler – the latter in particular giving the machine a cobby look.

Other features included a rear chainguard, now in two sections, and bright chrome plating. A steering damper was standard equipment, the Road Sports retained shrouds on its rear shocks (chromed), whilst the Road Scrambler featured fully exposed chrome springs. Wheels and tyres were as the previous Stateside model; 19in (48cm) front, 18in (46cm) rear. The carburettors had been changed from 389 Monoblocs to 930 Concentrics, with open bell mouths.

ABOVE LEFT: *A new model, the 1A, arrived in 1967; this was built at the Westwood, Bradford-on-Avon factory of the Enfield Precision Engineers. This is a British-registered bike with the larger fuel tank and Norton-type front brake.*

LEFT: *This 1,472cc (two 736 Interceptor Mark 1 engines) was built by an American who became the first to exceed 200mph (322km/h) on a naked motorcycle, in the mid-1970s at Bonneville Salt Flats, Utah. The engines were connected by gears, not chains.*

The previous toolbox/battery cover had been ditched, leaving the 12V battery exposed to the elements. Under the seat, and behind the battery, were two ignition coils – the magneto having been finally retired in the 1968 season. The ignition system for the latest bikes had been designed to have the ability to run without battery or lights, thanks to a capacitor discharge system. The contact breaker points lived in a circular housing, where previously the magneto had resided.

With a dry weight of 414lb (188kg) for both bikes, the Interceptor 1A was a purposeful looking motorcycle; some 1,000 examples were manufactured before it was replaced by the final Interceptor series, the Series 2.

Changes at the Top

In April 1962, the death occurred, at the age of 73, of Major Frank Walker Smith. It would be true to say that, as with many family-run motorcycle companies, AMC (Britain) and Moto Guzzi (Italy) being two good examples, the passing of the original family of pioneers was to signal problems ahead. And so it was to be in Royal Enfield's case; not helped by the beginning of a sales slump that continued throughout the 1960s, and the rise of the Japanese industry in the former British export markets.

Only seven months after Major Smith's death, the Enfield board of directors accepted a take-over bid (one of several it was rumoured at the time), and became part of the E. & H.P. Smith group of companies. It should be noted that these Smiths were no relation to the original Royal Enfield family.

The Smith Group was a much bigger enterprise than the Enfield Cycle Co., and owned a considerable number of industrial enterprises, several with motorcycle interests, the latter including gearbox specialists Albion and Alpha Bearings.

At first things looked promising, with the necessary motorcycling experience and, perhaps more important, enthusiasm coming from one of the E. & H.P. Smith's directors, Leo Davenport, himself a former TT and Grand Prix racing star. Davenport not only became Royal Enfield's joint managing director, but also their new competition manager.

Leo Davenport's fellow joint MD was Major Vic Mountford (Royal Enfield's former 1950s sales manager). Mountford was also put in charge of a design committee, that included works manager Gilbert Baker, chief designer Reg Thomas, Tony Wilson-Jones (now consultant engineer) and Jack Booker (development manager).

Reg Thomas, having been largely responsible for the redesign of the 736cc Twin Interceptor, was employed solely on the Royal Enfield motorcycle, whereas both Wilson-Jones and Booker had to take on work for the entire range of powered products of the newly formed Enfield Industrial Engines division, which meant working on both industrial diesel and marine power units.

A major blow – and probably the decisive one as far as Royal Enfield's future as a volume motorcycle manufacturer – occurred in November 1964 with the death of the marque's joint managing director, Major Vic Mountford.

This left Royal Enfield's only voice at the highest level of the E. & H.P. Smith group as Leo Davenport. He was soon to be blamed for spending what the rest of the Smith board felt was excess money on projects such as the GP5 racer and the Continental GT.

Some eighteen months after Major Mountford's death, the last Royal Enfield motorcycle was built at the famous old Hewell Road, Redditch site, and only small batches of the Interceptor (all for export) were thereafter constructed at the Westward, Bradford-on-Avon underground factory of Enfield Precision Engineers.

But in truth, at least as a major force in the motorcycle industry, Enfield died when production ceased at Redditch. The plant was later sold to the local Development Corporation – the words 'asset stripping' come very much to mind.

With the closure also came the death of several interesting projects – not only the Davenport-inspired racing and motocross machines, but also several exciting prototypes including a four-valve version of the unit 250 and overhead-cam 175.

13 Interceptor Series 2

In late 1968 Royal Enfield, or more correctly, Enfield Precision Engineers, caused quite a surprise by bringing out what amounted to virtually a brand new motorcycle: the Interceptor Series 2. This was the work of designer Reg Thomas, who also had been largely responsible for the Interceptor Series 1 and the unit singles.

A Wet Sump System

Of all the changes, the most notable was without doubt the use of a car-type wet sump lubrication system – and this from the marque that over half a century earlier had pioneered the dry sump lubrication system for motorcycles. The oil – still 4 pints capacity – was to be found in a massive, finned sump. This circulated at some four times the previous rate via a two-stage pressure system, with the lubricant being pumped at 60psi to the big ends and 15psi to the rockers in the cylinder head. This was achieved thanks to a new, larger oil pump. This pump was located under a cover, attached by half a dozen allen screws to the rear of the equally new timing cover. This timing cover was triangular and closely resembled one from a Triumph Bonneville. It was given wide joint faces to prevent oil leakage and was a neater looking component than before.

A New Crankcase

The pair of crankcases, with the integral sump at their base, were taller than before; the design was very similar to Ducati's bevel V-twin that was to come in the following decade.

An Interceptor Series 2 with Swedish enthusiast Sven Hjalmarsson aboard. This machine is fitted with the 2gal (9ltr) 'export' tank.

An entirely stock Series 2 model on display in the National Motorcycle Museum near Birmingham. Note features such as braced handlebars, fork gaiters, enclosed rear shocks, Norton front end and aluminium wheel rims.

BELOW: Series 2 Interceptor engine. A major difference from earlier Enfield Twins was the wet sump lubrication system.

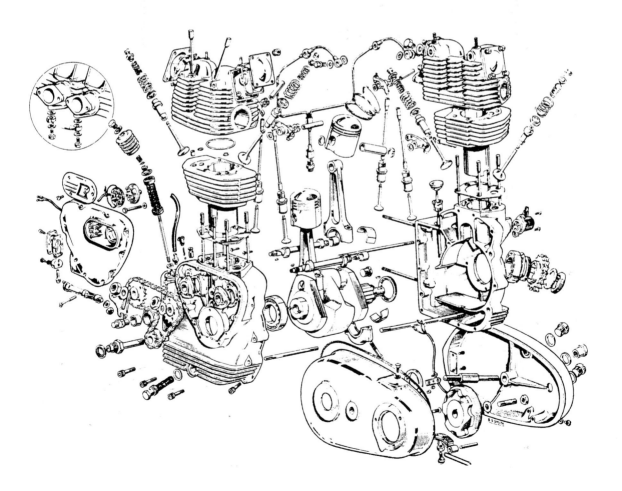

The revised crankcases and outer engine cover give the Series 2 power plant an entirely fresh appearance.

rocker oil feed, the spring-and-ball-bearing rocker oil release valve and oil pressure relief valve, and an unusual finned circular tower (chrome-plated). This latter item was topped by a hexagonal headed bolt, with a tubular mesh oil filter that had previously been used in the old engine. There was, in addition, a washable mesh filter in the sump, accessible from the offside central position. A finned aluminium oil cooler (used on the earlier Series 1 and 1A), but with the new internals to suit the revised lubrication system, was at first offered as an option, later fitted as standard. When plumbed-in, it was coupled by protected piping in the oil filter tower at the rear of the offside cylinder barrel.

All these measures at least meant that the Royal Enfield twin was amongst the most oil tight of all motorcycle engines – certainty of the British variety.

A Norton Front End

As discussed elsewhere, Enfield at this time had a link with Norton Villiers. The major change to the cycle parts of the Interceptor 2 was in the adoption of a complete Norton front end, including the famous Roadholder telescopic fork assembly. Originally the brake was the SLS 8in (20cm) Atlas type, but it is still an excellent

Another area of change was the clutch. The original milled slots around the clutch centre had been replaced by splines, as on the Norton Commando. However, although an improvement in theory over the one it replaced, there are reports that the drums, or at least some batches, were not hard enough, causing premature wear.

The contact breakers were operated by a cam situated on the end of the exhaust camshaft. In the area behind the cylinder barrels, where the points had previously been housed, was now the oil filter cap, flush to the casting in the style of the Continental GT single. At first this component was equipped with an adaptor for its collar, but the adaptor was discontinued from engine number IBI333. There was in addition a pipe for the

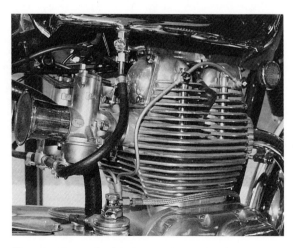

Top end with twin Amal 900 Series Concentric carburettors. Size was 32mm (coded 932).

The wet sump Series 2 engine is taller than earlier Enfield Twins. This engine has the optional oil cooler mounted at the front of the crankcase, low down.

Close-up of the oil baffle on top of the crankcase and external oil piping on Interceptor Series 2.

brake (at least when compared with other drums). Several owners have subsequently substituted the twin leading shoe brake plate from the Commando.

A stop-light switch was now a standard fitment. Fork gaiters (but of a different design from those fitted to the Series 1 Enfield forks) were standard. A pair of chromed 'cups' supported the matching speedo and tacho, with the drive for the latter being taken from the exhaust camshaft via the nearside front of the crankcase.

Many of the electrical components, such as the lighting equipment, were the latest Lucas ware, and so very much like those found on the Norton Commando.

Two-leading-shoe, full-width aluminium drum front brake, as used on the Interceptor Series 2; it is the same as found in the early Norton Commando.

In line with Stateside laws, side reflectors were standard equipment (even on non-US bikes).

Compression ratio on all Series 2 engines was standardized at 8.5:1, power output being unchanged at 52.5bhp. Both 2¼gal (10ltr) and 4¼gal (19ltr) tanks were fitted, depending on market/model, whilst the all-shrouded chrome-bodied rear shocks from the 1A Road Sports were chosen.

Dry weight had increased to 426lb (193kg). Items such as air cleaner assembly, a sump bash plate and a chrome-plated passenger grab handle were all cost options.

Some testers considered the Concentric carbs a retrograde move as far as smooth running and low down pick-up were concerned, and certainly the Series 2 was no quicker than the 1/1A on either maximum speed or acceleration. What it was, however, was more reliable and oil-tight than its predecessors.

Revised Gearing

The revised gearing of 4.44, 6.05, 8.19 and 12.4 still did not fully answer the over-wide gap between third and top.

On price the Enfield was competitive: the UK figure was £455, against that of the Norton 750 Commando Fastback at £466.

Unless maximum engine revolutions were used on a regular basis, the Series 2 engine was a tough nut. However, full bore for long periods could cause problems, even breakages of the crankcase were known to have occurred. Sensibly driven it was reliable, as evidenced by one owner's 12,000 mile (19,308km) overland trip to Australia on a machine that had already clocked up in excess of 50,000 miles (80,450km).

1970 Specification

For the 1970 model year, the company decided to make several previous extras standard equipment. So the oil cooler, bash plate, air cleaner and grab rail were included in the price that had risen to over £500.

Crankcases were changed slightly from engine number IB2002. Then on 3 July 1970 engine production at the Westwood works ceased, at number IB2200.

Some 546 Series 2 Interceptors were sold in 1969, with approximately 600 further engines being sold to the American Floyd Clymer for fitment to his Indian Enfields – these used frames made by the Italian Italjet concern, with the majority of other components also of Italian origin.

In something of a rerun of the 1950s American Indian Enfield saga, publisher and bike enthusiast Floyd Clymer relaunched the Indian marque in the late 1960s. The 1970 Clymer Indian Interceptor 2 used Italian cycle parts with the British parallel-twin engine. Very few were sold, due in part to Clymer's unfortunate death in 1970.

In addition, a further 137 motorcycles were subsequently built by Rickman using the Interceptor Series 2 engine (for the story of this venture *see* box overleaf). But after this there were to be no more British made Enfields. Why was this so? Well, the reason why the Redditch works was closed is given in Chapter 12 (*see* page 161), and it seems that the E. & H.P. Smith Group were having all sorts of problems, as not only was the Redditch bike operation axed but also Enfield Industrial Engines that, being housed on the same site, was also disposed of – this time to a Greek shipping magnate. In addition, the Royal Enfield motorcycle spares operation was sold off around the same time in early 1967 to Velocette, themselves also by now in terminal decline.

It is interesting to note that when Velocette eventually expired in early 1971, the spares and rights to the Royal Enfield name, and later the Interceptor tooling and spares, joined the remains of Scott and Vincent as the property of Aerco, headed by entrepreneur and motorcycle buff, Matt Holder, who died a decade later in 1981.

Manganese Bronze

1966 had seen the fall of the giant AMC (Associated Motor Cycles). This was to result in Dennis Poore's Manganese Bronze empire taking over AMC. Complicated behind-the-scenes moves saw a March 1967 press story emerge that the Enfield Cycle Company's share capital had been purchased for £82,500 by the newly formed Norton–Villiers concern (the Poore amalgamation of the various AMC motorcycle brands including Norton and the Poore's other recent acquisition, Villiers Engines of Wolverhampton). This became even more complicated, because Norton–Villiers' parent group, Manganese Bronze Holdings, already owned a 30 per cent interest in Enfield India Ltd, the subsidiary in Madras who had been producing large quantities of the pre-1956 Bullet single for many years under licence from the Redditch factory (*see* Chapter 14 for the full story).

Westwood Works

Meanwhile Royal Enfield, or at least the Interceptor Twins, continued to be built at the Westwood works (actually there were two sites) at Bradford-on-Avon. These motorcycles were built under the auspices of Enfield Precision Engineers, which at that time was still under control of E. & H.P. Smith, not Norton–Villiers.

Then came an agreement between Smiths and NV for the latter to market the former's machines in the USA. However, it appears that Dennis Poore and Smiths fell out, and thereafter Enfield Precision marketed their motorcycles through P. Mitchell & Co., a large import/export agency who not only had valuable contracts abroad, but did considerable business with Elite Motors of Tooting, South London and as the Rickman box reveals (*see* page 169), it was the London company who ended up marketing those particular machines.

But in 1968 this was all in the future. Meanwhile, Enfield Precision brought out the Interceptor Series 2 and were also well on the way to a production version of an 800cc prototype. This venture had some £1 million spent on tooling alone, and some 400 orders outstanding from just the USA, when Interceptor 2 production came to an end, thus bringing the whole venture to an end.

Enfield Precision did not close, but simply ceased its motorcycle production, from then on concentrating upon Ministry of Defence contracts for the British Government.

By the late 1980s Enfield Precision was under the control of a Norwegian engineer who, it was rumoured, used it as a 'shell' for his investment company.

By the time the last Rickman Enfield Interceptor had been sold during the early 1970s, the engine tooling, spares and manufacturing rights were in the hands of Matt Holder and no more were to be built, even though both Elite Motors and Rickman Engineering were keen to build more bikes.

The end had come for the British Enfield motorcycle; from now on it had to be left to the Tiruvot-Tiyur factory outside Madras to continue a proud name and tradition.

Rickman

The Rickman brothers, Don and Derek, had first sprung to fame during the early 1960s by building a series of motocross machines using their own frame design (after originally employing a BSA chassis) with a series of British engines, including the Triumph T100 and Matchless G80. Christened the Metisse, a French term for a female mongrel, they gained countless race victories.

By 1964, half of all off-road racers in Britain were using Rickman-built Metisse machining. Then came a long association with the Spanish Bultaco marque and an entry into road racing in 1966. A new development late in the decade was the Rickman eight-valve conversion for the Triumph 650 engine, this coming about thanks to a tie-up between Rickman and the Weslake company.

Then in 1969, the Rickman brothers became involved with the Enfield marque. The result was the Rickman Interceptor, using a Series 2 engine. Its public debut came at the London Sporting and Racing Show in January 1970. The combination of the 736cc engine and superb Metisse chassis produced a generally excellent motorcycle that, with less weight than the standard Enfield-made Interceptor, was capable of 118–120mph (190–193km/h).

The frame was of an all-welded construction with duplex tubes throughout and was finished, as was Rickman practice, in bright nickel plating.

The swinging arm was mounted on an eccentric pivot to provide a more reliable method of rear chain adjustment and the front forks were of the well-known Rickman road-racing pattern.

During the early 1970s, Rickman Engineering built the Rickman Enfield, using their Metisse frame kit with an Interceptor Series 2 engine. This was an excellent machine, offering the combination of a torquey motor and race-bred chassis.

Both wheel hubs carried Lockheed hydraulically-operated single disc brakes, unusual at that time on street bikes – if a disc was present (as on Honda's CB750 four), it was duly found at the front only.

The tank, seat and mudguarding were manufactured in fibreglass and were produced by Rickmans themselves, at their New Milton, Hampshire base.

The dual ignition coils for the 12V system nestled just aft of the Albion four-speed gearbox, with the area over them boxed in for the battery and tool kit.

One of the more controversial features was the method of mounting the rider's footrests, each being clamped into a small vertically-mounted tube welded to the outer side of its respective exhaust pipe. Although this system functioned without fuss and bother, one has to question what would happen in the event of the motorcycle being involved in a crash.

Marketing was handled by Elite Motors of Tooting, South London, who sold 137 machines between the spring of 1971 and the end of 1972.

Having ridden a Rickman Interceptor there is no doubt that vibration (at least on the example that I rode) was worse than a standard Enfield-produced Mark 2 Twin; the Albion gearbox was its biggest drawback. Even so, the few bikes actually built (restricted due to the decision of Enfield Precision, Bradford-on-Avon, to cease production) and the Rickman name means that surviving examples are highly prized by collectors and enthusiasts alike. One example is on permanent display at the National Motorcycle Museum in Birmingham, to remind everyone just what they missed when deciding not to buy a Rickman Interceptor when Elite advertised them in the motorcycling press of the 1970s. Instead, most ended up purchasing a Honda CB750, Norton Commando or a BSA/Triumph triple.

continued overleaf

Single disc, Girling-made rear shock and welled alloy rim of the Rickman Enfield. A total of 137 examples were built of this now classic motorcycle.

Rickman *continued*

This shows how the Rickman machine made the Interceptor
Series 2 engine appear smaller than when it was mounted in
the Enfield frame. This was due to the motor being placed
lower (between the bottom frame tubes) and because the
Rickman fuel tank hid the top of the cylinder head from view.

Lockheed twin-piston caliper and single disc of the Rickman
Enfield Interceptor.

Racer Steve Linsdell made a name for
himself on Royal Enfield Twins (an early
Interceptor is seen here at Oulton Park in
1980), plus the Bullet single.

14   The Madras Connection

During 1954, Royal Enfield's Redditch works received a massive order from the Indian army, to supply a total of 800 350 Bullet ohv singles. The specification was little changed from the model being made at that time for civilian use, but the consignment was to be finished in a matt sand colour. However, because the army was then currently at war with Pakistan, the bikes had to be 'ready for action'. This meant that each engine needed to be 'seize-proof'; so the British factory had to give each bike a full and rigorous road test, which entailed a stint of full-throttle work. Any engine that suffered a full or partial seizure was subsequently removed and the barrels and pistons exchanged for new ones, which then went through an identical test procedure. The completion of this contract saw much of Royal Enfield's staff working around the clock, seven-days-a-week for some months.

The very reasons why the Bullet had been chosen by the Indian military – performance, reliability and ease of maintenance – also saw the beginning of 'the Indian operation'.

During the mid-1950s, the Indian government decided that a policy should be adopted where its countrymen should be actively encouraged (and supported by legislation) to manufacture many products, rather than import them. This was to result, in 1956, in a joint venture between the Madras Motor Company and the British Enfield Cycle Company. With the Indians holding a controlling 51/49 per cent interest (the deal was negotiated in India by Enfield's Major Vic Mountford), the Madras Motor Company began by having shipped in the Bullet, in knocked-down kit (KDK) form.

The next stage was for the Indian operation to begin manufacturing the chassis components (frame, swinging arm, tin-ware and the like). After this, Enfield went from shipping complete engine assemblies to supplying the components for the engines to be assembled locally in India. Eventually, Madras Motors was also manufacturing the engines – which meant that it was a bike builder in the true sense. In any case, the mother company back in Great Britain was by now in terminal decline (together with the rest of the industry).

The owner of Madras Motors even sent two of his sons to the English factory to serve apprenticeships with Royal Enfield during the late 1950s. That this was a wise move was to be proved, not only by the great success of the Bullet model but also by the fact that in the late 1970s another facility was opened at Runipet to manufacture German Zündapp lightweight two-stroke motorcycles, under a similar licence agreement to that made with the Enfield Cycle Company. Since then several other concerns, including BMW, have attempted to muscle into the lucrative Indian motorcycle market, but the Enfield Bullet was there first – and has successfully seen off all attempts to unseat it as India's most popular large-displacement motorcycle.

The basis of the long-running Indian Bullet has been the 1955 350 model with AC electrics and, in some ways, this has led to a 'time warp' machine, which means that even the latest Bullet has much of the charm and, unfortunately, the servicing requirements of the original. However, as is to be revealed later, things are at last changing, with the adoption of innovations such as 12V electrics, 5-speed gearbox and electric start.

Coals to Newcastle

In early 1977 came the news that the Bullet 350 was to be re-imported and sold on the British market, by the Herefordshire-based Slater Brothers' operation headed by Roger Slater – a real coals-to-Newcastle story.

From that time onwards, via a succession of importers, the Indian-made Bullet has proved a consistent seller, albeit in relatively some numbers in the UK market. Slaters gave up the concession during the early 1980s, when they struck financial troubles. In the early/mid 1980s imports were handled by Evesham Motorcycles. Then came Raja Naryan, head of the Banavar organization. Based in Purley, Surrey, Naryan held the concession for over a decade. During this time he generally did his best to improve the quality of the machines. Originally he began, in the mid-1980s, as not just the importer for the British Isles, but also for Continental Europe. This eventually was changed by the Indian factory, to only Britain, simply because they wanted separate importers in each country as they felt this would give them increased sales potential.

One of these Europeans was the Swiss engineer, Fritz Egli, who had already built a formidable reputation in racing and superbike circles for a succession of high-speed motorcycles from the late 1960s, when he had produced a frame kit for the venerable Vincent V-twin.

Egli was later to become a consultant for the Indian factory, but his policy of rebuilding the bikes totally and selling them at a very high price (because of the work he had put into them) did not go down too well in India, so eventually Egli reverted back to simply being the Swiss importer.

During his time as consultant, Egli developed a 624cc version of the Bullet engine. This was never to reach production, in the author's opinion probably due to concerns about the additional stress this would place on the engine's bottom end; after all, the original post-war Bullet power unit had been designed as a 350. The largest production version of the engine has in fact been the 535cc, in which the bore size of the 500 power unit was increased from 84 to 87mm, the stroke remaining unchanged at 90mm. Although available on the domestic market, the 535 is not currently available in UK. However, this, together with other recent developments, shows the Indians are looking ahead.

When the first exports began in the late 1970s, the Bullet was exactly as it had been back in 1955.

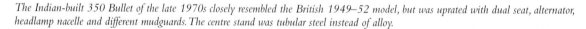

The Indian-built 350 Bullet of the late 1970s closely resembled the British 1949–52 model, but was uprated with dual seat, alternator, headlamp nacelle and different mudguards. The centre stand was tubular steel instead of alloy.

So it did not benefit from the annual updates found in the British-built versions until production ceased in the early 1960s. However, in the last few years, Enfield India (now owned by the Eicher Group and called Royal Enfield Motors) has begun to introduce significant changes. Outlined in Chapter 15, these include 12V electrics, an electric start option and, for the immediate future, a five-speed gearbox and a new Lean Burn engine.

Now under a new owner (Eicher) and with a new, young and dynamic managing director, the Indian Royal Enfield Motors operation seems set to make progress during the twenty-first century in a manner that has not been seen before, and just maybe, further on into the future, the name Royal Enfield will once again mean innovation, as it did in the first few decades of the twentieth century. There is certainly no reason why this should not come about in due course. And, of course, the motorcycles have one of the most famous names, in Royal Enfield.

An attempt by British importers Slater Brothers to make a more glamorous version of the Indian Bullet, circa 1978.

By the late 1980s, Banavar Products of Purley, Surrey, had become British importers. They even offered the 500 Bullet with the option of a Brembo front disc brake.

View showing the road between Chennai (formally Madras) and the factory.

Diesel Power

The first 'production' diesel-powered British motorcycle just had to be an Enfield and was the culmination of a decade's work, when it arrived in the early 1990s.

Arch diesel enthusiast, Ernie Dorsett, who had built his home-brewed, diesel-engined Matchless G3 and five other similar bikes, approached the Blixworth, Northamptonshire Redbreast concern, the British importers for the Japanese Fuji Robin diesel unit. This came after Dorsett had problems in locating AMC frames. Then a deal was arranged between Redbreast's Paul Holdsworth and partner Roger Kimbell, and the then Enfield India's UK importers Bavanar Products to supply engineless Bullet rolling chassis.

Returning an amazing 200mpg (1.4ltr/100km), the Enfield Robin D-R 400D was propelled by an all-alloy air-cooled Fuji single-cylinder diesel, a unit more usually found on the likes of generators, pumps and mini excavators.

Part of the Indian Enfield factory.

A line-up of Bullets awaiting delivery at the Indian works.

The bore and stroke of 82 × 78mm gave a displacement of 412cc. The power output was a modest 8.5bhp at 3,600rpm, with a 21:1 compression ratio and a Bosch fuel injector firing diesel directly into the combustion chamber. The necessary air supply was fed separately into the head via a cylindrical oil–bath air cleaner.

Although the traditional Enfield kickstarter was retained, it was actually much easier to use the additional electric starter – the first electric button found on an Enfield! Because the fuel–air mixture ignited under compression, there were no spark plugs, coils or contact breaker points to worry about.

Some of the staff at the factory's training college.

The Enfield Robin's engine casing was machined to accept the standard Enfield primary drive, clutch and four-speed Albion-type gearbox. The rolling chassis was also modified to accept the new power unit. It was stripped by the Redbreast organization and refinished with black powder coating and a two-pack finish.

So far everything sounds fine. But then things began to go pear-shape for the Enfield Robin. For starters, at £4,500 in 1993 it was almost double what a standard 346cc ohv four-stroke Enfield India would have cost. It was also lacking any real performance, even by Enfield India 350 Bullet standards. A *Classic Bike* test stated 'performance is gentlemanly' and that 'a calendar is more appropriate for measuring increases in the machines rate of velocity – "acceleration" is an overstatement'. The *Classic Bike* tester concluded:

Apart from those who like the kudos of owning a highly individual machine, the Robin is best suited to admirers of the landscape. Sitting astride its comfortable seat at a stately pace, you have plenty of time to reflect on a green and pleasant land.

LEFT: Frame construction taking place at the Chennai plant, very much as the same procedures would have been done back in the Redditch factory almost half a century earlier.

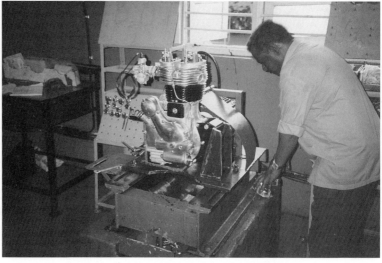

A Bullet engine on the factory's test rig.

An engine on a dynamometer in a section of the Indian factory complex.

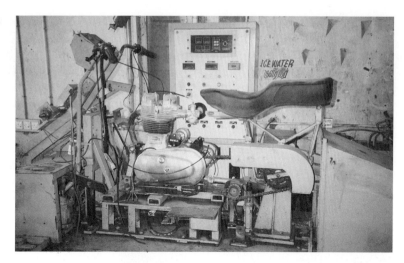

Another problem the Robin faced, and one it shared with machines such as the Suzuki RE5 and Hercules W2000 rotaries, was the unfamiliar-to-the-eye engine shape. Even so, the Robin's existence alone proved that someone, somewhere, will want to own even the most unusual of motorcycles.

The Enfield Robin was not, however, unique. India's *Car & Bike International* magazine reported in August 1992 that Sooraj Automobiles of Saharonpur in Utter Pradesh had already put a 325cc diesel-powered bike into production. Powered by an imported Italian Lombardini unit, it also used the Enfield Bullet chassis. The magazine commented: 'The majority of buyers are all inevitably from rural areas, farmers predominately, who understand the value of low operating costs and are hardy souls who can withstand all the vibrations and noise that a diesel can throw up.' This motorcycle, the Taurus, was marketed through the official Indian Enfield (later Royal Enfield Motors) domestic dealer network until the 2001 model year, when it was finally discontinued.

But the Enfield diesel bike is not dead! Far from it in fact, as Coleville, Leicestershire dealership Charnwood Classics is currently marketing a 350cc model powered by a German Hatz engine.

Retailing in the UK in spring 2002 at £4,250, the Charnwood machine employing a standard Bullet set of cycle parts with the following modifications and changes:

Petrol tanks arriving at the factory. India is a country of great contrasts, but how long will scenes like this remain?

Enfield Robin Model D-R 400D 412cc 'Yellow Peril' record-breaker of 1995 – a team of riders achieving an around-Britain journey of 3,609.88 miles (5,808.3km) in 168 hours, averaging 201.89mpg (1.4ltr/100km).

- frame modified from single to twin front down-tube;
- modified primary chaincase;
- wiring loom altered to suit new engine;
- heavy duty 12V battery (needed for electric start);
- different exhaust.

As with the previous Enfield diesel-powered motorcycles, the main feature is incredible fuel economy. In the Charnwood Hatz/Enfield's case this averages between a low of 165mpg (1.7ltr/100km) to a high of 220mpg (2.3ltr/100km). Maximum speed is 65mph (105km/h), but currently one example is being tested with a supercharger, which will give it a definite advantage over the standard version.

Charnwood Classics' new owner, Jim Darcy, revealed that a pair of his creations had travelled to the Dragon Rally – held in North Wales – in truly atrocious weather conditions. Not only did both bikes perform admirably, but fully loaded and often having to travel in low gears due to head winds and driving rain, the two machines still averaged 145mpg (2ltr/100km), when a conventional petrol engine Bullet would have been hard pressed to record a third of these figures in similar conditions.

The Indian Enfield Taurus diesel. Built by the Madras (Chennai) factory, it used an Italian Lombardini engine of 325cc. Production ceased in 2001.

The only Enfield diesel-powered motorcycle still available is the Hatz Enfield built by Charnwood Classics. It is powered by a 350cc German Hatz engine and can reach 65mph (105km/h) and better 200mpg (1.4ltr/100km).

15 Enfield Today

When the first Royal Enfield motorcycle appeared in 1901, few would have thought that over a century later it would be the marque that would effectively have outlived all the other British companies (if one discounts the rebirth of Triumph). And that, even more controversially, the bikes would latterly have been built in India, not Great Britain. But that is exactly how things have panned out.

Survivors

So, just why has Royal Enfield survived when great names such as Sunbeam, Matchless, Ariel, BSA, Velocette and Vincent all went to the knacker's yard years ago? Well, part of the reason was explained in the previous chapter, which outlined how and why the Indians got involved. However, to explain just why the rest of the world is still attracted to a motorbike with its roots firmly stuck in the middle of the twentieth century, it is important to read the following words, which greet a prospective owner when they apply for information to the current British importers, Watsonian–Squire Ltd:

> Buying a Royal Enfield is an attractive proposition. You are getting a classic bike with good looks, low running-costs and insurance, plus a full warranty and nationwide dealer support – all at a very affordable price.

It then goes on to point out a few things that the owner of one of today's expensive fuel-burning plastic rocketships certainly won't have to take account of:

> You need to remember that the Royal Enfield is basically a 1955 motorcycle that requires a greater level of care and attention than modern motorcycles, as was

the case in that period. For example, the Bullet needs running in and gets noticeably better with time; the gear change gets smoother, the engine frees off and overall performance improves. Even when run-in, to retain reliability, these machines need to be ridden with sensitivity and not thrashed in the way a modern bike can be. Its design predates motorways, therefore it will not (and nor will you) like using them. The variation in speed and conditions that come with using typical 1950s type A and B roads is both enjoyable and are ideal conditions for Royal Enfields. As an owner you will need to keep a check on electrical connections as well as various nuts and bolts for tightness. Valve clearances, drive chain tension, brake and clutch controls all require regular adjustment. To keep the appearance in peak condition the chrome needs to be protected against bad weather.

Low Costs

But of course being a machine from 1955, it can be maintained by the owner, will comfortably exceed 70mpg (4.4.ltr/100km) and costs little more than many 50cc scooters. Being a newly built classic bike means that you do not have to restore an old heap that will soak up money like a sponge.

Another thing to remember is development. Strangely, for many years, little or no development took place at the Indian works. However, recently, there has been an active ongoing programme. Already this has seen benefits such as 12V electrics, a 2LS front brake and, perhaps most important of all, an electric start option (with Japanese Denso components). The latter has proved extremely popular and now over two-thirds of the Bullets sold in Britain feature the electric thumb.

New Developments

With the appointment of a new, young, dynamic (28-year-old) managing director, Siddhartha Lal, other innovations are currently being introduced, including a new five-speed gearbox and a Lean Burn engine. The five-speed 'box has been developed by the British company Criterion engineering, and will be available on all models from 2003.

As far as the Lean Burn engine, this is the work of Austrian engineering specialists AVL; this engine also features electronic ignition, whereas points have been used up to now. As if all this were not enough, it seems likely that disc brakes will soon be introduced. This will solve, currently, the Bullet's biggest weakness, a less than effective front stopper. Even so, oval brake drums are not such a problem on Indian-made Bullets as they were a few years ago. And the brakes, like the rest of the machine, definitely improve as the miles go by.

Currently three engine sizes are manufactured:

- 346cc 70 × 90mm;
- 499cc 84 × 90mm;
- 535cc 87 × 90mm.

An Indian-made 350 Bullet photographed at Snetterton race circuit in March 2002 in a sea of modern hi-tech superbikes.

The new managing director of the Indian Royal Enfield company is 28-year-old Siddhartha (Sid) Lal. Son of the chairman, he rides to work every day on a 350 Bullet, instead of the usual company car.

OPPOSITE: The British importer's advertisement proclaims the qualities of the latest Bullet: 'Real Motorcycles Realistic Prices'. One cannot argue.

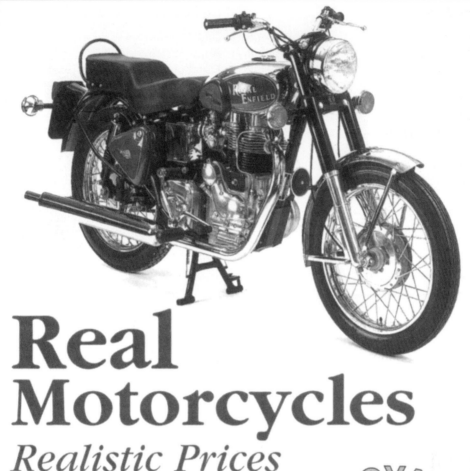

2002 Models

In autumn 2002, when this book was being completed, the official model range from the Indian factory was as follows:

- Bullet Lightning 535cc
- Bullet Euro Classic (346, 499 and 535cc);
- Bullet US Classic (346, 499 and 535cc);
- Bullet Military (346 and 499cc);
- Bullet Police (346 and 499cc);
- Bullet Machismo (new 346cc Lean Burn engine).

(The 535cc engine size is for India only.)

Lightning 535 (535cc)

The Lightning 535 is styled very much in the American custom mould so beloved by Harley-Davidson and the big four Japanese producers. It is an attractive bike, but would it sell in overseas markets such as the USA, Great Britain and Continental Europe? This is a dilemma for the Indian factory. Do they continue to improve the existing classically styled Bullet series or do they try to compete head-on with the likes of the Japanese over the next few years? The author's feeling is that it would be better to concentrate upon improvement and evolution, rather than try an all-new approach. The latter would probably be a big financial gamble.

Peter Rivers-Fletcher of the British importers Watsonian–Squire Ltd, with a Bullet 500 and Watsonian sidecar at the company's Blockley, Gloucestershire headquarters, c.2003.

Even BMW misjudged the domestic Indian market. They set up a local manufacturing plant to build and sell a variant of their successful F650 4-valve single. However, the idea bombed, not helped by a purchase price some four times higher than the 350 Bullet at that time. The plant is now closed.

Currently, Kawasaki are faring little better with a version of their 250 Eliminator twin.

Financial Considerations

Another factor to consider is that in 2001 the Indian Enfield operation lost money for the first time ever – a worrying development. Currently some 25,000 machines are produced annually (of which most are 350s). However, in export markets that account for less than 10 per cent of the production, the 500 outsells the 350 by over three-to-one.

As for the UK market, Peter Rivers-Fletcher of importers Watsonian–Squire has seen sales steadily climb since his company took over in mid-1999. Going from 75 in the first six months, to 250 in 2000, 430 in 2001 and a projected 600 in 2002, that would make the UK the biggest market outside India.

RIGHT: Johnny Szolddrak's much modified 500 Bullet single at Daytona, March 2002. It gave a good account of itself against the likes of Manx Nortons and Matchless G50s.

It is possible to buy the Army version of the Bullet, complete with a khaki paint job and panniers.

German Peter Lohr with one of the 500 Clubman S models. It successfully captures the spirit of the 1960s.

Another 'nostalgia' model built by Watsonian–Squire for the UK market is the 350 Trials. It is an affordable way of recapturing Royal Enfield's mud-plugging past heroics by men such as Brittain and Stirland.

Peter Rivers-Fletcher also views current developments as proof positive that at last the Indians see that it is important to improve both the quality and function of their motorcycles. For example, the electric start has opened up a whole new customer base, making the Bullet (particularly in 500 form) much easier to start.

Details of the 2002 Bullet, including side panel with Bullet logo.

Headlamp with speedo, ammeter, ignition switch and sidelights.

Ignition (still contact breaker points).

12 volt electrical system.

Two leading shoe front drum brake.

The Denso motor driving through gears and a sprag clutch (the latter a one-way bearing), has proved most effective and reliable in service. Additionally the whole machine has undergone a re-tooling exercise, as has the casting, machining, materials and functions of some component parts.

Improving Quality

To improve quality, a new chrome-plate facility has been installed, likewise a new paint shop. Stainless steel spokes have been introduced and special attention has been given to the problem of oval brake drums, which has plagued some machines in the past. Inspection procedures have been tightened up; whilst each export machine is packed in a wooden crate, with only the front wheel removed.

Watsonian–Squire's engineering director, Mike Williams-Raahauge, has spent time at the Indian works, satisfying himself that the manufacturing standards are improving. What he found was that since the Eicher takeover, considerable investment has taken place.

Models for the UK differ from those sold on the domestic market. Tyres, lighting, exhaust systems, handlebar controls and emission levels are all to EEC specification. It should also be noted that carburation and ignition settings may also differ from country to country. All machines brought into the UK are checked and prepared at the Watsonian–Squire works before delivery to the dealer network, which currently stands at forty-one (October 2002).

UK Range

The 350 and 500 Bullet models were both available in classic and de luxe guises, the latter featuring chrome tank, mudguards and chainguard. Besides the traditional black with gold pin-striping, there are several other options including dark green, royal blue and bright red. Another option is the Army version in khaki green. Then there are the UK-built 500S Clubman (café racer) and 350/500T (Trial/Trail); for the latter, the customer has the option of a 21in (53cm) front

wheel for an additional £90 (only on a new, factory-supplied machine). The T models feature a single sprung saddle and a silver paint job.

The UK price list as at October 2002 is:

- 350 Classic £2,485;
- 350 De Luxe £2,585;
- 350T Trials £2,995;
- 350 Army £2,585;
- 500 Classic £2,768;
- 500 Classic Electric Start £3,018
- 500 de Luxe £2,918;
- 500 de Luxe Electric Start £3,168;
- 500S Clubman £3,995;
- 500 Army £2,918.

Black is standard (silver on T models), with red, green and blue optional at £50 extra.

All the above prices include VAT and are OTR (On The Road), including delivery to the dealer, first registration, road fund tax, number plates and 12 months recovery scheme.

Sidecars

Watsonian–Squire can supply specially tailored sidecar outfits using both the 350 and 500 Bullet models:

- 350 Classic (black) and Stratford chair £4,326;
- 500 Classic (black) and GP Manx chair £5,136;
- 500 de Luxe (black) and GP Jubilee chair £6,070.

Testing the 500S Clubman

When *Motor Cycle News* tested an example of the 500S Clubman in the 28 March 2001 issue, the headline read: 'Luckily, some things never change'. This was in reference to the machine's café racer looks, when 'Rockers wore leathers, rode bikes customized with go-faster goodies and congregated at venues such as London's legendary Ace Café'. And it was that look that the British importer, Watsonian–Squire, have attempted to re-create.

Eicher

Since the late 1990s, the Indian Enfield operation has been owned by Eicher Goodearth Ltd. With headquarters in New Delhi, the Eicher group of companies is a major player in the burgeoning Indian industrial scene, and has a strong global presence as well, with working relationships in the UK, Germany, Japan, Italy and Finland.

Eicher's production includes tractors, gear manufacturing, light commercial vehicles, ladies' footwear and, of course, motorcycles. Eicher is also involved with product development and management consulting for other firms. World-wide, Eicher employs over 6,000 staff, has ten manufacturing plants and a massive dealer network.

The Eicher Group began in 1948, when the Goodearth Company was set up to sell and service imported tractors. Then perceiving an urgent need to mechanize Indian agriculture, it set up a tractor manufacturing facility. The Goodearth Company established Eicher tractors in 1959 and, in doing so, became India's first tractor manufacturer. The first production example rolled out of Eicher's Faridabad factory in 1960. Other products and services were added to Eicher's portfolio in subsequent years. It acquired Royal Enfield Motors in 1996, after having first taken a stake in its operation back in 1994. They see the Royal Enfield brand name as a valuable asset, viewing it in much the same way as the Americans see Harley-Davidson or the Italians MV Agusta. Harnessing this brand name will, the management feel, play a vital role in the projection of Royal Enfield in future years.

Eicher's chief executive is Vikram Lal, the father of the new Royal Enfield boss, the young and dynamic Siddhartha Lal. With this combination, Enfield has in effect been given a heart transplant. Not only are developments taking place on the existing Bullet series, but there is even talk of the Interceptor Twin making a comeback. As journalist Kevin Ash observed in the June 2002 issue of *Classic Bike*: 'Consider the success of the Hinkley Triumph Bonneville, now its best selling model, and think what could be done with a modern Interceptor. With Eicher's money to turn this bold talk into reality, and Lal's vision to direct it, Enfield's future in India looks very strong indeed.' I couldn't agree more – and I can't wait for such a machine to arrive and await the day when an example sits in my Wisbech garage!

Lightning 535, using a larger bore version of the existing 500 Bullet engine. It is currently only sold on the home market.

Royal Enfield created a new world record by transporting 201 people at the same time on a team of Bullets.

Much of the style came directly from Mick Walker's previously published book *Café Racers of the 1960s*, which Peter Rivers-Fletcher used for inspiration. Working in conjunction with specialist Norman Hyde, the result is a successful attempt to re-create the era. As *Motor Cycle News* related:

It's a perfectly innocent question – 'How old is it, mate?' asks the passer-by, intrigued by the mint-looking antique I've just parked in the High Street. 'Er, about a year actually,' I reply, before his bemused expression forces me to explain that his query is not as simple as it sounds. Yes, the Royal Enfield 500S Clubman looks just like a café racer from the 1950s or 1960s. But this model first appeared in 2000!

Considering the *Motor Cycle News* tester's lot is usually getting his leg over such awesome modern metal as a Fireblade, 996, RI or GSX-R1000, he ended up being very enthusiastic about the Enfield Clubman, concluding the test by saying, 'This is a gem from the golden days of biking, put in a time capsule to be enjoyed again in 2001', and: 'It's difficult to describe the feeling of blurring past the dry-stone-walled lanes of the Cotswolds on a bike like this. A combination of the timeless countryside, old-style racer riding position and wonderful, raw exhaust note really made me feel like I had stepped back in time.'

That *Motor Cycle News* test really summed up what the Royal Enfield experience is all about – pure nostalgia. And, as I said earlier, if the Indians were to go instead for a new, fresh, modern design it would have to be as good as the very latest Japanese models – a super difficult task. Otherwise the road testers of the day would throw the newcomer to the journalistic sword, and I know that *Motor Cycle News* would not be anywhere as kind when reviewing any such newcomer, unless it really was perfection on wheels.

At present, the Bullet series has a joint role, providing affordable, reliable, respected transport back home, whilst on the export markets it has a niche as the old/new classic motorcycle. If the status quo is maintained, there is absolutely no reason why in 2048 the Bullet (in swinging arm form), or 2033 in the case of the original Bullet, should not be celebrating its centenary!

RIGHT: The first 'Lean Burn'-engined machine after being uncrated at the British importers in May 2002; note also the equally new five-speed gearbox.

BELOW: The electric starter has made the Bullet even more popular; the revised primary cover with Japanese Denso starter motor are shown.

BELOW RIGHT: Making its debut in 2002, the new 'lean burn' engine pointed the way ahead for the Indian Royal Enfield concern.

Index